THE ORG
DIRECTORY

THE ORGANIC DIRECTORY

YOUR GUIDE TO BUYING ORGANIC FOODS

2000-2001 edition, compiled by Clive Litchfield

FOREWORD BY PATRICK HOLDEN

GREEN BOOKS
WITH THE SOIL ASSOCIATION

Acknowledgements

Ever since I started work on the first edition of this Directory in 1991 I have had enormous amounts of help and encouragement from a variety of people and organisations. A list follows, and if I have missed anyone out I apologise.

My partner Annie, our daughters Sophie, Lydia and Ella, Mark Redman, Paul Adams and everyone at the Soil Association, Basil Caplan, Alan and Jackie Gear at the HDRA, Robert Sculthorpe at Organic Farmers and Growers, James Anderson at the BDAA, Dr. Mae-Wan Ho at the Open University, Genetics Forum, Gene-Watch, G.P. Lawson and Jan Hurst for Mac and website help, and John Elford at Green Books for taking on this project.

Published in June 2000
by Green Books Ltd, Foxhole, Dartington,
Totnes, Devon TQ9 6EB
greenbooks@gn.apc.org
www.greenbooks.co.uk

with the Soil Association
Bristol House, 40-56 Victoria Street
Bristol BS1 6BY
info@soilassociation.org

Cover design by Rick Lawrence

Typeset in Sabon at Green Books

Printed in Great Britain by
J.W. Arrowsmith Ltd, Bristol, UK

Text printed on Cyclus Offset 100%
recycled paper, manufactured from
waste paper. 100% of residuals
from production are reused.
Non-chlorine bleached.

A CIP record for this book is available from the British Library.

ISBN 1 870098 84 6

(6-copy counterpack for retailers: ISBN 1 870098 85 4)

CONTENTS

FOREWORD

by Patrick Holden, Director of the Soil Association

I am delighted to have been asked to write the foreword to this, the latest edition of *The Organic Directory*, which sees a unique collaboration between two like-minded organisations. Green Books is a well respected environmental publisher. The Soil Association has been at the centre of the organic movement since 1946, until now producing its own guide called *Where to Buy Organic Food*. This year we have decided to amalgamate our book with *The Organic Directory*, to bring you the most up to date, most comprehensive listing of organic produce ever.

More and more people have been buying organic food during the last few years and it has now become a mainstream activity. Media interest is unprecedented. All the major supermarkets stock an ever increasing range of organic products. There are even signs that the Government may have to bow to public pressure and come up with extra funding for organic farming.

It may seem that we have won the battle for food you can trust. It is true that people are questioning the quality of the food they eat, and are using their consumer power to shake the very foundations of the conventional food industry. But there is still much work to do!

Despite the word 'organic' being constantly in the press in the last few years, there are still only 2,000 certified organic holdings in Britain (a mere 2.5% of farmland), although many more farms are now converting.

At the same time we are also seeing the rebirth of local food economies as consumers, caterers and local retailers begin to re-establish close connections with local organic farmers and growers. We took these connections for granted until 30 years ago, but by the end of the century they had largely disappeared, and our culture is the poorer for that.

By using *The Organic Directory* to find and buy organic food in your locality, you can support these new enterprises as well as your own health. Supporting these local growers will encourage them to produce more, and their neighbours to convert to organic methods. Only this way can we meet the enormous demand for organic food currently supplied mostly by imports. The more farmers and growers that convert, the fewer there are trapped in the destructive cycle of industrial farming.

Organic foods can be certified by a number of different companies, all with slightly different standards—a fact that can be confusing when buying. For the first time, *The Organic Directory* will put the symbol of the appropriate body by each listing, for rapid and easy reference. Using this book to buy organic food may not only improve the food on your plate, but open up new links in to your local community.

If you are not already a member, I hope that you will also end up wanting to support the Soil Association's work further by joining us. In doing so you will be helping us to increase the scale of organic farming in the UK which will bring so many benefits not only to your health but also to the diversity and vitality of our countryside.

INTRODUCTION

Organic Standards

Organic farmers work to the stringent standards set down by UKROFS (the United Kingdom Register of Organic Food Standards), and have to be registered and inspected annually—whereas it is estimated that chemical farmers can expect to be inspected once every thirty-five years! Organic farmers work to the principle that healthy soil produces healthy crops and that building the health of the soil is paramount to the whole operation. This involves the careful management of animal and plant wastes to prevent nutrient loss; by stabilising these nutrients and returning them to the system in the form of compost and manure, the soil will be fed, building up fertility and organic material in the soil, thereby enhancing soil structure as well as aeration and water retention. The aim is to cultivate the soil in a manner which maximises biological activity and provides the best growing environment. Rotation of livestock and crops is a major tool in the control of weeds, pests and diseases and improving soil fertility. Leguminous crops are grown for their nitrogen-fixing qualities, and trace elements are provided by deep rooted herbs, seaweed and rock minerals. Pest outbreaks are prevented by encouraging healthy predator populations in a diverse environment. Stress-free conditions are provided for both crops and animals, and of course no routine or prophylactic treatments are used, though there is an approved range of mostly plant-based pesticides and homeopathic medicines. The health and wellbeing of animals is a major concern: upon veterinary instruction, conventional medical intervention would take place to prevent any suffering, though this often requires increased withdrawal periods and in severe circumstances can result in the loss of organic status for the particular animal or crop. Animals, of course, are born and reared free range.

Bio-dynamic farmers apply organic standards but in addition use special preparations for field sprays, and compost and manure treatments. Close attention is also paid to practical rhythms in husbandry, concentrating on closed systems. Bio-dynamics is a contemporary organic philosophy, following the ideas of Rudolf Steiner; it sees the whole earth as a living organism interrelating with the universe. Bio-dynamic produce is certified by the Demeter Standards Committee and carries their symbol, which is their trademark.

Permaculture (from permanent agriculture) has similar principles, in that it is based on an ecologically sustainable way of living, optimising our environmental impact, co-operating with nature and again caring for the earth's resources. Permaculture stresses the need for local connections, to eliminate where possible such follies as the Food Miles issue (where food often travels hundreds of miles to end up on a supermarket shelf a few miles from its original source), and debt-burdened third world countries growing cash crops for supermarkets.

Forest Gardening is a form of agro-forestry devised by British pioneer Robert Hart. It is a way of working with nature that is highly productive, requires minimal maintenance, and creates great environmental benefits. A forest garden is a small scale imitation of natural forest, with seven principal 'layers': the rhizosphere (root vegetables and roots), the soil surface (e.g. dewberries and creeping herbs), the vertical layer (climbing berries and vines), herbaceous (herbs such as comfrey), shrubs (e.g. currants and berries), the low tree layer, and the canopy (largest trees).

Organic Food & Farming:
Some Questions Answered

What is organic farming?

"Sustainable agriculture is a form of food production which builds biodiversity and provides people with wholesome, healthy food for all time"—Jonathon Porritt, patron of the Soil Association

Organic agriculture is a safe, sustainable farming system, producing healthy crops and livestock without damage to the environment.

It avoids the use of artificial chemical fertilisers and pesticides on the land, relying instead on developing a healthy, fertile soil and growing a mixture of crops. In this way, the farm remains biologically balanced, with a wide variety of beneficial insects and other wildlife to act as natural predators for crop pests and a soil full of micro-organisms and earthworms to maintain its vitality.

Animals are reared without the routine use of the array of drugs, antibiotics and wormers which form the foundation of most conventional livestock farming.

Organic is a term defined by law and all organic food production and processing is governed by a strict set of rules. The Soil Association Symbol is awarded to organic products which have been inspected and conform to our "Standards for Organic Food and Farming".

So why is it so important?

There are many important beneficial effects of organic farming. It is totally different to conventional agriculture. Four key areas of difference are Animal Welfare, Environment, Health and Resources.

Animal Welfare

The Soil Association insists on stringent animal welfare standards in its "Standards for Organic Food and Farming". The rules are constantly under review by a group of experienced organic farmers, vets and scientists to ensure that all the farm animals are reared in optimal conditions on organic farms.

Animals have access to fields and are allowed to express their natural behaviour patterns. Animals always have comfortable bedding, usually straw, and plenty of space when they are housed.

Organic livestock farmers can manage their animals without the routine use of antibiotics and other drugs because they run a healthy, balanced system; not keeping too many animals on a given area, keeping a mixture of species wherever possible and using natural organic feedstuffs. Grazing animals like cows and sheep are fed mainly on herb and clover rich grass.

Homeopathy and herbal remedies are used widely in organic livestock management. In a case of acute illness, where the animal might otherwise suffer, a conventional drug treatment would be used.

Human Health

The best reason for buying organic food is simply that it tastes extremely good, but undoubtedly there are also sound health reasons for doing so. It has been shown in some studies to have more vitamins and trace elements than conventionally grown food and, of course, it will not have been treated with noxious chemicals.

There is a vast array of pesticides used in conventional agriculture, many of which are extremely toxic to humans, causing cancers as well as other illnesses. So-called acceptable levels are calculated for each of these chemicals and their risks to human health evaluated. However, surveys consistently show much higher residues occurring in a proportion of food samples than government regulations allow. There is also little knowledge of the long term effects of these compounds or of the 'cocktail' effect (the way in which their toxicity may be increased by mixing them together).

Intensive agriculture methods also cause high levels of pesticides and nitrates to filter through into drinking water via the water courses. Not only does this present a serious health risk but the cost of reducing the levels in the water has to be met by the tax payer.

Genetically Modified Food

If you want to be sure that you are not eating foods containing any genetically modified (GMO) material, you have to choose organic food. In organic systems, genetically modified soya, maize and other products are banned for use in animal feed as well as in human food products.

"The Soil Association believes that genetically modified organisms have no place in organic food or farming and they are therefore prohibited under the Standards for Organic Food and Farming"—Soil Association policy statement on genetically modified organisms.

BSE

Organic beef comes from the safest possible form of farming. The Soil Association banned the inclusion of animal proteins in ruminant feeds in 1983 long before the emergence of the BSE crisis. There has not been a recorded case of BSE in any herd which has been in full organic management since before 1985.

Environment

"Wildlife is not a luxury for the organic farmer, but an essential part of the farming system." —Soil Association handbook 1991

Extensive research has shown that organic farming can be better for the environment than conventional agriculture.

Surveys by, among others, the Ministry of Agriculture and the British Trust for Ornithology, have shown the beneficial effects of organic farming on wildlife. It's not difficult to see why; the pesticides used in intensive agriculture kill many soil organisms, insects and other larger species. They also kill plants considered to be weeds. That means fewer food sources available for other animals, birds and beneficial insects and it also destroys many of their habitats.

In contrast, organic farming provides a much wider range of habitats; more hedges, wider field margins, herb and clover rich grassland and a mixed range of crops. Conservation is an integral part of the Soil Association's standards.

Earth's resources

The avoidance of artificial chemicals means organic farmers minimise health and pollution problems. They also reduce the use of non-renewable resources such as fossil fuels which are used to produce fertilisers and other agrochemicals.

How do I know it's Organic?

Organic Standards and what the Symbols mean

'Organic' is a term defined by law and all organic food production and processing is governed by a strict set of guidelines.

Producers, manufacturers and processors each pay an annual fee to be registered and are required to keep detailed records ensuring a full trail of traceability from farm, or production plant, to table. Any major infringement of this results in suspension of licence and withdrawal of products from the market. All organic farmers, food manufacturers and processors are annually inspected, as well as being subject to random inspections.

The standards are stringent and cover every aspect of registration and certification, organic food production, permitted and non-permitted ingredients, the environment and conservation, processing, packaging and distribution. The standards are regularly updated and are then enforced by certification bodies— most of which operate higher standards than are required by law.

The governing body is the independent UK Register of Organic Food Standards (UKROFS), which sets the basic standards to which the various organic bodies and producers have to adhere to. UKROFS standards in turn, conform to the European Community directive on organic production.

Each certification body has its own symbol and EU code number. These are the marks you should look for on organic products, and are visible proof that they have met the required UKROFS standards and any others set above those by that certification body.

The Organic Certification Bodies

UKROFS
Largely funded by MAFF, UKROFS is the government authority responsible for the approval and supervision of the other certification bodies. Any produce bearing the UKROFS label will have been produced to UKROFS standards. Producers registered with the following certification bodies may also use the UKROFS logo if they wish to.

Soil Association Certification (SA Cert)
The country's leading certification body, certifying approximately 70% of organic food produced in the UK. It operates its own set of standards, which are more specific and generally stricter than those laid down by UKROFS.

The Organic Food Federation (OFF)
A trade federation set up primarily to help its members, who comprise of producers, manufacturers and importers to market organic foods. Its standards conform to those of UKROFS.

Organic Farmers and Growers Ltd (OF&G)
The second largest organic certification body in the UK. Its standards conform to those of UKROFS.

Bio-Dynamic Agricultural Association (Demeter)
Demeter is the written symbol used for the Bio-Dynamic Agricultural Association (BDAA). Central to the Bio-dynamic philosophy is that man, earth and the universe are bound together and that cosmic forces can effect plants, animals and soil.

The Irish Organic Farmers and Growers (IOFGA)
Has its own standards additional to those laid down by UKROFS.

The Scottish Organic Producers Association (SOPA)
Standards conform to those laid down by UKROFS.

All organic food sold in shops must be clearly marked with the appropriate certification body. Labelling regulations are strict. They are the same for all organic certification bodies, are governed by the EU standards and also apply to imported EU and other pre-packaged organic foods.

The easiest way to tell if a manufactured product is organic is to look for the symbol of certification on the packaging. This takes the form of that certification body's logo, as shown above, or the equivalent European Certifying Authority code numbers, listed on page 16.

Imported Produce
Each EU country has its own national organic certification authority which conforms to EU standards, much like UKROFS, and within each there are various certification bodies. As in the UK, each certification body may apply additional

specifications on top of the EU standards. EU standards, in turn, are subject to those laid down by the International Federation of Organic Agricultural Movements (IFOAM).

For food imported from outside Europe into the EU, the situation is slightly more complicated, but is still subject to the same rigorous checks and guarantees. Imported produce must come from countries recognised as applying equivalent standards and inspection procedures, or where national standards do not exist, importers may apply on behalf of specific organic producers. They are then inspected by one of the EU recognised certification bodies and thereafter subjected to annual inspections in the usual way. Storage facilities for imported produce must be open to inspection at all times.

If in doubt . . .

To avoid any confusion with non-organic produce, most organic food is sold pre-packaged. Always check for the symbol and/or number of recognised certification bodies. Where produce is sold loose, proof of certification must be available to consumers. If the retailer cannot prove certification of the produce being sold, then find out who their supplier is and contact them to find out about their certification.

All manufacturers must be registered with a certification body. Some shops pay a certification fee to register as organic in their own right. This gives an added assurance to customers. Any shop that repackages goods out of sight of customers, or cooks its own food and labels it 'organic', must also have its own licence to do so.

Box Schemes

What is a vegetable box scheme?

Vegetable box schemes have grown rapidly in the last few years and seem to be the fastest growing form of direct market in the country. There are now over 200 certified organic vegetable box schemes operating in the UK. A number of different models exist, but all are based around the central principle of delivering a box of fresh, seasonal organic food either directly to the customers' home or to a central drop off point. The customer pays a standard price for a box. Most schemes are very local. Some are larger businesses buying from wholesalers and delivering more widely, also supplying fruit, dairy produce, meat, wines and wholefoods.

Benefits to consumers

In the face of increasing globalisation of the food industry there has been an enormous amount of public concern about food quality and food production methods. Food scares, genetic engineering, over-processed and over-packaged food—food which travels thousands of miles around the country or globe before it reaches our plates. Box schemes are one type of local food scheme that offer consumers access to fresh, healthy local produce at reasonable prices. What could be more convenient to have a box of seasonal produce delivered to your home or neighbourhood? Customers value the personal contact and receiving vegetables usually picked the same day. They never know exactly what will be in the box and enjoy the element of surprise. Many of them discover the seasonality of British vegetables for the first time.

Benefits to producers

There any many benefits for the producer. Establishing direct contact with customers removes the sense of isolation that is often associated with modern industrial agriculture. Growers can also respond directly to customer requests and there is less wastage because they know what they harvest will be sold. Gone is the heart-break of picking perfect vegetables which must rot because the supermarket has changed its order. There is no need to grade out good food because it doesn't fit the packaging. A secure and loyal market is established and financial returns are increased as the middle-man is cut out. Direct marketing provides producers with an economically and environmentally sustainable business.

Supermarkets

Supermarket chains have responded to growing consumer demand by increasing their ranges and quantities of organic foods. The attitude of each company to selling organic food is very different: some are adopting positive policies to develop their organic ranges, others take a more cautious approach. As a result the experience of shopping organic in a UK supermarket can vary between being confronted with a gratifying range and variety of products and total frustration, even in different branches of the same retailer!

Asda

Asda stocks a growing range of organic foods. In order to expand this range further, they would welcome more feedback from their customers.

The Co-op

The Co-op has a general policy of including organic food in its shops, but their range is quite restricted and fresh produce is not currently stocked in all stores.

Iceland

The first major multiple to ban all GMOs in their own produce, they also market own brand and other branded organic produce.

Marks & Spencer

M&S have recently developed and expanded their organic food range to meet growing customer demand. They now regard organic food as "a major priority for the company".

Safeway

Safeway were the supermarket pioneers in the organic food market, first introducing organic fruit and vegetables in 1981. They are committed to offering a range of staple foods, including fruit, vegetables, dairy products, processed foods and beverages.

Sainsbury's

Sainsbury's have been stocking organic foods since 1985. They are committed to providing their customers with a wide choice of organic food. They are working in partnership with organic producers to extend the range of organic fruit and vegetables grown by UK farmers and to achieve a consistency and continuity of supply.

Tesco

Tesco are keen to make organic food more widely available in their stores. They have stated their commitment to supporting commercial growers who want to convert to organic production, and to increasing their range of organic suppliers.

Waitrose

Waitrose have a positive policy to develop sales of organic food in all areas, based on their perception of the customer demand and also the availability of different products.

LABELLING OF ORGANIC FOOD

Strict EC regulations cover the labelling of organic foods, with the aim of ensuring that consumers are not misled. Natural products such as potatoes and lettuce may only be described as 'Organic' if they have been grown by a registered organic producer; they will probably be labelled 'Organically Grown Lettuce' or just 'Organic Lettuce'. The inspection system for organic producers is covered in the Introduction to this book. Manufactured goods such as bread are covered by the same regulations and will probably be labelled, e.g., 'Bread baked from Organic Flour'. Where it is not possible to manufacture goods from wholly organic ingredients, the manufacturer can use up to 5% non-organic minor ingredients—these are specified in the regulations and are recognised as not being available in sufficient quantities in organic form. So products labelled 'Organic' will be between 95% and 100% organic.

Products containing between 70% and 95% organic ingredients cannot be labelled 'Organic'. These products may use the term 'Organic' only in their ingredients list in descending weight order, e.g. Organically grown wheat (55%), Organically grown barley (15%), Organically grown oats (7%).

Products containing less than 70% organic ingredients may not use the term 'Organic' or any derivative of the term anywhere on the label. Percentages refer to agricultural ingredients; non-agricultural ingredients (e.g. water and salt) are not included in the calculations. No genetically modified or irradiated organisms are allowed in organic food products.

Below are the logos and acronyms of the seven certification bodies (including themselves) that are approved by the United Kingdom Register of Organic Food Standards (UKROFS):

 United Kingdom Register of Organic Food Standards (UKROFS)   UK1

 Organic Farmers and Growers (OF&G)   UK2

 Scottish Organic Producers Association (SOPA)   UK3

 Organic Food Federation (OFF)   UK4

 Soil Association Certification Ltd (SA Cert)   UK5

 BioDynamic Agricultural Association (BDAA)   UK6

 Irish Organic Farmers and Growers Association (IOFGA)   UK7

UKROFS also recognises all other EC certification bodies and a limited number of non-EC certification bodies that have an equivalent standard and inspection system. For all other countries, importers must demonstrate, either to UKROFS or an equivalent body in another EC country, that the food has been produced to equivalent standards and inspection systems in order for them to be allowed to use the term 'Organic' or its derivatives. A list of worldwide organic logos is available from the International Federation of Organic Agricultural Movements (IFOAM)—see under Associations.

HOW TO USE THIS DIRECTORY

The heart of this Directory (pages 18-167) comprises the entries for suppliers of organic goods and services: producers, wholesalers, retailers, bed & breakfast, restaurants & cafés, and garden and farm sundries. This is followed by (pages 168-179) a listing of a wide range of associations working in the field. There is also an alphabetical list of Farmers' Markets . Finally there is an index by name of the companies and organisations listed.

The symbols for the various kind of entries are shown before each company name. Where the company offers several services, the symbol for its primary activity is shown first. Sets of symbols with their meaning are scattered throughout the Directory, depending on the space available, but it may be easier to refer to the enclosed bookmark, or to the front cover.

Please telephone suppliers before making a special journey to visit them! Inevitably, some companies in the Directory will move premises, or even go out of business. The world of organics is changing fast.

There have been changes in recent years as regards the naming of Welsh and Scottish counties. We have used the new (some would say original) Welsh county names in this book, rather than the many unitary authorities as we feel they are irrelevant to this publication. For Scotland, we have used the county names as advised by the Scottish Office.

As with the previous edition, where there is space available we have also inserted some quotations. They are taken from a number of other titles published by Green Books:

Backyard Composting by John Roulac
Biopiracy: The Plunder of Nature and Knowledge by Vandana Shiva
Creating Sustainable Cities by Herbert Girardet (Schumacher Briefing No. 2)
The Ecology of Health by Robin Stott (Schumacher Briefing No. 3)
The Ecology of Money by Richard Douthwaite (Schumacher Briefing No. 4)
Genetic Engineering, Food, and Our Environment by Luke Anderson
No Destination: An Autobiography by Satish Kumar
Off the Map: Around the Dart, Avon and Salcombe-Kingsbridge Estuaries by Jane Fitzgerald
The Organic Baby Book by Tanyia Maxted-Frost
The River's Voice: An Anthology of Poetry edited by Angela King and Susan Clifford
Transforming Economic Life by James Robertson (Schumacher Briefing No. 1)

We hope these quotations will be of interest to users of the Directory.

DISCLAIMER

All the information in this Directory regarding the producers, retailers etc. and the products they grow and sell has been gathered from the entrants themselves, and from information supplied by the Soil Association and the Bio-Dynamic Agricultural Association. We have not verified any claims as to whether any produce described as such is 100% organic. Please note therefore that we cannot be held responsible for any claims made as to the quality of the produce or goods offered. There has recently been a proliferation of 'Green' labelling schemes and we advise you to satisfy yourself as to the validity of any such claims.

BEDFORDSHIRE

A. & D.J. CATLIN
CHURCH FARM, CHURCH LANE,
FLITTON MK45 5EL
Tel & Fax: 01525 861452
Contact: Mr D. Catlin
Producers of high quality vegetables to
wholesale and retail markets. At present we
have 4,000 hectares in conversion to start
production in April 2001. Soil Association
Licence Number G4481.

DAIRYBORN FOODS LTD
DAIRYBORN WAY, EATON GREEN RD.,
LUTON LU2 9XF
Tel: 01582 457979 Fax: 01582 400957
Contact: Billy O'Riordan
Soil Association organic standard licence no.
P4450. Cheese products for food
manufacturers.

DIVINE WINES
PO BOX 6059,
LEIGHTON BUZZARD LU7 8ZN
Tel & Fax: 01525 218100
Contact: Julie Pearson (MD)
Email: drink@divinewines.co.uk
Website: www.divinewines.co.uk
Selling a full range of organic wines, beers,
spirits and cordials. Suppliers to the trade
and by mail order. All products are 100%
organic. Free brochure, online ordering,
delivery UK-wide, friendly efficient service.
Local postcode delivery areas: LU, MK, HP.
See display ad.

EARTHWISE BABY
ASPLEY DISTRIBUTION LTD, PO BOX 1708,
ASPLEY GUISE, MILTON KEYNES MK17 8YA
Tel: 01908 585769 Fax: 01908 585771
Contact: S. Erlick
Email: sales@earthwisebaby.com
Website: www.earthwisebaby.com
Natural parenting, re-usable nappies and
sanitary pads.

JOHN HARE LIMITED
HENLOW MILLS, HENLOW SG16 6AJ
Tel: 01462 816188 Fax: 01462 815466
Contact: Jess Anderson
Email: jh@johnhare.com
Website: johnhare.com
Specialist miller producing bakery and
food ingredients including flours, flakes,
cut grains from malted and non-malted
cereals, seeds and pulses. Soil Association
P1846.

W. JORDANS (CEREALS) LTD

HOLME MILLS, BIGGLESWADE SG18 9JY
Tel: 01767 318222 Fax: 01767 600695
Contact: Philip O'Leary
Website: www.jordanscereals.co.uk
Soil Association accredited, family owned
business since 1855 producing a range of
standard and organic materials. Delivery
worldwide.

SHERRY'S HEALTH FOODS
58 HIGH ST., BIGGLESWADE SG18 0LJ
Tel: 01767 220020
Contact: Christine Soulsby
Email: sheradbrit@aol.co.uk
Health food shop with wide range of
organic foods, vitamins & mineral
supplements, herbs, homeopathy,
aromatherapy.

WHOLEFOODS & HEALTH (BEDFORD)
1 THURLOW ST. (BUS STATION SQUARE),
BEDFORD MK40 1LR
Tel: 01234 219618 Fax: 01234 213929
Contact: Paul Martin (Owner)
Well established family-run health food
shop specialising in a range of quality
products including natural foods, herbs
and spices, special dietary products,
organic foods, vitamin and mineral
supplements, herbal remedies, sports
nutrition and aromatherapy oils.

BERKSHIRE

 BROCKHILL FARM
ORGANIC SHOP
BROCKHILL FARM, WARFIELD,
BRACKNELL RG42 6JU
Tel & Fax: 01344 882643
Contact: Silvana Keen
Over 1200 lines of organic food in stock all
at competitive prices. Fresh fruit and
vegetables, fish, meat, poultry, dairy
produce, bread, cakes, groceries, snacks,
wine, beer and much more.

DOVES FARM FOODS LTD
SALISBURY RD., HUNGERFORD RG17 0RF
Tel: 01488 684880 Fax: 01488 688235
Contact: Clare Marriage
Email: mail@dovesfarm.co.uk
Website: www.dovesfarm.co.uk
Established in 1978, well known
manufacturer of organic cereal-based foods
including breakfast cereals, home baking
flours, sweet and savoury biscuits, bread
and cakes. Soil Association certified UK5.

   ELLIS ORGANICS
5 LEA RD., SONNING COMMON,
READING RG4 9LH
Tel & Fax: 0118 972 2826
Contact: Aidan Carlisle
Email: ellis-organics@clara-net
Website: www.eatorganic.co.uk
Full range of organic foods: fruit, veg,
breads, wholefoods, meat, poultry etc. Visit
website to see our current range. Soil Assn.
certified (E06S + RE06S). Delivery to most
RG post codes, also S.

  MR & MRS K. FORDER
HOLME DENE FARM, CRAVEN ROAD,
INKPEN, HUNGERFORD RG17 9DX
Tel: 01488 668664 Fax: 01488 668664
Contact: Mrs K. Forder
Email: kevin@holmedene.freeserve.co.uk
Small organic beef herd, member of the
Soil Association.

GARLANDS ORGANIC FARM SHOP
GARDENERS LANE,
UPPER BASILDON RG8 8NP
Tel: 01491 671556 Fax: 01491 671999
Contact: Gabriel Hutchings
Soil Association retailer and grower (no.
G1619). Complete farmshop/grocer. Fresh
produce grown on site, meat, dairy, gluten
and dairy alternatives, alcohol, wholefoods.
Delivery service—call for details.

   THE KULIKA
CHARITABLE TRUST
WARREN FARM, RECTORY RD.,
STREATLEY RG8 9QE
Tel: 01491 872149 Fax: 01491 873719
Contact: Alastair Taylor
Organic smallholding with various livestock
and vegetables. Training centre teaching
sustainable agriculture to African students.
Box scheme available in immediate area,
visitors welcome. Members of Soil
Association and WWOOF.

THE ORGANIC BEEF CO
THE OLD CRAVEN ARMS, INKPEN,
HUNGERFORD RG17 9DY
Tel & Fax: 01488 668429
Contact: Bernard Harris (Partner)
Email:
enquiries@theswaninn-organics.co.uk
Website: www.theswaninn-organics.co.uk
Organic BSE-free beef supplied to the
Organic Beef Company and butchered,
packed and labelled for direct sale to
public from farm shop at The Swan Inn
(see below).

RANGER CHICKENS LTD
HOLMES OAK FARM, COLLINS END,
GORING HEATH, READING RG8 7RJ
Tel: 01491 682568 Fax: 01491 681694
Contact: Theresa Whittle
Email: RangerChickens@virgin.net
Soil Association registered (no. G2549).
Organic Food Award winner (poultry) in
1999. Gourmet chickens and geese.
Producer of organic cordials, blackcurrant,
lime, orange, lemon and ginger.

SHEEPDROVE ORGANIC FARM
WARREN FARM, SHEEPDROVE,
LAMBOURN, HUNGERFORD RG17 7UU
Tel: 01488 71659 Fax: 01488 72677
Contact: Peter Molesworth
Email: manager@sheepdrove.com
Website: www.sheepdrove.com
See display ad.

THE SWAN INN
CRAVEN RD., INKPEN,
HUNGERFORD RG17 9DX
Tel: 01488 668326 Fax: 01488 668429
Contact: Mary Harris
The Swan Inn Bar and Restaurant menus
are almost 100% organical. Beef is a
speciality. The organic farm shop and
butchery sells over 1000 certified organic
lines: all meats, dairy, dry goods wines,
vegetables. Soil Association G887.

VINTAGE ROOTS LTD
FARLEY FARMS, BRIDGE FARM,
READING RD., ARBORFIELD RG2 9HT
Tel: 0118 976 1999 Fax: 0118 976 1998
Contact: Neil Palmer
Email: info@vintageroots.co.uk
Website: www.vintageroots.co.uk
Huge range of organic wines, beers, spirits,
ciders and juices from around the world,
all available by mail order. 100% organic—
contact the specialists for a free list. Trade
enquiries also welcome. See display ad.

WALTHAM PLACE FARM
CHURCH HILL, WHITE WALTHAM,
MAIDENHEAD SL6 3JH
Tel: 01628 825517 Fax: 01628 825045
Contact: John Healy
Soil Association (no. G557) since 1989.
Shop sells farm's own produce: beef, pork,
lamb, eggs, dairy produce, baked goods,
vegetables, jams, chutneys and more!
Friday 1.30-5.00, Saturday 10.00-1.00.

WILTON HOUSE
33 HIGH STREET,
HUNGERFORD RG17 0NF
Tel: 01488 684228 Fax: 01488 685037
Email: welfares@hotmail.com
Bed and breakfast in elegant listed 15th
century town house full of history—
flagstones, panelled rooms, period
furniture, attractive en suite bedrooms.
Delicious organic English breakfast. Three
miles M4, Heathrow one hour.

WISTBRAY LTD
PO BOX 125, NEWBURY RG20 9LY
Tel: 01635 278648 Fax: 01635 278672
Contact: Kate Gallop
Email: wistbray@dial.pipex.com
Website: www.rooiboschtea.com
We import Organic Eleven O'Clock
Rooibos Tea: caffeine-free, low tannin and
high in antioxidants. Available in all good
health food shops, speciality stores
including Holland and Barrett, Health and
Diet Centres and GNC. See display ad.

Genetically engineered foods have the
potential of introducing new allergies.
They also carry the risk of 'biological
pollution', of new vulnerability to
disease, of one species becoming
dominant in an ecosystem, and of
gene transfer from one species to
another.

Vandana Shiva, *Biopiracy* (1998)

BRISTOL COUNTY BOROUGH

  BART SPICES LTD

YORK ROAD, BRISTOL BS3 4AD
Tel: 0117 977 3474 Fax: 0117 972 0216
Contact: Robert Sanders
Email: robertsanders@bartspices.com
Website: www.bartspices.com
Bart Spices produces a range of organic herbs and spices destined for multiple retailers. We also sell bulk organic herbs and spices to other food manufactureres. Bart Spices is a member of the Soil Association.

THE BETTER FOOD CO

UNIT 1, WALLIS ESTATE, MINA ROAD, BRISTOL BS2 9YW
Tel: 0117 904 1191 Fax: 0117 904 1190
Contact: Phil Houghton
Email: betterfood@compuserve.com
Website: www.betterfood.co.uk
Soil Association certified. Personal home delivery service. Fruit, vegetables, meat, dairy, alcohol, dry foods, fine foods, household products. Delivery to the following areas: BS1-BS48, BA1-BA6, SN14-16 and GL..

THE ESSENTIAL TRADING CO-OPERATIVE LTD

UNIT 3, LODGE CAUSEWAY TRADING ESTATE, FISHPONDS, BRISTOL BS16 3JB
Tel & Fax: 0117 958 3550
Over 5500 vegetarian lines, unrivalled organic choice, working towards a company free of genetically modified food. Free trade catalogue available.

THE GREEN WHEEL

45 SHERBOURNE ST., ST. GEORGE, BRISTOL BS5 8EQ
Tel & Fax: 0117 955 9264
Contact: Billie Lane
We deliver to households in the Bristol area: two sizes of nets of organic vegetables, two sizes of bags of organic fruit, plus organic free range eggs . We aim to provide produce that is fresh and locally grown.

HARVEST NATURAL FOODS

224 CHELTENHAM RD., BRISTOL BS6 5QU
Tel: 0117 942 5997
Contact: Andy Billington (Manager)
We are a wholefood retailer specialising in organic and fair traded goods, including fresh produce, chocolate, ice cream, tea, coffee and the usual staples.

JEKKA'S HERB FARM

ROSE COTTAGE, SHELLARDS LANE, ALVESTON, BRISTOL BS35 3SY
Tel: 01454 418878 Fax: 01454 411988
Contact: Jekka McVicar
Email: farm@jekkasherb.demon.co.uk
Website: www.jekkasherbfarm.co
This farm grows over 350 different varieties of herb; also native wild flowers and vegetable plants. The transplants are grown to Soil Association Standards. The herb displays have won RHS Gold Medals at the Chelsea Flower Show in 1995, 1996, 1997 and 1999.

Hundreds of man-made toxic chemicals—many of them from food—have been found in human breastmilk samples around the world, and some breastfed babies in the UK are getting over forty times the 'acceptable' dose of some of them. The effects of these persistent, non-biodegradable chemicals on tiny foetuses and embryos in the womb is expected to be even worse—especially at key developmental stages.

Tanyia Maxted-Frost, *The Organic Baby Book* (1999)

LEARY'S ORGANIC SEED POTATOES

11 CALEDONIA PLACE, CLIFTON,
BRISTOL BS8 4DJ
Tel: 0117 923 8940 Fax: 0117 973 5158
Contact: Laurence Hasson (Proprietor)
Email: lhasson@bigfoot.com
Website: www.organicpotatoes.co.uk
Grower and supplier of organic seed
potatoes, eating potatoes, organic onion,
shallot and garlic sets. Sell mainly to
farmers, growers and by mail order.

NEAL'S YARD REMEDIES

126 WHITELADIES RD., CLIFTON,
BRISTOL BS8 2RP
Tel & Fax: 0117 946 6034
Contact: Graham Ibell
Stockists of a wide variety of natural
remedies and cosmetics. Many certified
organic, including herbs and tinctures,
homeopathic and flower remedies, e.g.,
essential oils, bath and body products,
massage oils and books.

R & B (BRISTOL) LTD

UNIT 4, BRISTOL DISTRIBUTION PARK,
HAWKLEY DRIVE, BRADLEY STOKE,
BRISTOL BS32 0BF
Tel: 01454 456700 Fax: 01454 456 710
Contact: Peter Wallis
Email: peterwallis@hwrm.com
We are a Soil Association certified site
(P2492), and produce organic pasta sauces
for retail.

RADFORD MILL

41 PICTON STREET, MONTPELIER,
BRISTOL BS6 5PZ
Tel: 0117 924 5360
Stockists of a wide variety of organic
produce including fruits, vegetables, eggs,
meats and wholefoods, along with home
made vegan take-aways. Market stall at
Bristol Farmers' Market every Wednesday.

STONEGROUND

5 THE MALL, CLIFTON, BRISTOL BS8 4DP
Tel: 0117 9741260
Veggie, GM-free shop stuffed with pulses,
cereals and soya, plus 200 organic delights
and award winning fresh bread. Excellent
organic, veggie wines and beers. Also
vitamins and supplements, homeopathic
and herbal remedies.

WILD OATS NATURAL FOODS

9-11 LOWER REDLAND ROAD, REDLAND,
BRISTOL BS6 6TB
Tel: 0117 973 1967 Fax: 0117 923 7871
Contact: Mike Abrahams
Email: info@wildoats.force9.co.uk
Organic and natural foods, groceries, plus
skincare, books, natural medicines, food
supplements and aromatherapy. We sell
over 4500 lines.

WINDMILL HILL CITY FARM SHOP

PHILIP STREET, BEDMINSTER,
BRISTOL BS3 4EA
Tel: 0117 963 3233 Fax: 0117 963 3252
Contact: John Purkiss
Email: info@windmillhillcityfarm.org.uk
Website: www.windmillhillcityfarm.org.uk
We sell locally produced food including
organic meat, free-range eggs, goat's milk,
and vegetables grown by organic methods
on our inner-city farm. Open Tuesday to
Saturday, 10am to 5pm.

In 1997 the British Agrochemical
Association predicted that the sales of
herbicide in the US would actually
benefit from the expanded use of
transgenic herbicide-resistant crops.

Luke Anderson, *Genetic Engineering,
Food, and Our Environment* (1999)

BUCKINGHAMSHIRE

CAPESPAN INTERNATIONAL PLC
FARNHAM HOUSE,
FARNHAM ROYAL SL2 3RQ
Tel: 01753 817917 Fax: 01753 736720
Contact: Lucy Crawford (Mrs)
Email: crawfol@capespan.co.uk
Website: http://172.16.12.16/
Member of Soil Association (UK-P4128).
We import fruit from around the world and
market it in Europe.

   FULLER'S
PURVEYORS OF FINE ORGANIC PRODUCE
MANOR FARM, BEACHAMPTON,
MILTON KEYNES MK19 6DT
Tel: 01908 269868 Fax: 01908 262285
Contact: George Fuller
Lamb, pork, beef, vegetables and soft
fruit. Soon opening a smokehouse, curing
room and commercial kitchen for
manufacture of pork pies etc. OF&G
registered. See display ad.

GREAT HUNDRIDGE MANOR FARM
THE ESTATE OFFICE, GREAT HUNDRIDGE
MANOR, GREAT MISSENDEN HP16 0RN
TeL: 01494 794551 Fax: 01494 794552
Contact: C. Mullins
Farm producing mainly organic arable
crops. Registered with the Soil Association,
Licence no. G2520.

  HEALTHRIGHT
27 HIGH ST., CHESHAM HP5 1BG
Tel: 01494 771267
Contact: Mrs T. Oliver (Manager)
Member of Soil Association. We stock a
variety of organic products including dried
fruits, bread, cakes, cereals, rice, soya milk,
lentils, millet and soy sauce.
Also at 48c FRIARS SQUARE,
AYLESBURY HP20 2SP
Tel: 01296 397022 Contact: Roger Oliver

 ONLY NATURAL
41 ST. PETERS COURT,
CHALFONT ST. PETER SL9 9QQ
Tel: 01753 889441 Contact: Mrs Sachdev
Small volume of pre-packed organic
products, including frozen organic ready
meals.

ORGANIC & FRESH LTD
296 WATERSIDE, CHESHAM HP5 1PY
Tel: 0800 0962897
Fax: 01494 582642
Contact: Simon Kitchener
Soil Association no. P4743. We provide a
box scheme service to Herts, Bucks, Oxon,
Berks and NW London. We are also a
wholesale supplier to independent
retailers, hospitals and children's day care
facilities.

ORGANIC CONCENTRATES LTD
3 BROADWAY COURT, CHESHAM HP5 1EN
Tel: 01494 792229 Fax: 01494 792199
Contact: Chris Green
Email: organic6x@6-x.co.uk
Website: www.6-x.co.uk
The production and sale to garden
centres/gardeners of '6x' organic fertiliser
and associated products.

 ORGANIC TRAIL
10 ST PAUL'S COURT, STONY STRATFORD,
MILTON KEYNES MK11 1LJ
Tel & Fax: 01908 568952
Contact: Jim Lawlor (Proprietor)
Email: jim@organictrail.freeserve.co.uk
Website: www.organictrail.freeserve.co.uk
Box scheme delivering fresh harvested
produce from local farms to the Milton
Keynes, Towcester, Olney, Buckingham and
Leighton Buzzard areas. A nationwide
service (next day delivery) is also available.

REDFIELD COMMUNITY
BUCKINGHAM RD., WINSLOW MK18 3LZ
Tel: 01296 713661 Fax: 01296 714983
Contact: Chris Reid (Secretary)
Email:
redfield_community@compuserve.com
Website:
ourworld.compuserve.com/homepages/
   redfield_community/redhome/htm
Intentional community in its 21st year,
which includes a 17-acre organic
smallholding. We hold regular events on
communities and co-operative living. See
display ad.

**THE SUSTAINABLE LIFESTYLES
RESEARCH CO-OP LTD**
POND COTTAGE EAST,
CUDDINGTON RD., DINTON HP18 0AD
Tel: 01296 747737 Fax: 01296 748278
Contact: Mike George
Email: mike.george@euphony.net
70-acre permaculture farm run by a
workers co-op. Organic box scheme, free
range eggs, subscription livestock,
community orchard, public access and
involvement. Developing eco-housing,
craft workshops, education facilities,
permanent wetlands alongside river
Thamé.

Sustainable agriculture is based on the recycling of soil nutrients. This involves returning to the soil part of the nutrients that come from it and support plant growth. The maintenance of the nutrient cycle, and through it the fertility of the soil, is based on an inviolable law of return that recognizes the earth as the source of fertility. The Green Revolution paradigm of agriculture substituted the regenerative nutrient cycle with linear flows of purchased inputs of chemical fertilizers from factories and marketed outputs of agricultural commodities. Fertility was no longer the property of soil, but of chemicals. The Green Revolution was essentially based on miracle seeds that needed chemical fertilizers and did not produce plant outputs for returning to the soil. The earth was again viewed as an empty vessel, this time for holding intensive inputs of irrigated water and chemical fertilizers. The activity lay in the miracle seeds, which transcended nature's fertility cycles.

Vandana Shiva, *Biopiracy* (1998)

To persuade people to give up suburbs and their quasi-rural ambience, they have to be offered urban qualities that are absent in sprawling cities: vitality, diversity, options for a wide mix of activities, social amenities and cultural facilities.

Herbert Girardet, *Creating Sustainable Cities* (1999)

An effective bait for trying to get those crabs and shrimps out from under the rocks in the human hand. Put your hand in the water, be very still and patient and wait. Soon, the curious inhabitants will venture out to investigate and feed off those delicious dead skin cells on your hand.

Jane Fitzgerald, *Off the Map* (2000)

CAMBRIDGESHIRE

 BARLOWS

UNIT 1 FENGATE, PETERBOROUGH PE1 5XB
Tel: 01733 315007 Fax: 01733 343804
Contact: Keith Mawson
Produce merchants and pre-packers
specialising in potatoes. Certified by the
Soil Association (licence no. P2103).
for packing and pre-packing of vegetables.

RUSSELL BURGESS LTD

STANLEY'S FARM, GREAT DROVE,
YAXLEY PE7 3TW
Tel: 01733 240253 Fax: 01733 243214
Contact: Andrew Burgess
Email: andrewb@burgess.co.uk
Soil Assn. registered, we are growers and
packers of root vegetables for large volume
retail and processing outlets.

 DAILY BREAD
CO-OPERATIVE (CAMBRIDGE) LTD

UNIT 3, KILMAINE CLOSE,
CAMBRIDGE CB4 2PH
Tel: 01223 423177 Fax: 01223 425858
Contact: Andrew Hibbert (Manager)
We retail and wholesale wholefoods with a
good and increasing range of organic
flours, grains, cereals, pulses, fruit and
vegetables.

DELFLAND NURSERIES LTD

BENWICK ROAD, DODDINGTON,
MARCH PE15 0TU
Tel: 01354 740553 Fax: 01354 741200
Contact: Jill Vaughan
Email: delfland@ndirect.co.uk
Website: www.delfland.co.uk
Soil Association no. G2428. All kinds of
outdoor vegetables, herbs and glasshouse
salad plants in plastic cell trays and semi-
discrete blocks. Also organic onion sets.
Deliveries made all over the UK. See
display ad.

G'S MARKETING LTD

BARWAY, ELY CB7 5TZ
Tel: 01353 727200 Fax: 01353 723021
Contact: Rowen Markie
(Organic Product Manager)
Email: rowen.markie@gs-marketing.com
Website: www.gs-marketing.com
Established organic suppliers of a wide
range of fresh and processed salads and
vegetables to the multiples. Organic
producers (2001), currently working
closely with organic growers. Strengths
include a strong procurement, technical
and marketing team.

NATURALLY YOURS

THE HORSE AND GATE, WITCHAM TOLL,
ELY CB6 2AB
Tel: 01353 778723
Contact: R.A. Finn (Partner)
Soil Assn. Reg. Nos. G1919 and P1919. All
livestock is raised out of doors and fed
cereal-based diets without growth
promoters, antibiotics or animal waste. The
majority are rare or old fashioned breeds
which mature slowly. A small
slaughterhouse is used and the meat is
properly hung. A full range of meat, home
cured and smoked bacon and wide
selection of sausages; also organic
groceries, fruit and veg. Free delivery
service in our own refrigerated vans direct
to the customer's door. Box scheme.

NORGROW INTERNATIONAL LTD

GRANGE FARM LODGE, LEVERINGTON
COMMON, WISBECH PE13 5JG
Tel: 01945 410810 Fax: 01945 410850
Contact: Henri Rosenthal
Email: sales@norgrow.com
Website: www.norgrow.com
Soil Association no. P2665. See our full
company details on our website, and see
display ad.

 **PETERBOROUGH HEALTH FOOD CENTRE**

25 THE ARCADE, WESTGATE,
PETERBOROUGH PE1 1PZ
Tel & Fax: 01733 566807
Contact: H. Walji (Partner)
Email: baaiw@mcmail.com
We stock organic beans and pulses, dried fruit, teas, honey, cooking oils, juices, cereals, flour, chocolate and soya milk.

 RUSSELL SMITH FARMS

COLLEGE FARM, GRANGE ROAD,
DUXFORD, CAMBRIDGE CB2 4QF
Tel: 01223 839002 Fax: 01223 837874
Contact: Andrew Nottage
Email: rsmithfarms@farmline.com
Arable and field scale vegetables—producer. Soil Association licence no. G2440.

 S PA FARM WHOLEFOODS

SPA FARM, APETHORPE,
PETERBOROUGH PE8 5DD
Tel: 01780 470250 Fax: 01780 470252
Contact: Liz Ogilvie-Davis
Email: spafarm@aol.com
Demeter certified farmers (UK6 no. 287) producing vegetables, fruit, meat and poultry. Box scheme (20 mile radius) with full organic grocery selection (over 500 lines) including, wines, beers and spirits.

 WATERLAND ORGANICS

QUAYSTONE COTTAGE, THE HYTHE,
REACH CB5 0JQ
Tel: 01638 741426 Fax: 01638 741426
Contact: Paul Robinson
Member of Soil Association (G1709). Run local box scheme around Cambridge. Supply local shops and restaurants with fruit and vegetables. Mail order strawberry and soft fruit bushes.

Crop plants are now being genetically engineered to produce pharmaceuticals and industrial chemicals. These plants could cross-pollinate with related species and contaminate the food supply, and could expose foraging animals, insects and seed-eating birds to a wide range of drugs, vacinations and chemicals. Unfortunately, in the 1995 joint consultation between the World Health Organisation and Food & Agriculture Organisation on the safety issues raised by genetic engineering, the potential dangers posed by these crops were judged to be "unrelated to food safety", and therefore outside the remit of the consultation.

Luke Anderson, *Genetic Engineering, Food, and Our Environment* (1999)

Key

Producers	Wholesalers	Import/Export
Retailers	Mail Order	Restaurants	Day Visits/B&B
Farm Gate Sales	Box Schemes/ Delivery Service	Garden/Farm Sundries	Manufacturers & Processors

CHANNEL ISLANDS

GRASS ROOTS ORGANIC
GREENACRES FARM, SION, ST. HELIER,
JERSEY JE2 3FL
Tel: 01534 865303 Contact: Brian Adair
Organic market garden.

  LA HOUGUE FARM
LA HOUGUE FARM, LA GRANDE ROUTE DE
ST. PIERRE, ST. PETER, JERSEY JE3 7AX
Tel: 01534 482116 Fax: 01534 483416
Contact: K. Le Feuvre
Email: lahougue@ukonline.co.uk
Producer of organic vegetables. Retail shop
includes large grocery range, organic
cheese and yoghurts, and organic meat to
order. Deliveries available. Soil Association
G2579.

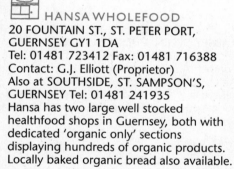

GUERNSEY ORGANIC GROWERS
LA MARCHERIE, RUETTE RABEY,
ST. MARTIN'S, GUERNSEY GY4 6DU
Tel: 01481 237547 Fax: 01481 233045
Contact: Anne Sandwith or Jeremy Clegg
Soil Association certified (G1000). We
grow over 50 different varieties of fruit and
vegetables and have run a box scheme/
delivery service for 6 years, with over 100
customers.

  THE ORGANIC SHOP
68 STOPFORD RD., ST. HELIER,
JERSEY JE2 4LZ
Tel: 01534 789322
Contact: Graham Falle (Proprietor)
Good range of groceries, wines, toiletries,
herbs and spices, bread, fruit and veg,
dairy products. Also offer island-wide
delivery service.

  HANSA WHOLEFOOD
20 FOUNTAIN ST., ST. PETER PORT,
GUERNSEY GY1 1DA
Tel: 01481 723412 Fax: 01481 716388
Contact: G.J. Elliott (Proprietor)
Also at SOUTHSIDE, ST. SAMPSON'S,
GUERNSEY Tel: 01481 241935
Hansa has two large well stocked
healthfood shops in Guernsey, both with
dedicated 'organic only' sections
displaying hundreds of organic products.
Locally baked organic bread also available.

RIVERSIDE VINERIES LT D
ROBERGERIE FARM, ST. SAMPONS,
GUERNSEY GY2 4NG
Tel: 01481 49293 Fax: 01481 45166
Contact: Roger Higgs
We are in our second year of conversion.
Six acres of glass growing mainly cherry
tomatoes. Soil Association licence no.
G2996.

  LA FRUITIERE
1-6 BERESFORD MARKET, ST HELIER,
JERSEY JE2 4WX
Tel: 01534 720052 Fax: 01534 507945
Contact: Brian Langdon
We are a grocery shop selling a
comprehensive range of organic produce
including vegetables, fruit, eggs, pasta,
pulses and snacks.

> Sustainable development at the local
> level must be implemented in a
> holistic process which inspires city
> people and which gives them a sense
> of ownership and direct involvement.
>
> Herbert Girardet,
> *Creating Sustainable Cities* (1999)

CHESHIRE

  ALEMBIC PRODUCTS LTD
UNIT 2, BRYMAU ESTATE, RIVER LANE,
SALTNEY, CHESTER CH4 8RQ
Tel: 01244 680147 Fax: 01244 680155
Contact: Andrew Robinson
Email: andrew@alembicproducts.co.uk
Website: www.alembicproducts.co.uk
Soil Association licensed (no P2978)
manufacturer of pasta dressing, full fat
mayonnaise, tomato ketchup, yoghurt
dressing, full fat seasoned mayonnaise,
coleslaw, oil-free dressing.

  ASHFIELD ORGANIC FARM
ASHFIELD FARM, CHESTER HIGH ROAD,
NESTON CH64 3RY
Tel: 0151 356 8788
Website: www.ashfieldfarm.8m.com
Farm shop selling solely organic produce
including potatoes, vegetables, fruit,
wholefoods and some dairy products. 10%
discount for subscribing Friends of Ashfield
Farm. Open Thursdays p.m., Fridays &
Saturdays a.m. Soil Association G4214.

BOOTHS SUPERMARKETS
STANLEY ROAD, KNUTSFORD WA16 0BS
Tel: 01565 652522 Fax: 01565 652504
Contact: Mr Matthews
Supermarket with broad range of organic
food, clearly labelled in store. Fresh
produce, meat, dairy, Village Bakery
products, and many other groceries.

THE CHEESE SHOP
116 NORTHGATE STREET,
CHESTER CH1 2HT
Tel: 01244 346240 Fax: 01244 314651
Contact: Carole Faulkner
Cheese, wine, chutneys, biscuits, eggs,
flour—we try to promote organic produce
as I believe in it. We use organic produce
in our restaurant (Elliott's—see next
column).

DEER PARK FARM
FORTY ACRES LANE, KERMINGHAM,
HOLMES CHAPEL, CREWE CW4 8DX
Tel: 01477 532188 Fax: 01477 571512
Contact: Martin Steer
Email: martin.steer@lineone.net
Soil Association registered.

DEMETER
12 WELLES ST., SANDBACH CW11 1GT
Tel: 01270 760445
Contact: Phillip Shallcross
Email: phillipdemeter@cs.com
A shop full of organic grains, flakes, fruits,
nuts, honey, yoghurts, cheese, snacks and
sometimes vegetables. Also essential oils,
selected supplements (Solgar etc), books,
cards and prints (Woodmanstern, Prime
Arts).

ELLIOTT'S RESTAURANT
2 ABBEY GREEN, CHESTER CH1 2JH
Tel: 01244 329932 Fax: 01244 314651
Contact: Ann Faulkner
We try to promote organic produce as I
believe in it. We use organic produce in
our restaurant. (See also The Cheese Shop
above.)

J. F. ERLAM
SUGARBROOK FARM, MOBBERLEY ROAD,
ASHLEY, NR. ALTRINCHAM WA14 3QB
Tel: 0161 928 0879
Soil Association producer (no. G4603). In
conversion year two, producing cereals,
beans, potatoes and lamb.

GOODLIFE FOODS LTD
34 TATTON COURT, KINGSLAND
GRANGE, WARRINGTON WA1 4FF
Tel: 01925 837810 Fax: 01925 838648
Contact: Fran Sawyer
Website: www.goodlife.co.uk
Manufacturer of frozen vegetarian foods.
Soil Association certified (no. P2241). See
display ad.

THE GREEN GOURMET

PO BOX 25, CONGLETON CW12 4FG
Tel: 01477 500703/697
Fax: 01477 500703 Contact: June Hales
Email: ggfood@aol.com
Website: www.greengourmet.com
Organic vegetarian hampers and gift boxes by mail order and through local farm gate sales. Member of Soil Association and Vegetarian Society. Delivery to UK and Ireland, have secure ordering facility on website. All organic: alcohol, non alcohol, cakes, chocolates, biscuits, cheese, preserves.

LES JARDINIERS DU TERROIR

4 HOLLINS GREEN, BRADWALL,
MIDDLEWICH CW10 0LA
Tel: 01270 764 960 Fax: 01270 764 960
Contact: Richard Smedley Dip.Hort.(Kew), MI Hort.
Email: info@lesjardiniersduterroir.org.uk
Website: www.lesjardiniersduterroir.org.uk
Organic and permaculture design and consultancy service. Involved in writing and lecturing on organic gardening, edible landscaping and garden history. Organic vegetable box scheme. Delivery to CW 10-12.

OAKCROFT ORGANIC GARDENS

OAK CROFT, CROSS 'O' THE HILL,
MALPAS SY14 8DH
Tel: 01948 860213
Contact: Ms M.S. Fardoonji
Soil Association certified (F08M). Grow large variety of veg and soft fruit, but also offer fruit not grown, bread, cheese and eggs. All 100% organic. Delivery to CW5, SY14, CW8, CW4, CH3 and WA1.

ONLY NATURAL

10 TIME SQUARE, WARRINGTON,
Tel: 01925 444885
Contact: Mrs B Arrowsmith
Healthfood shop stocking wide range of organic foods.

THE ORGANIC SHOP

64 CHESTERGATE, MACCLESFIELD SK11 6DY
Tel & Fax: 01625 503466 Contact: B Eadie
Wide range of organic fruit, vegetables, meat, fish, wholefoods, dairy, wine, beer, toiletries, cleaning products, garden sundries, clothing. Soil Association R1985, member of the Organic Retail Guild.

THE ORGANIC SHOP (ONLINE) LTD

CENTRAL CHAMBERS, LONDON RD.,
ALDERLEY EDGE SK9 7DZ
Tel: 0845 674 4000 Fax: 0845 674 1000
Email: info@theorganicshop.co.uk
Website: theorganicshop.co.uk
Have a healthy environmentally friendly lifestyle delivered to your door! Choose from over 900 organic products including fresh fruit and vegetables, meat and poultry, groceries, dairy, wines and beers. Approved by *Which?* and the Soil Association. See display ad.

THE ORGANIC STORES

BROOKLYN FARM, SEALAND ROAD,
CHESTER CH5 2LQ
Tel & Fax: 01352 740075
Retailers of organic fruit, vegetables, fish, poultry, meats, pies and cakes. We also have a dietary consultancy service. Free home delivery service to order. Facility for prepared vegetables.

ORGANIC WAREHOUSE LTD

BANK FARM, SEALAND ROAD,
CHESTER CH1 6BS
Tel: 01244 398486
Fax: 01244 398484/485
Contact: George Pithers
Email: orgwh@aol.com
Website: fresh-foods.co.uk
Members of the Soil Association and OF&G. Deliver to CH and LL postcodes, Cheshire and North Wales.

RAVENS OAK DAIRY
BURLAND FARM, WREXHAM ROAD,
BURLAND, NANTWICH CW5 8NO
Tel: 01270 524624/524210
Fax: 01270 524724
Contact: Sandra Allwood
Fresh and soft Brie-type cheeses made
from farm's own milk, organic from July
2000. Shop stocking wide range of organic
goods opening end April 2000. Farm
grown veg. Soil Assn. member. Fruit, veg,
bread, dairy, eggs, wholefoods, meat &
poultry. Specialist cheeses.

 UNITED SNACKS LTD
GOLD TRIANGLE, HARRISON ST.,
WIDNES WA8 8TN
Tel: 0151 420 1144 Fax: 0151 424 5454
Contact: D. Visko
Manufacturers of organic potato crisps and
extruded maize products for snack foods.
Registered with the Soil Association (no.
P2543).

UNIVERSAL INGREDIENTS LTD
UNITS 10-15, MEADOW LANE,
MEADOW LANE INDUSTRIAL ESTATE,
ELLESMERE PORT CH65 4TY
Tel: 0151 357 2655 Fax: 0151 355 0299
Contact: Graeme Hartley
Manufacturer of organic flavourings for the
snack food industry. Member of the Soil
Association (no. P2746).

H.J. UREN & SONS LTD
WOODPARK, NESTON,
SOUTH WIRRAL CH64 7TB
Tel: 0151 353 0330
Fax: 0151 353 0251/1938
Email: james.uren@uren.co.uk
Website: www.uren.com
Importers, processors, repackers and
distributors of organic ingredients for the
food industry in the UK and EEC. Factory in
Poland certified by BCS and factory in UK
certified by Soil Association. Deliver
throughout UK and Ireland. See display ad.

At the social level, the values of biodiversity in different cultural contexts need to
be recognized. Sacred groves, sacred seeds, and sacred species have been the cultural
means for treating biodiversity as inviolable, and present us with the best examples
of conservation. Community rights to biodiversity, and farmers' and indigenous
peoples' contributions to the evolution and protection of biodiversity, also need to
be recognized by treating their knowledge systems as futuristic, not primitive. In
addition, we need to recognize that non-market values, such as providing meaning
and sustenance, should not be treated as secondary to market values.

Vandana Shiva, *Biopiracy* (1998)

Key

 Producers

 Wholesalers

 Import/Export

 Retailers

 Mail Order

 Restaurants

 Day Visits/B&B

 Farm Gate Sales

 Box Schemes/ Delivery Service

 Garden/Farm Sundries

 Manufacturers & Processors

CORNWALL

A & N HEALTH FOODS
62 FORE ST., SALTASH PL12 6JW
Tel: 01752 844926 Contact: L. Law
Wholefoods and organics, veggie box
scheme, herbal and homeopathic
remedies, vitamin supplements, mail order
service.

BOSWEDNACK MANOR
ZENNOR, ST. IVES TR26 3DD
Tel: 01736 794183
Vegetarian B&B and self-catering cottage
in wonderful West Cornwall. Meditation
room, occasional retreats, organic garden
and meadows, sea sunsets, guided wildlife
walks. Organic produce used when
available.

THE BRANTUB
7 MARKET HOUSE ARCADE,
BODMIN PL31 2JA
Tel: 01208 76625 Contact:Tony Jennings
Fresh vegetables, pulses, flour. Delivery to
PL23 & PL31.

MICHAEL & MARIANNE BROOKMAN
JOPES PARK, LUCKETT,
CALLINGTON PL17 8LG
Tel: 01579 370770 or 370807
Fax: 01579 370807 Contact: Michael
Email: natpartner@aol.com Website:
www.nenvers.aol.com/natpartner/home
Enjoy B&B in peaceful 300-year-old
country cottage with gardens, own woods
and river. All organic breakfast, local and
own produced. Proprietors are also
herbalists, using own formulated products
for humans and animals.

 CARLEYS
34-36 ST AUSTELL STREET,
TRURO TR1 1SE
Tel: 01892 277686 Fax: 01872 277686
Contact: John Carley
Over 3000 certified organic foods—grains,
flakes, flours, pulses, oils, nuts, fruits, seeds,
dairy, meat, poultry, wines, ciders, beers,
herbs and spices. Delivery area covered: TR
postcodes (not Scilly).

RICHARD CARLISLE
TREGANNICK FARM, DRAKEWALLS,
GUNNISLAKE PL18 9ED
Tel: 01822 833969 Fax: 01822 834285
Contact: Richard Carlisle
Organic free range table chickens,
traditionally reared. Soil Association
registered (no. P0036).

CHURCHTOWN FARM
CHURCHTOWN FARM,
LANTEGLOS BY FOWEY PL23 1NH
Tel: 01726 870375 Fax: 01726 870376
Contact: M. & C. Russell
National Trust coastal farm selling organic
beef, lamb and chicken. Extensive range
available in any quantity, including
delicious barbecue products. Phone first.
Soil Association certified (no. G1784).
Holiday flat also available.

The assumption that we need to create new crop varieties through the use of genetic
engineering technologies overlooks the fact that there is untapped potential within
the wealth of existing varieties.

Luke Anderson, *Genetic Engineering, Food, and Our Environment* (1999)

CUSGARNE ORGANICS
CUSGARNE WOLLAS, CUSGARNE,
NR. TRURO TR4 8RL
Tel: 01872 865922
Contact: Teresa & Greg Pascoe
Email: cusgarne@freenet.co.uk
104 acre holding (certified organic for 10 years). Wide range of vegetables, organic free range eggs, grass/silage, corn (animal feed) beef, suckler and young stock herd. Wholesale deliveries between Hereford and Cornwall. Box scheme covers Redruth, Falmouth, Lizard and Truro. OF&G registered 31-UKF060140.

GOOD NATURE
2 ESPLANADE, FOWEY PL23 1HY
Tel: 01726 832110 Contact: Inge
General groceries, including box scheme with home delivery.

THE GRANARY
NEWHAM ROAD, TRURO TR1 2ST
Tel: 01872 274343 Fax: 01872 223477
Contact: Jill Thomas
Wholesale distributors of health foods, natural foods, delicatessen products throughout Cornwall, Devon, Somerset, parts of Wiltshire and Dorset. Certified by the Soil Association.

GREAT MORETON FARM
GT. MORETON, LAUNCELLS, BUDE EX23 9LY
Tel & Fax: 01288 381216
Contact: J. Gladnell
Email: jem@Great-Moreton.Freeserve.co.uk
Farmers and veg growers in field & polytunnel. Soil Assn. registered (no. G1795). Members and suppliers of Holsworthy Organics box scheme. North Devon beef traditionally prepared. Available at farm gate. Ring for availability.

 HESKYN MILL
TIDEFORD, SALTASH PL12 5BG
Tel: 01752 851481 Contact: Frank Eden
We are an old mill restored to offer restaurant facilities. We use what organic produce is available locally as much as possible. We also offer some organically produced wines.

JILLY ORGANIC WHOLEFOODS
BISCOMBE'S LANE, CALLINGTON PL17 7LB
Tel: 01579 384356
Contact: Jilly Johnson (Owner)
Retail shop stocking extensive range of certified organic foods including Village Bakery breads and cakes, plus homeopathic remedies, natural supplements, vitamins and toiletries. Friendly service. Opening times Monday to Saturday 9.30 a.m. to 5.30 p.m.

KENEGIE ORGANICS
KENEGIE HOME FARM, GULVAL,
PENZANCE TR20 8YN
Tel & Fax: 01736 333457
Contact: Joff Rorke
Soil Association certified (G1933). Organic vegetable boxes and supplies to catering trade in West Cornwall. Also organic beef.

KENIDJACK FARM
ST. JUST IN PENWITH, TR19 7QW
Tel: 01736 788675
Contact: Mike Bratt (Owner)
Soil Association symbol holder, Dexter cattle, early potato production.

MAKING WAVES VEGAN GUEST HOUSE
3 RICHMOND PLACE, ST. IVES TR26 1JN
Tel: 01736 793895 Contact: Simon Money
Beautiful eco-renovated 19th century house. Ocean views, peaceful, minutes from shops, beaches and harbour. Delicious organic food. Special diets catered for. Children welcome. Voted "Best Vegan Guest House" (*Vegan* magazine).

THE NATURAL STORE

16 HIGH ST., FALMOUTH, TR11 2AS
Tel: 01326 311507 Fax: 01326 565848
Contact: Paul Johnson (Proprietor)
Organic fresh fruit and vegetables, organic meat, dried fruit, nuts, seeds, flakes, flours, breads, general wholefoods and chilled food. Also natural remedies and essential oils.
Also at TRENGROUSE WAY, HELSTON TR13 8RT (no meat).

PLANTS FOR A FUTURE

THE FIELD, HIGHER PENPOL, ST. VEEP,
LOSTWITHIEL PL22 0NG
Tel: 01208 873554
Contact: Elaine Avery (Coordinator)
Day visits and tours, courses on woodland gardening, permaculture, nutrition, research, information, demonstration and supply of edible and otherwise useful plants. Plants for a Future is a registered charity researching and demonstrating ecologically sustainable vegan organic horticulture in the form of woodland gardening and other permacultural practices.

C.L.& B.E.PUGH

GOONGILLINGS FARM, CONSTANTINE,
FALMOUTH TR11 5RP
Tel: 01326 340 630 Contact: C.L. Pugh
Email: barbpugh@aol.com
Website: www.goongillings.co.uk
Soil Association certified as suckled beef producer. Holiday cottages on beautiful riverside farm.

THE PURE WINE COMPANY

UNIT 18, THE WOODS-BROWNING ESTATE,
RESPRYN ROAD, BODMIN PL31 1DQ
Tel: 01208 79300 Fax: 01208 79393
Contact: Jim White
Email: service@purewine.co.uk
Website: www.purewine.co.uk
Wine merchants specialising in the import and distribution of organic, vegetarian and vegan wines to both the general public and trade outlets. All major cards accepted. Complete UK coverage.

STONEYBRIDGE ORGANIC NURSERY & FARMSHOP

TYWARDREATH, PAR PL24 2TY
Tel: 01726 813858
Contact: David Pascoe (Proprietor)
Soil Association certified producer (P22W) of over 70 crops: vegetables, soft fruit and herbs. Also retail SA-certified organic meat. Farm shop open Tuesdays to Saturday noon, from Easter to the end of October.

R.V.& K.H.THOMAS

POLGEAR FARM, NINE MAIDENS,
REDRUTH TR16 6NB
Tel: 01209 831535 Fax: 01209 831535
Contact: K Thomas
Email: kimthomas@uk.hotmail.com
Organic milk and beef producer. Soil Association registered (no. G2159).

Key

 Producers   Wholesalers   Import/Export

 Retailers   Mail Order   Restaurants   Day Visits/B&B

Farm Gate Sales   Box Schemes/ Delivery Service   Garden/Farm Sundries   Manufacturers & Processors

TREE OF LIFE ORGANICS
SCALA NIJ, MITHIAN, ST. AGNES,
TRURO TR5 OQE
Tel: 01872 552 661 Contact: Marie/Silvia
Email: adzom@compuserve.com
Soil Association registered (nos. P2068 &
G2068). We are a small company that is
committed to the sustainable, organic way
of life. We can supply top quality fresh fruit
and vegetables and eggs produced locally.
Delivery area: Truro and 10 mile radius.

TRENANT FARM
TRENANT FARM, GREAT BOSULLOW,
MADRON, PENZANCE TR20 8NP
Tel: 01736 364572 Contact: Kevin Reed
Email: kevin.trenant@talk21.com
Soil Association registered (no. G1932)
smallholding. Production and direct sale of
Angus beef with small scale vegetable
growing. Self-contained holiday let in
converted barn.

W.D. & B.D.TRENBERTH
TREVALLARD FARM, MOUNT HAWKE,
TRURO TR4 8DL
Tel: 01209 890253 Contact: D Trenberth
Autumn and winter vegetables, beef and
cereals. Soil Association licence no. G2763.

WIDDICOMBE FARE
4 WEST ST., MILLBROOK,
TORPOINT PL10 1AA
Tel: 01752 822335
Contact: Jo Widdicombe (Proprietor)
Email: jaewidd@compuserve.com
Retail greengrocery and wholefoods—range
of organic products including fruit and
vegetables.

It is unlikely that the planet can accomodate an urbanised humanity which routinely
draws resources from ever more distant hinterlands, or routinely uses the biosphere,
the oceans and the atmosphere as a sink for its wastes. Can cities transform
themselves into self-regulating, sustainable systems—not only in their internal
functioning, but also in their relationships to the outside world? An answer to this
question may be critical to the future well-being of the planet, as well as of humanity.

Herbert Girardet, *Creating Sustainable Cities* (1999)

People are also becoming aware that the future direction of agricultural research is
being dictated by commercial interests. In 1998, for example, the British goverment
spent £52 million on research into agricultural biotechnology and a mere £1.7
million on research into organic farming, despite the fact that the organic sector is
growing rapidly. In the United States, a study by the Organic Farming Research
Foundation found that out of 30,000 federally financed research projects, those
determined to be organic represent less than 0.1 percent.

Luke Anderson, *Genetic Engineering, Food, and Our Environment* (1999)

CUMBRIA

ALSTON WHOLEFOODS LIMITED
KINGS ARMS LANE, FRONT STREET,
ALSTON CA9 6HU
Tel: 01434 381588 Contact: Carol Sutton
Small retail shop run by co-operative. Wide
range of wholefoods, choice cheeses,
delicious ice creams, breads, snacks, herbs
and spices, teas, soaps, and vegetables as
available. Emphasis on organic produce.

E.H. BOOTH & CO. LTD
THE OLD STATION, VICTORIA ST.,
WINDERMERE LA23 1QA
Tel: 015394 46114 Fax: 015394 88918
Contact: Mr E. McCabe (Manager)
Organic fruit and veg, fresh meat, dairy,
frozen burgers, frozen veg, wines,
preserves, flour, bread and cakes.

CHILTERN SEEDS
BORTREE STILE, ULVERSTON LA12 7PB
Tel: 01229 581137 (24hrs)
Fax: 01229 584549
Contact: A. Bushell
Email: odir@chilternseeds.co.uk
Website: www.chilternseeds.co.uk
The seed catalogue you won't want to put
down! Seeds of every kind including new
organic vegetable section.

HALF MOON WHOLEFOODS
14 FRONT ST., BRAMPTON CA8 1NG
Tel & Fax: 016977 3775
Contact: Sandra & Annette Howe,
Sandra Ambler
Small but comprehensive wholefood store
in north Cumbria. Stockists of Watermill
organic flours. Order service for products
not in stock.

HOWBARROW ORGANIC FARM
CARTMEL, GRANGE-OVER-SANDS LA11 7SS
Tel & Fax: 015395 36330
Contact: Julia Sayburn   Email:
enquiries@howbarroworganic.demon.co.uk
Website:
www.howbarroworganic.demon.co.uk
Soil Association symbol no. G2060. 13 acre
smallholding producing meat (pork, lamb,
chickens), eggs, vegetables and soft fruit to
supply local market stall, box scheme and
farm shop. Demonstration farm, walks and
display. B&B available.

KAN FOODS

9 NEW SHAMBLES, off MARKET PLACE,
KENDAL LA9 4TS
Tel: 01539 721190 Home: 01539 738116
Contact: Elizabeth Kan
Wholefood shop supplying organic foods,
local vegetable box scheme. Specialising in
vitamins, minerals and herbal remedies
(advice given). Magnetic and far infra-red
technologies, sleep systems to insoles—very
exciting. Non-food products sold
throughout Britain.

LAKELAND PAINTS
UNIT 19, LAKE DISTRICT BUSINESS PARK,
KENDAL LA9 6NH
Tel: 01539 732866 Fax: 01539 734400
Contact: Ian West
Organic odourless solvent-free paints,
varnishes and other related products.

LITTLE SALKELD WATERMILL
LITTLE SALKELD, PENRITH CA10 1NN
Tel: 01768 881523
Contact: Nick Jones (Partner)
Email: nj&j@aol.com
Website: www.cumbria.com/watermill/
Specialist organic flours milled the traditional
way by water power in our 18th century
watermill, to BDAA & SA standards. Soil
Association licence no. P632. Baking courses.

MUNCASTER WATERMILL
RAVENGLASS CA18 1ST
Tel: 01229 717232 Contact: Pam Priestly
Stoneground organic flour milled in 17th
century watermill. Mill, shop, mill tours,
tea shop and B&B.

SUNDANCE WHOLEFOODS
33 MAIN STREET, KESWICK CA12 5BL
Tel: 01768 774712
Contact: Julian Holdsworth
We stock a rapidly increasing selection of
organic products.

THE VILLAGE BAKERY
MELMERBY, PENRITH CA10 1HE
Tel: 01768 881515 Fax: 01768 881848
Contact: Andrew Whitley
Email: admin@village-bakery.com Website:
www.village-bakery.com
Specialist bakers of organic bread and
cakes in wood fired brick ovens.
Restaurant. Mail order. Bread making
courses. Soil Association licence no. P881.

WHITEHOLME FARM
WHITEHOLME, ROWELTOWN,
CARLISLE CA6 6LS
Tel: 016977 48058/48331
Contact: Mike Downham
Soil Association certified (no. G797A)
organic beef, lamb and pork, sold direct
from the farm to private customers locally.
Also sale of organically certified breeding
and store cattle. Organic resources centre
(for day or residential visits) opening
October 2000.

The revival of urban and peri-urban agriculture in the USA is particularly
remarkable because one would not expect it in such an affluent country. Clever
marketing, as well as the desire of consumers to know where their food comes from,
has a lot to do with it.

Herbert Girardet, *Creating Sustainable Cities* (1999)

Conventional economics has been based on a linear model of economic activities.
Material resources are extracted from Nature's supposedly unlimited pool, outside
the economic system; they are then processed stage by stage into the eventual
manufacture of consumer goods; those are then distributed and consumed, and the
final wastes are dumped in Nature's unlimited sink, again outside the economic
system. The capacity of Nature's resource pool and the capacity of Nature's waste
sink have been treated as free goods, of no value.

James Robertson, *Transforming Economic Life* (1998)

DERBYSHIRE

BEANO'S WHOLEFOODS
HOLME ROAD, MATLOCK BATH DE4 3NU
Tel: 01629 57130 Fax: 01629 57143
Contact: Anne Thorne
Email: sales@beanos.fsbusiness.co.uk.
Retailers of organic vegetarian foods for
over 15 years. Vast selection of organic
fruit, vegetables, wines,beers, grains,
pulses, milk, cheeses, convenience foods.
Box scheme. Free delivery service available.

HI PEAK FEEDS PROCTORS
(BAKEWELL) LTD
HI PEAK FEEDS MILL, 12 ASHBOURNE RD.,
DERBY DE22 3AA
Tel: 01332 342224 Fax: 01332 200497
Contact: John Walker
Email: info@hipeak.co.uk
Website: www.hipeak.co.uk
Manufacturers and distributors of organic
and UKROFS permitted animal feeds for all
farm livestock, horses and dogs.
Nationwide delivery and mail order. Soil
Association licence no. P2486, OF&G
licence no. 11UKP090258. We supply
farmers and smallholders.

HI PEAK ORGANIC FOOD LTD
12 ASHBOURNE RD., DERBY DE22 3AA
Tel: 01332 342224 Fax: 01332 200497
Contact: John Walker
Email: info@hipeak.co.uk
Website: www.hipeakorganics.co.uk
Eggs produced to Soil Association standards.
Meats including beef, pork, lamb, chicken,
turkey, bacon, sausage and burgers supplied
nationwide to homes, shops, restaurants and
schools. Soil Association licence no. P2488.
See display ad.

MANDY & ADRIAN HUNTER
TURLOW FIELDS FARM, HOGNASTON,
NR. ASHBOURNE DE6 1PW
Tel & Fax: 01335 370834
Contact: Mandy or Adrian Hunter
Email: hunters@turlow.co.uk
Farm shop selling home produced beef,
lamb, pork, chicken, sausage, bacon and
ham, mainly frozen. Also home cured
fleeces, craft ware and decorative
ironwork. Soil Association licence no.
G4062.

MEYNELL LANGLEY ORGANIC FOOD
LODGE FARM, LODGE LANE,
KIRK LANGLEY DE6 4NX
Tel: 01332 824815 Contact: Helen Meynell
Email: organic@meynell-langley.co.uk
Beef from our suckler herd of pedigree
Welsh blacks, lamb, chicken, eggs and
vegetables all produced on the farm. Soil
Association G1287. Farm shop open Fri 1-
6.30 p.m., Sat 10 a.m. - 2 p.m., and other
times (phone). Local deliveries possible.
Mail order (beef only).

MIMMO'S
1 ST. MARY'S GATE, WIRKSWORTH,
MATLOCK DE4 4DQ
Tel: 01629 826724
Contact: Melanie Glendinning
Mimmo's is an Italian restaurant
specialising in organic Sicilian pasta and
rice dishes, and home-made stone-oven
pizzas. Much of our produce is obtained
from a local organic farm.

Today America is losing over three billion tons of topsoil a year, with as much as
700 million tons washing into the Gulf of Mexico alone.

John Roulac, *Backyard Composting* (1999)

 NATURAL CHOICE

24 ST. JOHN ST., ASHBOURNE DE6 1EH
Tel & Fax: 01335 346096
Contact: Steve or Roy Parker (Partners)
Email: naturalchoice@lineone.net
Website: www.herbal.net-traders.co.uk
Wholefoods, natural remedies, therapy centre, fair trade products, gifts, cards, music, books, special diets catered for.

   NATURAL DELIVERY WHOLEFOODS

THE OLD KINGS, BUXTON ROAD, BAKEWELL DE45 1DA
Tel & Fax: 01629 814507
Contact: John Edgington
Email: ndwholefoods.free-online.co.uk
Website:
www.bbr-online.com/n-d-wholefoods
Home delivery service for wholefoods, organic fruit and vegetables (box scheme). Shop open Mon-Sat. Delivery to S. Yorks and Derbyshire. Organic Food Federation registered no. NDR/97.

 NEW HOUSE FARM

KNIVETON, ASHBOURNE DE6 1JL
Tel: 01335 342429
Contact: Bob & Mary Smail (Farmers)
Organic family farm producing and selling from the farm gate: beef, lamb, eggs and vegetables. B&B all year; farm walks during the summer (school visits welcome).

 NORTHERN TEA MERCHANTS

CROWN HOUSE, 193 CHATSWORTH RD., CHESTERFIELD S40 2BA
Tel: 01246 232600 Fax: 01246 555991
Contact: David & James Pogson
Email: rbr75@dial.pipex.com
Members of Soil Association. Packers and wholesalers of organic coffee and cocoa. Own label organic products quoted for packing on request.

    THE ORGANIC SHOP

3 SETT CLOSE, NEW MILLS SK22 4AQ
Tel: 01663 747550 Fax: 01663 741411
Contact: B. Eadie
Wide range of organic fruit, vegetables, meat, fish, wholefoods, dairy, wine, beer, toiletries, cleaning products, garden sundries, clothing. Soil Association registered (no. R1985); member of the Organic Retail Guild.

 SUNFLOWER HEALTH STORE

20 MARKET PLACE, ILKESTON DE7 5QA
Tel: 0115 930 4750
Contact: Mr K. Clifford
Email: afi054@beeb.net
We sell a wide range of groceries, supplements and cosmetics, stocking as many organic and ethically produced goods as possible. We are pleased to order items not stocked if available.

    WELEDA (UK) LTD

HEANOR RD., ILKESTON DE7 8DR
Tel: 0115 944 8200 Fax: 0115 944 8210
Contact: Roger Barsby (Sales Manager)
Email: weledauk@compuserve.com
Manufacturers of homeopathic and anthroposophic medicines and natural toiletries. Gardens. Demeter certified.

> A society physically, socially and economically structured around motor transport means loss of opportunity, liberty and quality of life for people without cars—especially children, women and elderly people—for whom cars make the street unpleasant and dangerous.
>
> James Robertson, *Transforming Economic Life* (1998)

DEVON

ACLAND ORGANIC MEAT
EAST ACLAND FARM, LANDKEY,
BARNSTAPLE EX32 0LD
Tel: 01271 830216
Contact: Dr Charles Morrish
Email: chmorrish@tinyword.com
Traditionally reared organic beef and lamb,
local breeds, reared naturally. Delivery
possible. Farm has been organic since
1966 (Soil Association no. M12W).

ALAN'S APPLE
26 FORE STREET, KINGSBRIDGE TQ7 1NY
Tel: 01548 852308 Contact: Alan Knight
Traditional greengrocer, stocking organic
vegetables, organic dairy produce, organic
ice cream and organic meat and poultry.

THE ARK WHOLEFOODS SHOP
38 EAST STREET, ASHBURTON TQ13 7AX
Tel: 01364 653020
Contact: Christine Wilkinson
Small is beautiful: this shop is crammed full
of a huge variety of lines including many
organic ones. Vegetables are sourced from
Riverford Farm and Woodlands Organics.
Baked goods are home-made or come
from a local vegetarian bakery. Organic
lines are represented in most dry goods
and dairy sectors too.

BEDPORT FARM
BEDPORT FARM, BURRINGTON,
UMBERLEIGH EX37 9LE
Tel: 01769 560592 Fax: 01769 560592
Contact: Mr or Mrs Tyler-Upfield
Inspection by OF&G has taken place—
awaiting written confirmation). 6000
organic laying hens producing eggs.

BEE ORGANIC
MARKET GARDEN, FOXHOLE CENTRE,
DARTINGTON HALL ESTATE,
TOTNES TQ9 6EB
Tel: 01803 840140
Contact: Paul Hutchings
Growing seasonal vegetables, fruit and herbs
on 3 1/2 acres of land. Utilising intensive
raised bed system and permaculture
principles. Certified by the Soil Association
since 1996 (licence no. G1402).

BIRCH FARM ORGANIC BAKERS
BIRCH FARM, STOKE RIVERS,
BARNSTAPLE EX32 7LE
Tel: 01598 710854
Contact: David Karniewicz
Hand made organic breads and cakes.
Organic Farmers and Growers licence no.
UKF020400 for mainland Britain; other
areas by arrangement.

BUCKLAND FILLEIGH ORGANIC PRODUCE
BRAMLEY WOOD, BUCKLAND FILLEIGH,
BEAWORTHY EX21 5JD
Tel: 01409 281693 Contact: Jane Bartlett
Soil Association reg. no. G2237. Producer
of free range eggs, plant raising,
greenhouse crops, soft fruit, herbs,
vegetables, situated in mixed woodland
offering educational vists. Forestry
producer of charcoal. Delivery to areas
EX21, EX38 and EX39.

CHOPS AWAY
1 TICKLEMORE COURT, TICKLEMORE ST.,
TOTNES TQ9 5EJ
Tel & Fax: 01803 864404
Contact: Noni Mackenzie
Email: noni@chopsaway.com
Website: www.chopsaway.com
A co-operative of organic and Bio-dynamic
farmers and growers. We sell meat, herbs,
plants, seeds, crafts and fair trade
chocolate. Tea, coffee and cake are served
in our courtyard café.

CLIVE'S PIES (VEGIE WHOLEFOOD KITCHEN)

HAMLYN HOUSE, MARDLE WAY,
BUCKFASTLEIGH TQ11 0NR
Tel: 01364 642279 Fax: 01364 643888
Contact: Lucie Lowe
Organic bakery products: pies (mushroom, goulash, Arabian chickpea), soysage rolls, organic cakes. Soil Association certified P2974. Delivery areas: Devon, Cornwall, Bristol-Bath, London area (also Brighton).

THE COURTYARD

76 THE SQUARE, CHAGFORD,
NEWTON ABBOT TQ13 8BY
Tel: 01647 432571 Contact: Jo Hodges
The Courtyard serves fresh organic food and drink and sells organic wholefoods, fruit and veg and fair trade goods, and is a focus for the Lets scheme and Proper Job.

DARTINGTON TECH— THE REGIONAL CENTRE FOR ORGANIC HORTICULTURE

WESTMINSTER HOUSE,
38/40 PALACE AVENUE,
PAIGNTON TQ3 3HB
Tel & Fax: 01803 867693
Contact: Jenny Pidgeon (Project Manager)
Email: jpidgeon@rcoh.co.uk
Website: www.rcoh.co.uk
The RCOH is an education and resource centre for the promotion of organic gardening and horticulture. We offer courses for professionals and amateurs at our Soil Association certified site (G1402).

DARTMOOR DIRECT CO-OPERATIVE LTD

MITCHELCOMBE FARM,
HOLNE, TQ13 7SP
Tel: 01364 631528
Home delivery service of extensive range of organic produce, including from local producers, and Clearly Devon spring water.

DITTISHAM FARM

CAPTON, DARTMOUTH TQ6 0JE
Tel: 01803 712452 Fax: 01803 712452
Contact: Sue Fildes
Email: suefildes@supanet.com
Website: www.self-cater.co.uk/dff
Small organic farm (Soil Association licence no. G4070) producing pork from 100% free range pedigree Berkshire Pigs. Also eggs and herbs, some Pick-Your-Own Fruit in season. Also self-catering accommodation.

DRAGONFLY FOODS

2A MARDLE WAY,
BUCKFASTLEIGH TQ11 0NR
Tel & Fax: 01364 642700
Contact: Simon Boreham (Partner)
Supplies health food stores via wholesalers throughout UK, Ireland and Europe (own label). Dragonfly Foods produces chilled, vacuum-packed organic vegetable protein food including organic tofu (3 types), organic beany burgers and roasts (11 recipes). Certified by Soil Association (P1080), approved by Vegetarian Society, and gluten-free.

EUROVEG LTD

UNITS 37 & 38, TEIGNBRIDGE BUSINESS CENTRE, CAVALIER RD., HEATHFIELD, NEWTON ABBOT TQ12 6TZ
Tel: 01626 836350 Fax: 01626 836351
Contact: Kirstie Mills
Email: euroveg@breathemail.net
We process roasted organic vegetables and supply prepared vegetables for use in manufacture or retail. See display ad.

FERRYMAN POLYTUNNELS

BRIDGE RD., LAPFORD, CREDITON EX17 6AE
Tel: 01363 83444 Fax: 01363 83050
Contact: Hugh Briant-Evans
Email: polytunnel@sosi.net
Website: www.ferryman.uk.com
Manufacturer of polytunnels for gardeners and professional grower. Over 400 variations from 8' wide to 24' wide. Whole of UK supplied, export enquiries welcome.

GOLLAND FARM GARDEN PROJECT

GOLLAND FARM, BURRINGTON, UMBERLEIGH EX37 9JP
Tel & Fax: 01769 520263
Contact: Jon Lincoln-Gordon
Email: golland@btinternet.com
Website: www.marketsquare.co.uk/chulmleigh/bridleway
Small mixed organic farm with 2 holiday cottages and a horticulture therapy project producing organic vegetable boxes for local people.

GOURMET ORGANIX

3-4 QUEEN ST., LYNTON EX35 6AA
Tel: 01598 752228 Fax: 01598 752221
Website: www.gourmetorganix.com
For food lovers: a gourmet general store specialising in quality service, delicatessen, local and imported cheese, ham, dry goods, juices, local farm fresh veg, local meat fresh or freezer boxes. Vegan, allergy aware, fully licensed, weekly home deliveries in Devon & Somerset.

GRAYS FARM

MEMBURY, AXMINSTER EX13 7TZ
Tel & Fax: 01404 881481
Contact: Mr J.B. Foster
Organic hay, certified by the Soil Association, made from species-rich flower meadows. Delivery to east Devon, west Dorset, south Somerset.

GREAT CUMMINS FARM

TEDBURN ST MARY, EXETER EX6 6BJ
Tel & Fax: 01647 61278
Contact: David Garaway
OF&G member IIUKRF0-03084. Organic lamb and vegetables. Farm shop open Friday-Sunday. Local home deliveries to EX6.

GREENFIBRES

99 HIGH ST., TOTNES TQ9 5PF
Tel: 01803 868001 Fax: 01803 868002
Contact: William Lana
Email: mail@greenfibres.com
Website: www.greenfibres.com
Comprehensive range of clothing, bedding, fabric and household linen made from organic raw materials under fair and safe conditions. Feel and look good while supporting organic agriculture and ethical work practices. See display ad.

THE GREEN HOUSE

2A LOWER PANNIER MARKET, CREDITON EX17 2BL
Tel: 01363 775580 Contact: Loo Brown
Full range of wholefoods including large organic selection. Fresh organic fruit and veg. Small friendly cafe serving organic teas and coffees and yummy cakes! Environmentally friendly, fair trade gifts. Delivery for orders over £20.

GREENLIFE & GREENLIFE DIRECT

11-13 FORE STREET, TOTNES TQ9 5DA
Greenlife Tel: 01803 866738
Greenlife Direct Tel: 01803 866733
Fax: 01803 864948
Contact: Liz or Penny or Jamie
Natural health and wholefood, retail and mail order—one of the largest natural health shops in the South-West.

GRIFFIN WHOLEFOODS

120 EAST ST, SOUTH MOLTON EX36 3BU
Tel: 01769 572372
Contact: Graeme Wilkinson
Wholefoods retailer including many organic lines. Fresh fruit and veg, dairy, bread etc.

THE HEALTH FOOD STORE

GAMMON WALK, BARNSTAPLE EX31 1DJ
Tel: 01271 345624
Contact: Wilson Blackburne
Organic spreads, fruits, nuts, pulses, oats, flakes, oils and much more, with a friendly information service.

HEALTHWISE

81 FORE ST., KINGSBRIDGE TQ7 1AB
Tel & Fax: 01548 857707
Contact: Irene Jeeninga
We stock a wide range of organic foods:
muesli, dried fruit, seeds, nuts, tea, honey,
eggs, dairy and non dairy products,
Cranks' bread, fruit spreads.

HERBIE'S WHOLE FOOD VEGETARIAN RESTAURANT

15 NORTH ST., EXETER EX4 6Q
Tel: 01392 258473 Contact: Tony Mudge
Vegetarian restaurant using organic
ingredients where available and local
produce in season.

HIGHDOWN FARM HOLIDAY COTTAGES

HIGHDOWN FARM, BRADNINCH,
EXETER EX5 4LJ
Tel: 01392 881028 Fax: 01392 881272
Contact: Sandra Vallis
Email: highdownfarm@ukgateway.net
Registered organic dairy farm. Two
cottages ideal for families and a romantic
barn conversion for two. Spectacular
views, short breaks available.

HIGHER HACKNELL FARM

BURRINGTON, UMBERLEIGH EX37 9LX
Tel: 01769 560909 Contact: Jo Budden
Email: budden@hacknell.fsbusiness.co.uk
Website: www.higherhacknell.co.uk
Award winning organic beef and lamb
direct from the farm to your door—tasty,
top quality and affordable. Nationwide
delivery.

HIGHER SHARPHAM BARTON FARM

COACHYARD COTTAGE, SHARPHAM,
ASHPRINGTON, TOTNES TQ9 7UT
Tel: 01803 732324 Contact: Richard Smith
Bio-dynamic meat (beef and lamb—Demeter
symbol no. 208). Organic and Demeter
sheepskins, baby rugs (by post). Annual on-
farm family camp: this year 4th-13th August.
Meat for sale in Totnes: Ticklemore Street
Farm shop opening March/April.

HIGHFIELD HARVEST

HIGHFIELD FARM, CLYST RD.,
TOPSHAM EX3 0BY
Tel & Fax: 01392 876388
Contact: Ian Shears (M.D.)
Highfield Harvest organic farm shop,
award winning organic vegetables from
our 118-acre family farm plus organic
meat, dairy, wines, groceries. Open Tues to
Sat 9 to 6, Sun 10 to 1, closed Mondays.
Soil Association certified (no. S41M).

HOLSWORTHY ORGANICS

c/o LITTLE EAST LAKE FARM, EAST CHILLA,
BEAWORTHY EX21 5XF
Tel: 01409 221417 & 01288 381216
Contact: Mo Robley & Jemima Gladwell
Marketing co-op selling organic veg, fruit,
herbs, meat, eggs and other produce.
Producer member of Soil Assn. (no. PR30W).

GEOFF JONES

THE OAKS, YEOFORD EX17 5PP
Tel & Fax: 01363 84369
Contact: Geoff Jones (Proprietor)
Wholesale distribution of certified
vegetables, fruit and dairy products (local
and imported) to ensure 12-month supply
to retail outlets throughout the South-West.

KILWORTHY KAPERS

11 KING ST., TAVISTOCK PL19 0DS
Tel: 01822 615039
Contact: Mr & Mrs Kiely (Proprietors)
We stock a wide range of organically grown
foods including fruit, vegetables and eggs.
Also supplements, herbal remedies etc.

LEAFCYCLE

COOMBE FARM, COVE,
TIVERTON EX16 7RU
Tel & Fax: 01398 331808
Contact: Michael Cole
Leaf curd and Leafu production. Leaf curd is
a highly nutritional food ingredient made
from fresh green leaves grown in a non-
animal organic system. Soil Association and
Vegan Society symbol holder.

LINSCOMBE FARM

SANDFORD, CREDITON EX17 4PS
Tel: 01363 84291
Contact: Phil Thomas & Helen Case
Email: linscombe@exl.co.uk
Mixed organic farm specialising in production of a wide range of vegetables for direct sale via our local box scheme. Over 300 varieties including 20 types of potato. Small beef suckler herd. Soil Association registered (no. G2047).

LITTLE ASH ECO-FARM

THROWLEY, OKEHAMPTON EX20 2GQ
Tel & Fax: 01647 231394
Contact: Dr M. Kiley-Worthington & Alex Armstrong (Owner & Veg Grower)
Courses in animal welfare, animal minds, improved husbandry, self-sustaining small ecological agriculture. Farm walks and nature trail, Soil Association licensed beef, lamb, dairy products, cereals, vegetables, boxes, llamas and horses. Organic wool & fine fibres and garments.

LITTLE EAST LAKE FARM

EAST CHILLA, BEAWORTHY EX21 5XF
Tel: 01409 221417
Contact: M. Robley (Owner)
Producers and sellers direct to the consumer of Soil Association symbol standard eggs, vegetables and soft fruit. Produce delivered locally. Members of Holsworthy Organics veg box scheme.

LUNN LINKS KITCHEN GARDEN

GREENBRIAR, VICTORIA RD.,
BRIXHAM TQ5 9AR
Tel: 01803 853579 Fax: 01803 883892
Contact: Stephen Lunn
Email: llorganic@aol.com
Website: www.kitchen-garden.co.uk
Registered organic importer (UKP080074). Organic and fairtraded herbs and spices, non-GMO soya flour, TVP, soya coffee substitute; bulk organic ingredients supplied. Mail order on Website.

LUSCOMBE ORGANIC DRINKS

LUSCOMBE FARM, COLSTON ROAD,
BUCKFASTLEIGH TQ11 0LP
Fax: 01364 644498 Contact: Gabriel David
Email: luscombeltd@freeserve.co.uk
Highly acclaimed traditional organic drinks, Devon apple, pear and apple. Lemonades, ginger beer and ciders to Soil Assn. standards. Award winners at National level.

LLOYD MAUNDER LTD

WILLAND, CULLOMPTON EX15 2PJ
Tel: 01884 820534 Fax: 01884 821404
Contact: Richard Maunder
Email: richard@lloydmaunder.co.uk
Website: www.lloydmaunder.co.uk
www.meatdirect.co.uk
Lloyd Maunder procure UKROFS and Soil Association approved lamb, beef and pork from producers throughout the UK and across Europe in order to process for the wholesale and supermarkets chains. Soil Association licence no. P709. Organic poultry also available. New service—Meat Direct www.meatdirect.co.uk is nationwide throughout the UK. See display ad.

MARSHFORD ORGANIC PRODUCE

CHURCHILL WAY, NORTHAM,
BIDEFORD EX39 1NS
Tel: 01237 477160
Contact: D.G. & V.M. Ebdon (Proprietors)
Also at 14A BUTCHERS ROW, BARNSTAPLE (retail shop)
We sell the widest possible range of certified organic food from our farm shop. Our own vegetables are freshly picked daily, and we sell other local certified produce. Box scheme. Garden trail. S.A. Nos. E19W, PE19W.

MIDDLE CAMPSCOTT FARM (T/A INCLEDON LTD)
MIDDLE CAMPSCOTT FARM, LEE,
ILFRACOMBE EX34 8LS
Tel & Fax: 01271 864621
Contact: Karen Wright
We produce hard pressed ewe's milk cheeses using milk from our flock; wool from our naturally coloured shetland sheep, lamb and beef from our Ruby Devon cattle. Soil Association no. G1923. We welcome visitors to the farm; we offer educational access and accommodate WWOOFers.

MUNCH MANIA
20 HIGH ST., TOTNES TQ9 5RY
Tel: 01803 868899
Contact: Claire or Carole
Email: munchbox@themail.co.uk
Organic café and take-away. Sandwiches, toasties, jackets, soups, salads, munchies. Buffets and parties catered for. Organic juice bar—fruit and vegetable juices freshly made to order.

NATUREMADE
EAST JOHNSTONE, BISH MILL,
SOUTH MOLTON EX36 3QE
Tel & Fax: 01769 573571
Contact: Esme Brown
Email: sales@naturemade.co.uk
Website: www.naturemade.co.uk
Alternative dairy, i.e. goat's and sheep's milk and products. Organic vegetarian foods. Soil Assn no. P1471. Delivery throughout South West. Countrywide by courier. Also mail order.

NATURE'S ROUND
DART MILLS, OLD TOTNES RD.,
BUCKFASTLEIGH TQ11 0NF
Tel: 07957 472654 (mobile)
Contact: Brent Tebbutt
Box scheme and delivery service supplying fresh fruit and vegetables along with organic wholefoods. Deliver to approximately 200 households, will be looking at Bio-dynamic milk, meat and other dairy products to expand range in the near future.

HEATHER AND JOHN NICHOLSON
NORWEGIAN WOOD, BERRY POMEROY,
TOTNES TQ9 6LE
Tel & Fax: 01803 867462
Contact: H. Nicholson
We offer high quality service with top quality organic food at affordable prices. One double, one twin in a colourful, relaxing, refreshing house overlooking the edge of Dartmoor.

NICHOLSONS
12 FORE STREET, KINGSBRIDGE TQ9 1NY
Tel: 01548 854347 Fax: 01548 854335
Contact: Frances Stathers (Proprietor)
Extensive range of health foods including a wide range of organic products: dry goods (flours, pulses, cereal, fruit etc.), dairy and soya products, jams, honey and other grocery items.

OLD CUMMING ORGANIC FARM
OLD CUMMING ORGANIC FARM,
COLSTON ROAD,
BUCKFASTLEIGH TQ11 0LP
Tel: 01364 642672
Email: cummingorganic@lineone.net
We are a small family-run organic farm offering a doorstep delivery service of organic produce. All our orders are tailor-made to customer specification and delivered the next day.

ORCHARD WHOLEFOODS
5A MILL ST., OTTERY ST. MARY EX11 1AB
Tel: 01404 812109 Contact: Jane Collier
We sell a small selection of organic wines, no fresh produce but a good selection of organic fruit, cereals, pastas, flours, yoghurts etc.
Also at 16 HIGH ST., BUDLEIGH SALTERTON EX9 6LQ (no wine)
Tel: 01395 442508

ORIGINAL ORGANICS LTD

UNIT 9 LANGLANDS BUSINESS PARK,
UFFCULME, EX15 3DA
Tel: 01884 841515 Fax: 01884 841717
Contact: Clive Roberts
Manufacturer of the world famous
'Original Wormery' and Rotol Composter,
and publisher of the Green Gardens
Catalogue.

PROPER JOB

3 FERNLEIGH, NEW ST.,
CHAGFORD TQ13 8BD
Tel & Fax: 01647 432616
Contact: Jo Hodges
Email: properjob@chagfd.freeserve.co.uk
Community business, holistic co-op.
Covers waste and resource issues,
especially composting, collecting
compostables, education/consciousness
raising. Organic veg production, and sale
in our community shop/café. Setting up
training in related issues. Organic
collection round.

PROVIDENCE FARM ORGANIC MEATS

PROVIDENCE FARM, CROSSPARK CROSS,
HOLSWORTHY EX22 6JW
Tel: 01409 254421 Contact: Mrs P. Riggs.
Small mixed farm, full Soil Association
certificate since 1998 (no. G2207).
Producing quality chicken, duck, guinea
fowl, seasonal goose and turkey, pork,
bacon, sausages, eggs and lamb. Farm
gate sales, always open.

REAPERS

18 BAMPTON ST., TIVERTON EX16 6AA
Tel: 01884 255310 Fax: 01884 242757
Contact: Ray Rice
Email:rayrice@reapers-healthfoods.co.uk
Website: www.reapers-healthfoods.co.uk
Having expanded our premises we now
stock fresh, organic fruit and vegetables, as
well as more than 500 organic products.

RICHARD'S

64 FORE ST., TOPSHAM, EXETER EX3 0HL
Tel: 01392 873116 Fax: 01395 233373
Contact: Richard Tucker (Owner)
We have a small section of organic fruit
and vegetables in the shop subject to
seasonal availability.

RIVERFORD FARM SHOP

RIVERFORD, STAVERTON, TOTNES TQ9 6AF
Tel:01803 762523 Fax: 01803 762571
Contact: Deborah Nash
Email: rffshop@netscapeonline.co.uk
Organic Farmers and Growers (cert no.
UKP100357). Organic and locally
produced beef, lamb, chicken, pork, free
range eggs, cheese, wine, bread and pies,
dry goods and Riverford Organic Milk.

RIVERFORD FARM SHOP AT KITLEY

YEALMPTON, PLYMOUTH PL8 2LT
Tel: 01752 880925 Fax: 01752 880263
Contact: Hilary Hornby
Email: rffshop@netscapeonline.co.uk
Organic Farmers and Growers registered.
Farm shop, plant centre and café offering a
wide range of organic food (vegetables,
meat, dairy, wine, dry goods and plant
seeds etc.). Emphasis on quality food from
local producers.

RIVERFORD ORGANIC VEGETABLES

WASH BARN, BUCKFASTLEIGH TQ11 0LD
Tel: 01803 762720 Fax: 01803 762718
Largest organic vegetable producers in UK.
Soil Assn (W24W). We sell wholesale, local
and home deliveries. Also free range eggs.
See display ad.

ROCOMBE FARM FRESH ICE CREAM LTD

OLD NEWTON RD., HEATHFIELD,
NEWTON ABBOT TQ12 6RA
Tel: 01626 834545 Fax: 01626 835777
Contact: Peter Redstone (M.D.)
Email: info@rocomefarm.co.uk
Website: www.rocombefarm.co.uk
Luxury organic dairy ice cream, organic
frozen yoghurt and organic fruit sorbet.
Soil Association no. P1006.

ROWDEN FARM

ROWDEN FARM, WASHBOURNE, TOTNES TQ9 7UF
Tel: 01803 732217 Contact: G.M. Dixon
Beef and lamb producer—fully organic.

  SACKS

80 HIGH ST., TOTNES TQ9 5SN
Tel: 01803 863263
We are a Soil Association registered shop (no. R1907) selling a complete range of organic food. A wide range of fresh organic fruit and vegetables always in stock.

 SEASONS

8 WELL ST., EXETER EX4 6QR
Tel: 01392 201282 Contact: Parviz Kargar
Organic vegetables, grains, beans, pulses, dried fruit, and natural groceries.

SHARPHAM PARTNERSHIP LTD
SHARPHAM ESTATE, ASHPRINGTON, TOTNES TQ9 7UT
Tel:01803 732203 Fax: 01803 732122
Contact: M. Sharman
Email: info@sharpham.com
Website: www.sharpham.com
The family company is currently farming 200 acres of organic and in conversion land. We produce organic vegetables and will convert the 60 Jersey cows this year. Also produce non-organic cheese and English wine. Soil Association no. G2483.

   SKYSPROUTS

GOSWORTHY COTTAGE, HARBERTON, TOTNES TQ9 7LP
Tel & Fax: 01364 72404
Contact: Brett Kellett
Email: skysprouts@thenet.co.uk
Soil Association no. P10W. We have been supplying sprouted alfalfa, mung, aduki, lentil, radish, sunflower, chickpea etc. for more than twelve years to wholesalers, shops and veggie box schemes.

 SOUTH DEVON ORGANIC PRODUCERS LTD

SHARPHAM ESTATE, ASHPRINGTON, TOTNES TQ9 7UT
Tel: 01803 762100 Fax: 01803 762755
Contact: Joanna Field
Email: mail@sdopltd.co.uk
Website: www.sdopltd.co.uk
We market a wide range of vegetables from organic growers.

 STALLCOMBE HOUSE

SANCTUARY LANE, WOODBURY SALTERTON EX5 1EX
Tel: 01395 232373
Contact: Ms G. Ritchie Smith
Residential care home for people with learning difficulties, producing fresh organic garden produce, free range eggs and granola with maximum involvement from residents.

 TAMAR ORGANICS

UNIT 5A, WEST BRIDGE INDUSTRIAL ESTATE, TAVISTOCK PL19 8DE
Tel & Fax: 01822 618765/832242
Contact: C. Guilfoy (Proprietor)
Email: tamarorganics@compuserve.com
Seed and organic mail order company, plus Tavistock Friday Market for organic vegetables and plants. Soil Association registered (G1823 & P1823). NB: We shall be moving premises in the near future.

TIDEFORD ORGANIC FOODS LIMITED

5 THE ALPHA CENTRE, BABBAGE ROAD, TOTNES TQ9 5JA
Tel: 01803 840555 Fax: 01803 840551
Contact: Karen Hutchinson
We produce luxury fresh chilled organic pestos, soups and sauces. Fully licensed by the Soil Association (P2178), and Award Winners in the last 2 years. New range includes cassoulets and stews. Members of the Tastes of the West.

TORBAY HEALTH STORE
28 HYDE RD., PAIGNTON, TQ4 5BY
Tel & Fax: 01803 527251
Contact: Richard Shepherd (Proprietor)
Wide-ranging stocks of vitamin, herbal and
homeopathic remedies. Essential oils, Bach
flower remedies, organic wholefoods and
much, much more. Mail order service
available.

   **TOTNES HEALTH
SHOP & SEEDS BAKERY**
35 HIGH ST., TOTNES TQ9 5NP
Tel: 01803 862526
Contact: Barry Pope (Partner)
Health food retailer. Organic veg, bread and
other foods, organic essential oils, baking
fresh savouries and cakes with organic flour.

   D.J. & S.J. URSELL
ALLER FARM, DOLTON,
WINKLEIGH EX19 8PP
Tel: 01805 804414 Contact: David Ursell
Email: ursell@farmersweekly.net
Beef and cereals, wheat triticale, all
produced organically. Producer no. G791.
Day Visits.

PETER & MAGGIE WHITEMAN
LOWER TURLEY FARM,
CULLOMPTON EX15 1NA
Tel: 01884 32234
Contact: Peter & Maggie Whiteman
(Owners)
Vegetables sold locally through a box
scheme. Beef and lamb occasionally
available. Soil Association registered no.
W32/W. Fleeces, machine carded wool and
individually hand made felt hats for sale.
Yurts and yew longbows made to order.

   WIGHAM FARM LTD
WIGHAM, MORCHARD BISHOP EX17 6RJ
Tel & Fax: 01363 877350
Contact: Steve Chilcott
Email: info@wigham.co.uk
Website: www.wigham.co.uk
Soil Association certified (G2236) organic
farm and guest house, producing organic
eggs, table birds, lamb, beef, dairy
produce, pork and pork products (bacon,
sausage, etc.). See display ad.

   WILDWOOD
LOWER MANOR COTTAGE, THORNBY,
HOLSWORTHY EX22 7DD
Tel & Fax: 01409 261324
Contact: Lorna Howarth
Email: lorna@macace.co.uk
Wildwood is an organic nursery specialising
in wild, rare and interesting perennials, trees
and shrubs, including wild garlic, elderberry,
marshmallow, blueberry, ferns, dogwoods,
willows and much more. write or email for
catalogue. Soil Association no. G2256.

 **WILLOW VEGETARIAN
GARDEN RESTAURANT**
57 HIGH STREET, TOTNES TQ9 5PB
Tel: 01803 862605
Contact: Dani De Beaumont
Email: kimndani@aol.com
Willow is a popular fully vegetarian
restaurant. The delicious food is hand
prepared from natural ingredients which
are organic where possible. A good
selection of organic beers and wines can
be enjoyed.

WOODLAND ORGANICS
MOORFOOT CROSS, WOODLAND, NR.
DENBURY, NEWTON ABBOT TQ12 6EQ
Tel: 01803 813760 Contact: Mike Jones
Soil Association no. G2070. 7 acre organic
holding producing over 80 varieties of fruit
and vegetables plus organic free range
eggs. Operating direct delivery veg boxes,
plus supplying trade locally.

DORSET

 BARTON MEADOWS

BARTON MEADOWS FARM,
DORCHESTER RD., CERNE ABBAS DT2 7JG
Tel: 01300 341336
Contact: Dr & Mrs Gourley
Pedigree breeding of Aberdeen Angus and
Romney ewes (Soil Association symbol no.
956). Producer of organic beef and lamb
from high health status animals, suitable
for home freezers.

BECKLANDS FARM
WHITCHURCH CANONICORUM,
BRIDPORT DT6 6RG
Tel: 01297 560298
Contact: Hilary and Francis Joyce
Email: becklands.farm@wdi.co.uk
Eggs, beef, pork & cheese. Farmshop with
homemade jams and cakes. B&B in
thatched farmhouse, beautiful views, ponds,
river. Open days: 1st June-7th Sept
Tues/Thurs 10.45 a.m.- 3.45 p.m. Adults £3,
Children £1.50. Soil Association no. G4225.

BOSCOMBE HEALTH FOODS
8 ROYAL ARCADE, BOSCOMBE BH1 4BT
Tel: 01202 301947 Contact: Mrs S. Clark
Retail health food shop wide range of
foods & ingredients, dried fruit, nuts etc.,
drinks and alternative remedies, vitamins,
minerals.

CLIPPER TEAS LTD
BROADWINDSOR RD., BEAMINSTER,
DORSET DT8 3PR
Tel: 01308 863344 Fax: 01308 863847
Contact: Lorraine Brehme
Email: enquiries@clipper-teas.com
Website: www.clipper-teas.com
Importers and distributors of organically
produced teas. Our products are covered
by a range of certifying bodies.

DOWN TO EARTH
18 PRINCES ST., DORCHESTER DT1 1TW
Tel: 01305 268325 Contact: David Nesling
Retailers of a wide range of organic
produce including meat and poultry
products, butter, cheese, eggs, fruits and
vegetables, bread, dried foods. Frozen and
chilled produce. Specialists in British
cheeses.

MANDIE FLETCHER
SUNNYSIDE FARM, LOWER KINGCOMBE,
TOLLER PORCORUM,
DORCHESTER DT2 0EQ
Tel: 01300 321537
Email: MandieFletcher@Sunnyside95fsnet.co.uk

FOOTS EGGS
STONEY FARM, BISHOPS CAUNDLE,
SHERBORNE DT9 5ND
Tel: 01963 23033 Fax: 01962 23093
Contact: Mr J.R. Foot
Email: emmafoot@hotmail.com
Family run business for over 45 years.
Organic egg producers since 1997, we sell
our own produce. Registered with OF&G
(no. 01030197). Deliveries to Southern
England (London to Plymouth).

FOREST PRODUCTS (UK) LTD
BRIDPORT DT6 8BU
Tel: 01308 458111 Fax: 01308 420900
Contact: Gavin Brooking
Email: gavin@forestproducts.co.uk
Website: www.forestproducts.co.uk
Manufacturers of fine organic jam,
marmalades, chutneys and mustard.
Superb presentation, high quality, and a
full range. Members of the Soil Association
(no. P2758). Own label available on larger
orders.

GOLD HILL ORGANIC FARM
CHILD OKEFORD,
NR. BLANDFORD FORUM DT11 8HB
Tel: 01258 860293/861413
Fax: 01258 861413 Contact: Sara Cross
From May until March we sell up to 35
varieties of vegetables, fruit, organic beef,
milk and bread through our farm shop at
weekends only: Sat & Sun 9-1, 2-5.30. Veg
box scheme. Also at Castle Cary Market
(Tuesdays). Deliver to Blandford and
Shaftesbury.

J.R.A. & S. GOODBODY
BRIMSTONE COTTAGE, HOLWORTH,
OWERMOIGNE, DORCHESTER DT2 8NH
Tel: 01305 853045
Contact: J.R. Goodbody
Producer of organic seed (Soil Association
symbol holder for 10 years). Retail beef for
sale, slaughtered and butchered by organic
licence with Soil Association. Also sell
organic beef animals on hoof. Deliver
anywhere depending on size of orders.

THE HEALTH MINISTRY
16 HIGH ST., CHRISTCHURCH BH23 1AY
Tel: 01202 471152
Wide range of organic dried goods, e.g.
nuts, pulses, flour, etc.

HERITAGE PRIME—EARNESTLY BRITISH MEATS OF RARE QUALITY
SHEDBUSH FARM, MUDDY FORD LANE,
STANTON ST. GABRIEL, BRIDPORT DT6 6DR
Tel: 01297 489304 Fax: 01297 489531
Contact: Denise
Email: heritageprime@aol.com
Bio-dynamic farming—'food more carefully
produced than the highest organic
standard'. All animals and land treated
homeopathically: pork, lamb, beef. Mail
order only, nationwide.

LONGMEADOW ORGANIC VEGETABLES
GODMANSTONE, DORCHESTER DT2 7AE
Tel: 01300 341779
Contact: Hugh & Patsy Chapman
Soil Association registered (no. C60W).
Seasonal vegetables available from farm
gate shop, open 9.00-6.00 Wed-Sat; also
through box scheme.

MANOR FARM
GODMANSTONE, DORCHESTER DT2 7AH
Tel: 01300 341415 Fax: 01300 341170
Contact: Pam Best
Email: bestmanorfarm@compuserve.com
Mixed farm, organic since 1986 (Soil
Association reg. no. B27W). Pasteurised
whole and semi-skimmed milk and cream.
Unpasteurised wholemilk. Lamb and mince,
prepared for the freezer. Also wheat,
combed wheat reed and rearing calves.

MANOR FARM ORGANIC MILK LIMITED
MANOR FARM, GODMANSTONE,
DORCHESTER DT2 7AH
Tel: 01300 341415 Fax: 01300 341170
Contact: Will Best
Website: www.manorfarmorganic.co.uk
Organic milk from Dorset. Farms, whole and
semi-skimmed, pasteurised and cartoned in
500ml and 1 litre cartons, and cream in
240ml and 140ml pots and 2 litre containers.
Distribution over the South of England.

MARKUS PRODUCTS LTD
19 OLD MARKET CENTRE, STATION ROAD,
GILLINGHAM SP8 4QQ
Tel: 01747 823716 Fax: 01747 825692
Contact: Simon Clarke
Email: simon@markusproducts.co.uk
Website: www.markusproducts.co.uk
Manufacturer of flavoured batters, soft
cheese, stuffing and oils. Garlic spreads for
the pizza industry and fast food outlets.

ORGANIX BRANDS

KNAPP MILL, MILL RD.,
CHRISTCHURCH BH23 2LU
Tel: 01202 479701 Fax: 01202 479712
The only 100% organic baby food in the
UK. No bulking agents, just pure 100%
organic baby food.

RECTORY FARM

EAST CHALDON ROAD, WINFRITH
NEWBURGH, NR. DORCHESTER DT2 8DJ
Tel: 01305 852835
Contact: Annette Evans.
Pedigree Jersey herd producing milk,
cream and associated dairy products,
organic eggs and beef. Soil Association
registered (no. G2057). The farm lies
approx 2½ miles from Lulworth Cove.
Open free of charge to visitors.

SACRED PLANET

484 WIMBORNE ROAD, WINTON,
BOURNEMOUTH BH9 2EY
Tel: 01202 522026 Fax: 01202 537474
Contact: Penny Morgan
Email:sem.ace@virgin.net
Website: www.sacredplanet.co.uk
Ethical trading centre, wholefoods, health
products and groceries. Fresh take-away
foods, eco-household and cruelty-free
products, world crafts, new age gift store
and therapy treatment rooms.

N.R.S TOATE AND SONS

CANN MILLS, SHAFTESBURY SP7 0BL
Tel: 01747 852475 Fax: 01747 851936
Contact: Michael Stoate
Email: michaelstoate@lineone.net
Stoneground flour millers specialising in
organic wholemeal, brown and white flour.
Soil Association no. P1453.

STURTS FARM COMMUNITY

SHEILING TRUST, THREE CROSS ROAD,
WEST MOORS, FERNDOWN BH22 0NF
Tel: 01202 870572 (Farm) 01202 894292
(Shop) Contact: Markus Konig (Farmer)
Fully Bio-dynamic certified large market
garden, farm includes dairy, beed, poultry,
pigs, 90 acres. Farm shop includes full
range of fruit and veg, dry goods, health
products.

TAMARISK FARM

WEST BEXINGTON,
DORCHESTER DT2 9DF
Tel: 01308 897781/897784
Contact: Adam Simon
Email: organicfarm@tamariskfarm.co.uk
Website: www.tamariskfarm.co.uk
All home grown on family farm by the sea.
Order direct from the farm: beef, lamb,
mutton, sausages, wholemeal wheat and
rye flours and vegetables all year round
(Soil Association no. P07W).

UPLYME BUTCHERS

UPLYME RD., UPLYME DT7 3TQ
Tel: 01297 443236
Contact: Paul & Lisa Faiers (Owners)
Large selection of chilled dairy and dry
organic goods. Organic vegetables
delivered on Mondays. Stockists of quality
organic wines.

Today, Aveton Gifford is once more a thriving community, as it was in earlier days
when the harmonium was heaved aboard the village barge, and the Methodist Church
Sunday School set off down river singing their hearts out all the way to Bantham.

Jane Fitzgerald, *Off the Map* (2000)

COUNTY DURHAM

BOWLEES ORGANIC FARM
BOWLEES FARM, WOLSINGHAM,
WEARDALE DL13 3JF
Tel: 01388 528305 Contact: David Pike
Email: David@bowleesfarm.co.uk
Website: www.bowleesfarm.co.uk
Bowlees farm, the first registered organic
farm in County Durham, produces top
quality pork, bacon, hams, sausages, beef,
eggs, etc. in a truly unique free range
environment. Soil Association no. G2056.

EGGLESTON HALL GARDENS
THE COTTAGE, EGGLESTON HALL,
EGGLESTON, BARNARD CASTLE DL12 0AG
Tel: 01833 650115 Fax: 01833 650378
Contact: Mrs R.H. Gray
All vegetables, fruits and herbs sold from
the gardens when in season are organically
grown. We do not wholesale our produce.

THE HEALTH WAREHOUSE
15 POST HOUSE WYND,
DARLINGTON DL3 7LU
Tel: 01325 468570
Contact: Michael Barker
Retailing health foods and natural
medicines, fresh baked take-aways (on-site
bakery). Organic fresh produce, chilled
and dried goods.

MOLLYS WHOLEFOOD STORE
11 FRONT ST., FRAMWELLGATE MOOR,
DURHAM DH1 5EJ
Tel: 0191 386 2216
Contact: Fiona (Co-op Member)
Co-operative wholefood store, 100s of
organic lines including vegetables, fruit,
wines, beers, meat, bread, dairy produce
and eggs. Box scheme, café, books, also
homeopathic, Bach herbal and Ecover
products. Recycling scheme.

ORGANIC GROWERS OF DURHAM LTD (GROWING GREEN)
LOW WALWORTH MARKET GARDEN,
WALWORTH, DARLINGTON DL2 2NA
Tel: 01325 362466
Experimental work and education in
sustainable horticulture without using
animal products. Supported by 100+ local
subscribers who participate in the project
and receive a weekly bag of vegetables,
newsletter, etc.

There is growing scientific evidence that many diseases and susceptibility to illness in later life stem from exposure to toxins and poor quality food in childhood. "My daughter had rashes from allergies when she was just a few months old, and when we had her tested the practitioner said that her allergies to tomatoes, potatoes and dairy produce were due to the hormones given to the cows and the chemicals in the food. We changed to organic and now she can eat those foods."—Melissa Paulden, Berkshire

Tanyia Maxted-Frost, *The Organic Baby Book* (1999)

ESSEX

 JAMES ABBOTT
1 WATERFALL COTTAGES, PARK RD.,
RIVENHALL, WITHAM CM8 3PR
Tel & Fax: 01376 584576
Contact: James Abbott (Owner)
Growers of organically produced trees and
wild flowers on our own nursery. Planting
and design/landscaping advice service.

AURO ORGANIC PAINT SUPPLIES
UNIT 1, GOLDSTONES FARM, ASHDON,
SAFFRON WALDEN, ESSEX CB10 2LZ
Tel: 01799 584888 Fax: 01799 584042
Contact: Richard Hadfield
Email: auroorganicpaintsuk@cwcom.net
Website: www.auroorganic.co.uk
Importers of natural organic paints: 100%
free from petrochemicals and their
derivatives. The range includes emulsions,
glosses, eggshells, woodstains, floor
finishes, waxes, varnishes and adhesives, all
of which are uncompromising in their use
of natural ingredients.

 BUNTINGS
89 HIGH STREET, MALDON,
ESSEX CM9 5EP
Tel: 01621 853271 Fax: 01376 561233
Contact: Stephen Bunting
Retail fine food shop specialising in
butchery, delicatessen, home made pies,
cooked meats, patés. Soil Association
member/producer (no. P2704). Deliver to
CM8, CM9, CO6.

DALGETY ARABLE LIMITED
MORETON MILL, ONGAR CM5 0PD
Tel: 01277 890341 Fax: 01277 890541
Contact: Martin Veitch
Website: www.dalgety.co.uk
Agricultural merchants—Soil Association
organic certification no. P891. Grain
trading activity.

 FARMER KIT
LITTLE BOWSERS, LITTLE WALDEN,
SAFFRON WALDEN CB10 1XQ
Tel: 01799 527315 Fax: 01799 527315
Contact: Kim Barker
Organic eggs (reg. no. UKF060629);
organic strawberries, English and Chinese
vegetables (Soil Association reg. no.
G2143). Weekend stalls at Islington and
Borough Farmers' Markets. Wholesale
deliveries to New Covent Garden.

 FOOD FOR THOUGHT
4 CAMERON RD., SEVEN KINGS,
ILFORD IG3 8LA
Tel: 0181 597 4388 Contact: Peter Price
Strict wholefood shop supplying a
comprehensive range of fresh organic fruit
and veg, plus organic cereals, grains,
flakes, pulses, rice, dried fruit and nuts;
also proprietory organic products (Whole
Earth, Lima, etc), organic cosmetics and
beauty products.

THE HAPPY CATERPILLAR
92 LEIGH RD., LEIGH ON SEA SS9 1BU
Tel & Fax: 01702 712982
Contact: Peter Wilson (Proprietor)
Email: sales@happycaterpillar.co.uk
Website: www.happycaterpillar.co.uk
Shop and delivery service, fresh fruit and
vegetables, meat, bread, eggs, dairy, dried
produce, dietary specialities, books and
household goods. All GMO-free, all
certified organic produce. 9.30-5.30
except Weds 9.30-3.00.

 **HDRA,
THE ORGANIC KITCHEN GARDEN**
AUDLEY END, SAFFRON WALDEN CB11 4JG
Tel: 01799 520444
Open April-October 31st, Wednesdays to
Sundays plus Bank Holiday Mondays.
Everything to do with organic gardening.
Organic restoration of Victorian walled
kitchen garden.

HEPBURNS OF MOUNTNESSING
269 ROMAN ROAD, MOUNTNESSING,
BRENTWOOD CM15 0UH
Tel: 01277 353289 Fax: 01277 355589
Contact: Gordon Hepburn
Soil Association registered (no. P2695).
Traditional butcher and grazier with a
reputation for quality and service.
Established 1932. Highgrove organic beef,
lamb and pork when available.

HILLCREST FARM SHOP
HILLCREST FARM STOCK ROAD, STOCK,
NEAR INGATESTONE CM4 9QZ
Tel & Fax: 01277 840727
Contact: Brian Waterman
Email:
farmshop@hillcrestfarm.freeserve.co.uk
Website: www.hillcrestfarm.freeserve.co.uk
We provide high quality traditional and
organic pork, beef, lamb and poultry. We
are licenced members of the Soil
Association (no. P4495).

E. W. KING & CO LTD
MONKS FARM, PANTLINES LANE,
COGGESHALL ROAD, KELVEDON, ESSEX,
CO5 9PG
Tel: 01376 57000 Fax: 01376 571189
Contact: Mrs D. Haggett
Supplier of all horticultural seeds, including
many organically produced varieties for
both commercial and domestic use.

NAPIERS HERBS
COLCHESTER RD., TIPTREE,
ESSEX CO5 0EX
Tel: 01621 815238 Contact: Liz Adams
Email: lizadams@freeserve.co.uk
Website: www.napiersherbs.co.uk
I supply a range of over 200 varieties of
herb plants and also organically grown cut
herbs and salads to order. The shop is
open Thursday, Friday and Saturday.

PILGRIM'S NATURAL
41-43 HIGH ST., HALSTEAD CO9 2AA
Tel: 01787 478513
Also at 4 KING GEORGES PLACE, HIGH ST.,
MALDON CM9 5BZ
Tel: 01621 858605
Retailer and packer of a wide range of
organic food including butter and
yoghurts, ice cream, bread and cakes.
Meat available at Halstead shop only.

J. M. SAWDON
PELDON HALL, PELDON,
NR. COLCHESTER CO5 7PU
Tel: 0973 750367 Fax: 01206 735791
Contact: J. Sawdon
Email: j.sawdon@farmline.com
We store, bag, dress, clean, dry and blend
wheat, barley, triticale, oats, beans, peas,
maize, lucerne and bran.

SUNRISE HEALTHFOODS
18 SPA RD., HOCKLEY SS5 4PH
Tel: 01702 207017
Contact: Richard (Partner)
Healthfood shop carrying many organic
lines. Can obtain any organic requirements
to order. Special diets catered for. Natural
therapies daily. Special diet and natural
therapy centre.

TRADERS FAIR WORLD SHOP
10 HIGH ST., OLD HARLOW CM17 0DW
Tel & Fax: 01279 450908
Contact: Jokey Lloyd (Manageress)
Email: jokey@compuserve.com
Website: www.worldshops.org
Shop selling wide range of fairly traded
products including many organic dried
goods. Box scheme for mixed fruit and veg
from £7.50. Phone to order, collect Friday
p.m. or Saturday.
Also at UNIT 4, PORTAL PRECINCT, SIR
ISAAC'S WALK, COLCHESTER CO1 1JJ.
Tel: 01206 763380 Contact: Sue Fox
Email: foxnorth@tinyworld.co.uk

JENNY USHER

THE COTTAGE, THRESHERS BUSH,
NR. HARLOW CM17 0NS
Tel: 01279 444663 Contact: Jenny Usher
Soil Association registered grower/
wholesaler (no. U02E), fruit and veg. N.B
farm gate by arrangement only. Delivery to
E. Herts and W. Sussex.

WATER LANE NURSERIES

NAYLAND, COLCHESTER CO6 4JS
Tel: 01206 262880 Fax: 01206 262880
Contact: Simon Faithfull
Soil Association registered (nos. G3059
and P5211). Mixed vegetables, asparagus,
fruit, strawberries, medlars. Delivery to CO
postcodes area.

WELLGATE COMMUNITY FARM

COLLIER ROW RD, COLLIER ROW,
ROMFORD RM5 2BX
Tel: 01708 74750 Contact: Robert Gayler
We are a community farm on a small
acreage, producing eggs and goats milk all
year round, and vegetables, fruit and
flowers in season. We are talking about
small quantities only because of the size of
the plot. The farm opens at present on
weekdays 9.30 a.m.-3.30 p.m. and
weekends.

THE WHOLEFOOD STORE

26 HIGH ST., MANNINGTREE CO11 1AJ
Tel & Fax: 01206 391200
Contact: Jon or Sarah
Email: dyvig@hotmail.com
We are an independent and friendly
wholefood store selling an extensive range
of organic dried foods, fresh fruit and
vegetables, dairy products, drinks, bread
and pastries and meat to order. Soil
Association registered (no. R2355).

WRITTLE COLLEGE GARDEN CENTRE FARM SHOP

LORDSHIP RD., WRITTLE,
CHELMSFORD CM1 3RR
Tel: 01245 422011 Fax: 01245 424250
Contact: Emily Baker
Organic fruit and vegetables. Open 7 days
a week.

The close relationships between multinational corporations and national governments are increasingly becoming causes for concern. Between June 1997 and July 1998, for example, there were 56 official meetings between the biotech industry and the British government, compared to only six meetings with the environmental and consumer groups.

Luke Anderson, *Genetic Engineering, Food, and Our Environment* (1999)

Support for Citizen's Income continues to grow, especially in Britain and Western Europe. A recent study showed that a full Citizen's Income could be introduced in Ireland over a period of three budgets. It would result in nobody receiving less than the poverty line of income; all unemployment and poverty traps being eliminated; and it always being worthwhile for an unemployed person to take up a job.

James Robertson, *Transforming Economic Life* (1998)

GLOUCESTERSHIRE

ADEYS FARM ORGANIC MEATS
ADEYS FARM, BREADSTONE,
BERKELEY GL13 9HF
Tel: 01453 511218
Contact: Tim & Caroline Wilson
Soil Association licence no. G 1770. Adeys
Farm is a 500 acre mixed farm producing
superior quality organic beef, lamb, pork
and bacon. Professionally butchered for
direct sales to the public.

AMBERLEY VALE FOODS
UNIT 1-2 STATION ROAD, SOUTH
WOODCHESTER, STROUD GL5 5EQ
Tel: 01453 873400 Fax: 01453 873400
Contact: Mark Tyler
Specialist in organic fresh meats, especially
dry cured bacon, traditional sausage
products, hams and gammons. Winner of
Soil Association Award for Gluten-free Pork
sausage. Soil Association Symbol no. P2943.

THE AUTHENTIC BREAD CO
STRAWBERRY HILL FARM,
STRAWBERRY HILL, NEWENT GL18 1LH
Tel: 01531 828181 Fax: 01531 828151
Contact: Jane Davis
Wholesale bakers of speciality organic
bread, cakes, croissants, pasties, etc. 1996
Soil Association Organic Food Award
Winner, 1998 highly commended. Own
distribution within 60 mile radius; mail
order. Soil Association symbol no. P1912.
See display ad.

BODYWISE UK LTD, NATRACARE
UNIT 23, MARSH LANE INDUSTRIAL
ESTATE, MARSH LANE,
PORTBURY BS20 0NH
Tel: 01275 371764 Fax: 01275 371765
Contact: Susie Hewson
Email: info@natracare.com
Website: www.natracare.com
Natracare 100% cotton tampons with and
without applicator. Soil Association
L/N1303, Organic Farmers & Growers
UK120044, OCIA (USA). See display ad.

CAMPHILL VILLAGE TRUST— OAKLANDS PARK
OAKLANDS PARK, NEWNHAM GL14 1EF
Tel: 01594 516550 Fax: 01594 516821
Working community with people with
special needs. Soil Association V0IM,
Demeter 101. Involved with regional land
training (Bio-dynamic), vegetables, herbs
and fruit for wholesaling and box scheme.
Work opportunities for many levels of ability.

CHELTENHAM NUTRITION CENTRE
133 BATH RD., CHELTENHAM GL53 7LT
Tel: 01242 514150 Contact: D. Galpin
Also at 28 WINCHCOMBE ST.,
CHELTENHAM GL52 1LX
Tel: 01242 529934 Contact: D. Galpin
Also at 98 HIGH ST., TEWKESBURY
Tel: 01684 299620 Contact: D. Galpin
Retail health food stores—wide range of
organic products. Established 28 years,
advice always available from trained,
qualified, friendly staff.

Individual and societal health can only be improved if decisions are taken and
implemented by people who can: relate directly to each other; understand the
relevance of decisions to their lives; determine the size of the constituency which
needs to be involved in the decision-making; and therefore practise human scale
decision-making.

Robin Stott, *The Ecology of Health* (2000)

COTSWOLD HEALTH PRODUCTS LTD

5-8 TABERNACLE RD.,
WOTTON-UNDER-EDGE GL12 7EF
Tel: 01453 843694 Fax: 01453 521375
Contact: K. R. Davies
Email: sales@cotsherb.demon.co.uk
Website: www.cotsherb.co.uk
Soil Association no. P1926. Importers and
distributors of herbs and spices.

CROOKED END FARM

RUARDEAN, FOREST OF DEAN GL17 9XF
Tel: 01594 544482
Contact: Morag Norman
Small mixed organic farm (Soil Association
licence G2393). Close to Forest of Dean,
views across Wye Valley. Free range eggs,
vegetables in season, beef, lamb, pork. Self
catering holiday cottage.

D.M. & S.A.L.FOSTER

GROVE FARM, CHASTLETON,
MORETON-IN-MARSH GL56 0SZ
Tel: 01608 674214 Fax: 01608 676326
Contact: Sue Foster
Email: d.m.foster@btinternet.com
Forage and beef finishers. Soil Association
reg. no. G2271.

GILBERT'S

GILBERT'S LANE, BROOKTHORPE,
NR. GLOUCESTER GL4 0UH
Tel & Fax: 01452 812364
Contact: Jenny Beer
Email: jenny@gilbertsbb.demon.co.uk
Website: www.smoothhound.co.uk
Bed and Breakfast in highly acclaimed 16th
century listed timber framed house on
organic smallholding. Much of the
delicious English breakfast is home grown,
the rest as local and organic as possible.

GLOBAL ORGANIC MARKETS

UNIT 5, CANAL IRONWORKS,
HOPE MILL LANE, LONDON ROAD,
BRIMSCOMBE, STROUD GL5 2SH
Tel & Fax: 01453 884123
Contact: Andie Soutar
Email: globalorganicmarkets@fsmail.net
Organic fruit, vegetables and eggs.
Producer marketing: wholesale collection
and delivery in surrounding areas. Retail
market stalls in Stroud (Gloucester)
Shambles Market (Wednesday/Friday) and
Old Spitalfields, London (Sunday).

HEALTH-WISE

23 NORTH WALK, YATE BS37 4AP
Tel & Fax: 01454 322168
Contact: Mrs P. Dyer
Open 9-5.30 Mon-Sat supplying organic
cereal, nuts, seeds, jam, flour, vegetarian
food. Collection Point for Better Food Co.
box scheme.

HOBBS HOUSE BAKERY

UNIT 6, CHIPPING EDGE ESTATE,
HATTERS LANE,
CHIPPING SODBURY BS17 6AA
Tel: 01454 321629 Fax: 01454 329757
Contact: Clive Wells & Trevor Herbert
(Partners)
Soil Association registered. Organic
wholemeal and white bread distributed in
the Bristol, Bath and South Gloucestershire
area.
Also at 39 HIGH ST.,
CHIPPING SODBURY BS37 6BA
Tel: 01454 321629 Fax: 01454 329757
Contact: Clive Wells & Trevor Herbert
We are licensed by the Soil Association
(P1632), producing organic white and
wholemeal bread for our own shops and
wholesale outlets.

In order to assess the sustainability of human activity, the Canadian ecologist William
Rees and his colleague Mathis Wackernagel developed the concept of the ecological
footprint. This they define as the land areas required to supply a city or a nation with
food or timber products, and to absorb its output of waste gases such as CO_2.

Herbert Girardet, *Creating Sustainable Cities* (1999)

KITCHEN GARDEN PRESERVES
UNIT 15, SALMON SPRINGS TRADING
ESTATE, CHELTENHAM ROAD,
STROUD GL6 6NU
Tel: 01453 759612 Fax: 01453 755899
Contact: Barbara Moinet
A range of hand-made jams, marmalades
and chutneys. Our organic Seville orange
marmalade won its category in the 1999
organic food awards. Telephone for
stockists. Soil Association no. P2409.

KOLISKO FARM
BROOKTHORPE (between GLOUCESTER
AND STROUD) GL4 0UN
Tel: 01757 812722 Contact: Adriaan Luyk
Bio-dynamic farm: dairy, beef and
vegetables. Shop with full range of
groceries. Registered with BDAA (no. 239).
Milk round (local, Gloucester, Stroud).

   LA BODEGA

TAURUS CRAFTS, THE OLD PARK,
LYDNEY PARK ESTATE, LYDNEY GL15 6BU
Tel: 01594 844841 Fax: 01594 845636
Contact: Cliff Gorman
La Bodega stocks local produce and
organic foods, specialising in organic
wines, coffees and deli foods.We are part
of the Taurus Craft Centre, celebrating
living by bringing together wholesome
food, fine arts and handmade crafts.

LIVING EARTH PRODUCE
RUSKIN MILL, OLD BRISTOL RD.,
NAILSWORTH GL6 0LA
Tel: 01453 837510 Fax: 01453 835029
Contact: Andy Horton
Organic and Bio-dynamic food store.
Vegetables, fruit, frozen meat, milk,
cheese, yoghurts, herbs and spices, eggs
and a wide range of groceries.

MAD HATTERS RESTAURANT
3 COSSACK SQUARE,
NAILSWORTH GL6 0DB
Tel: 01453 832615
Contact: Mike & Carolyn Findlay
Since the use of GMOs in animal feeds we
use totally organic meat, milk, butter,
cream and cheese. Non-smoking.
Wheelchair access. Local seasonal organic
produce cooked classically without
additives or cheap substitutes by four
enthusiastic and idealistic chefs. Organic
wines, beers and soft drinks. Bright
informal décor. B&B.

  M.A.S.

9 BREVEL TERRACE, CHARLTON KINGS,
CHELTENHAM GL53 8JZ
Tel: 01242 234355 Fax: 01242 234355
Contact: William Evans (Owner)
We market nationally a comprehensive
range of grass seed and wild flower
conservation mixtures for amenity and
agricultural use. Seeds for the organic
grower, special grass leys for cattle, horses,
goats, hens and deer. Seed for fodder
crops and green manure crops.

  MOTHER NATURE

2 BEDFORD ST., STROUD GL5 1AY
Tel: 01453 758202
Contact: Trevor Searby (Co-owner)
Email: watertacks@cwcom.net
Food on three floors. Organic wine, meat,
bread, dairy products, hand made Dutch
chocolates, champagne and perry.

THE NATURAL GROCERY STORE LTD
142 BATH ROAD, CHELTENHAM GL53 7NG
Tel: 01242 243737 Fax: 01242 238872
Contact: Paul Lewis
Email: triple8.trading@virgin.net
Soil Association membership. Fresh fruit and
vegetables, dairy, meat, poultry, fish, bread,
cakes, wine, beer and cider; also canned,
dried & bottled groceries and provisions.
Open daily 8 a.m. - 10 p.m.

NEAL'S YARD REMEDIES

9 ROTUNDA PLACE, MONTPELIER ST.,
CHELTENHAM GL50 1SX
Tel: 01242 522136
Neal's Yard Remedies manufactures and
sells natural cosmetics in addition to
stocking an extensive range of herbs,
essential oils, homeopathic remedies and
reference material.

NORDEX FOOD UK LIMITED

WYNCHFIELD HOUSE, KINGSCOTE,
NR. TETBURY GL8 8YN
Tel: 01666 890500 Fax: 01666 890522
Contact: Claire Jackson
Email: dairyland@nordex-food.co.uk
Website: www.nordex-food.co.uk
Nordex Food UK is a Danish manufacturing
and dairy trading organisation selling and
developing organic dairy products for UK
retail/wholesale sectors. Marketed under
'Dairyland' organic brand and Soil
Association certified.

THE ORGANIC FARM SHOP

ABBEY HOME FARM, BURFORD ROAD,
CIRENCESTER GL7 5HF
Tel: 01285 640441
Fax: 01285 640441/644827
Contact: Hilary Chester-Master
Email: cargofco@aol.com
Website: www.theorganicfarmshop.co.uk
Farm trailer rides, educational visits, cookery
demos. 1999 Producer of the Year award
winning farm. 100% organic farmshop and
cafe with garden, and woodland walk. Our
own vegetables, meat, eggs. Home made
freezer dishes and general groceries. Open
Tues-Sat. Soil Association reg. no. G1715.

THE ORGANIC SHOP

THE SQUARE,
STOW-ON-THE-WOLD GL54 1AB
Tel: 01451 831004
Contact: Sheila Wye (Proprietor)
The first independently owned retail shop
in the UK specialising in the sale of Soil
Association symbol produce, including
meat. Open 9.00 a.m. to 5.30 p.m. every
day except Christmas and Boxing Day.

OUT OF THIS WORLD

6-8 PITTVILLE ST., CHELTENHAM GL52 2LJ
Tel: 01242 518300 Contact: Sheila Clifford
Small chain of ethical and organic
supermarkets in Newcastle upon Tyne,
Nottingham and Cheltenham (also organic
café). Selling over 4000 products, most
food products certified organic plus fairly
traded crafts, recycled paper, bodycare
products etc. Consumer co-op with over
17,500 members.

E. & J. PHILLIPS LTD

18-22 CHURCH ST., TETBURY GL8 8JG
Tel: 01666 502364 Contact: Teresa Francis
Bakers and confectioners who also produce
organic bread. Established 1870. Soil
Association reg. no. P1721.

PINETUM PRODUCTS DIRECT

PINETUM LODGE, CHURCHAM GL2 8AD
Tel: 0452 750554 Fax: 01452 750402
Contact: David Wilkin
Email: pinetum1@aol.com
We supply everything necessary to
promote a healthy fertile soil: a selection of
pest controls, useful gardening aids and
some popular vitamins as trace elements in
pill form. Member of Good Gardeners
Association.

   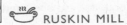

RUSKIN MILL

OLD BRISTOL RD.,
NAILSWORTH GL6 0QE
Tel: 01453 837500 Fax: 01453 837512
Contact: Julian Pyzer
Part of a special needs further education
college, with Bio-dynamic market garden
and mixed farm, and fish farm. Café and
shop; crafts, exhibitions, workshops,
concerts, storytelling and talks.

SHIPTON MILL LTD

LONG NEWNTON, TETBURY GL8 8RP
Tel: 01666 505050 Fax: 01666 504666
Contact: John Lister (M.D.)
Email: jlister@shipton-mill.com
Website: www.shipton-mill.com
We are a small flour mill in the heart of the Cotswolds, producing stoneground organic flours for the craft baker as well as supplying the home baker through our friendly mail order service. Members of the Soil Association.

SLIPSTREAM ORGANICS
34A LANGDON RD.,
CHELTENHAM GL53 7NZ
Tel: 01242 227273 Fax: 01242 227798
Contact: Nick McCordall
Email: nick@slipstream-organics.co.uk
Website: www.slipstream-organics.co.uk
Award winning box scheme established 1994, supplying localy grown organic food to over 400 households in Cheltenham, Gloucester and Stroud. Boxes range from £5-£15 at present. Small retail operation also (Fridays only). Please phone for more information. Soil Association no. R1732.

SUNSHINE CRAFT BAKERY
THE BRITISH SCHOOL, SLAD ROAD,
STOUD GL5 1QW
Tel: 01453 752592
Contact: Andrew Hill (Partner)
Bake and supply organic bread, cakes and savouries (vegetarian) for our own shop (see below) and Cheltenham Nutrition Centres.

    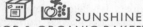 **SUNSHINE HEALTH SHOP & ORGANIC BAKERY**
25 CHURCH ST., STROUD GL5 1JL
Tel: 01453 763923
Contact: Ray Hill (Proprietor)
Food, herbals, supplements, fresh organic breads, cakes, savouries, fruit and vegetables. Mail order, local deliveries, specialist herbal and healthfood suppliers to practitioners and trade. Soil Association nos. R1557, P1615.

THORNBURY ORGANIC CO-OP
9 CROSSWAYS RD., THORNBURY BS35 2YL
Tel: 01454 415345 Contact: Judith Dale
Local delivery service for a comprehensive range of organic foods including fresh fruit and vegetables, dairy produce, bread, meat, fish and wine, locally produced whenever possible.

  G.S.& C.J.TOMLINSON

DOWN FARM, WESTONBIRT,
TETBURY GL8 8QW
Tel: 01666 880214 Fax: 01666 880266
Contact: G.S. Tomlinson (Partner)
Email: bpc@downfarm.fsnet.co.uk
Producer of organic beef and milk.

 WYEDEAN WHOLEFOODS

13 & 14 MARKET STREET,
CINDERFORD GL14 2RX
Tel & Fax: 01594 825455/826639
Contact: Barry or Heather
One-stop organic shopping with over 700 organic lines. Dairy and eggs, meat and poultry, bread, fruit, vegetables and commodity lines.

 WYEDEAN WHOLEFOODS

15 MARKET PLACE, COLEFORD,
GLOUCESTER GL16 8AW
Tel & Fax: 01594 810303
One-stop organic shopping with over 700 organic lines. Dairy and eggs, meat and poultry, bread, fruit, vegetables and commodity lines.

 WYEDEAN WHOLEFOODS

18 NEWERNE STREET, LYDNEY,
GLOUCESTER GL15 5RF
Tel & Fax: 01594 841907
One-stop organic shopping with over 700 organic lines. Dairy and eggs, meat and poultry, bread, fruit, vegetables and commodity lines.

HAMPSHIRE & THE ISLE OF WIGHT

BROUGHTON ORGANICS
THE ANCHORAGE, SALISBURY RD.,
BROUGHTON,
NR. STOCKBRIDGE SO20 8BX
Tel: 01794 301234 Contact: S.L. Tidy
Organic fruit, vegetables, eggs, poultry all
produced to Soil Association symbol
standard (no. T07S). Use permaculture
techniques. Camping on ECEAT-listed
ecological campsite.

M.J. & L.K. COLLINS
PARK FARM, HECKFIELD, HOOK RG27 0LD
Tel & Fax: 0118 932 6535
Contact: Martin Collins (Partner)
Organic beef, pork and lamb produced
with traditional breeds, also fresh fruit and
veg and dairy products. Visitors to the
shop are welcome to walk around the
farm—bring your wellies. Open Tuesday,
Wednesday a.m., Thursday, Friday &
Saturday. Tel: 0118 932 6650.

DEACONS NURSERY
MOOR VIEW, GODSHILL,
ISLE OF WIGHT PO38 3HW
Tel: 01983 840750 / 522243
Fax: 01983 523575
Contact: Grahame D. Deacon (Partner)
Producers of top and soft fruit species i.e.
apples, pears, plums, gages, peaches,
medlars, loganberries, kiwis, grapes, nuts,
hops, strawberries, horse radish etc. Trees
sent anywhere, all over UK and abroad. Free
Deacons Millennium apple tree on all orders
over £40 during 2000. See display ad.

  EARTHRISE
19-21 VICTORIA ROAD NORTH,
SOUTHSEA PO5 1PL
Tel & Fax 02392 755660
Contact: Neil Dickson
Email: info@all-seasons.demon.co.uk
Website: www.earthrise.com
Sole UK importer of Earthrise, the world's
best selling range of spirulina, chlorella,
barley and wheatgrass tablets and
powders. Sole importers of Pines
wheatgrass products.

GODSHILL ORGANICS
NEWPORT RD., GODSHILL,
ISLE OF WIGHT PO38 3LY
Tel & Fax: 01983 840723
Contact: Mrs R. Illman (Partner)
Soil Association certified smallholding,
retail shop and box scheme and delivery
service. Specialists in as wide a range of
organic produce as possible.

GREENACRES ORGANIC CO LTD
THE OLD GATE HOUSE, 27 THE DRIVE,
TOTTON, SOUTHAMPTON SO40 9EH
Tel: 023 8066 8137 Fax: 023 8066 8138
Contact: Stuart and Tara Tilley
Email: info@greenacresorganic.co.uk
Website: www.greenacresorganic.co.uk
Home delivery service covering Hampshire
and Surrey (plus parts of Berks, Wilts and
Dorset). Extensive range of organic
products: wholefoods, meat & fish, fruit &
veg, dairy, baby foods, non foods. Soil Ass.
reg. no. P5436.

Environmental sustainability . . . can generate jobs at the local level, by shifting the
emphasis from employment in extractive industries to work in resource conservation—
enhancing recycling and the energy efficiency of cities and individual buildings.

Herbert Girardet, *Creating Sustainable Cities* (1999)

HARROWAY ORGANIC GARDENS
KINGSCLERE RD., WHITCHURCH RG28 7QB
Tel & Fax: 01256 895346
Contact: Mandy Wright
We are an organic market garden producing a wide range of vegetables and soft fruit. Our farm shop is open 9-6 Thursdays to Sundays. Soil Association reg. no. G971.

L.V. HEATHCOTE & PARTNERS
WARBORNE FARM, WARBORNE LANE, BOLDRE, LYMINGTON SO41 5QD
Tel: 01590 688488 Fax: 01590 688096
Contact: George Heathcote
We have an organic vegetable box scheme (delivery service) and fresh and frozen meat sales (also delivered). We are also members of the Soil Association (licence no. G2404).

NATURALLY HEALTH FOODS
5 WATERLOO COURT, SHAWS WALK, ANDOVER SP10 1QJ
Tel: 01264 332375 Fax: 01264 392689
Contact: Nikki Dake
Under new management, small independent NAHS healthfood shop building up organic ranges. We also stock supplements, herbals, homeopathic remedies, essential oils, foods/ingredients. Special diets a special concern.

NORTHDOWN ORCHARD
SOUTH LITCHFIELD, BASINGSTOKE RG25 3BP
Tel & Fax: 01256 771477
Contact: Mike Fisher
Box scheme serving Basingstoke and the Winchester areas. Vegetables and eggs available from farm (phone for details). Soil Association organic certification P1217 and G1217. Delivery to RG20-27, SO22-24.

THE ORGANIC FOOD COMPANY
UNIT 2, BLACKNEST INDUSTRIAL ESTATE, BLACKNEST, NR. ALTON GU34 4PX
Tel: 01420 520530 Fax: 01420 23985
Contact: Sarah Gooding
Email: sarah@tofco.free-online.co.uk
We import and distribute ambient organic products: biscuits, tomato sauces and condiments, vegetable juices, fruit bars, sweet and savoury spreads, baby food. Warehouse open to the public for sales one day per week. See display ad.

PETTY, WOOD & CO
PO BOX 66, LIVINGSTONE RD., ANDOVER SP10 5LA
Tel: 01264 345500 Fax: 01264 332025
Contact: F.E. Fulat
Email: ffulat@pettywood.co.uk
The distributor of Epicure organics. A comprehensive range of fine food organic products ranging from meat, pasta, sauces, bakery, oils and confectionery. Also distributors of Baxters Organics, Duchy Originals, Salla and Lensi Pasta Pals. See display ad.

RASANCO LTD
OLD ESTATE OFFICE, SUTTON SCOTNEY SO21 3JN
Tel: 01962 761935 Fax: 01962 761860
Contact: Russell Smart
Email: rasanco@dial.pipex.com
Website: www.rasanco.com
Soil Association reg. no. P2960. Organic ingredients for food and drink manufacturers. Fruit, vegetables, seeds, pulses, starches, syrups, tomatoes, nuts, spices, herbs, oils, fats, cocoa, pasta, egg, dairy. Delivery UK, Eire, EU. See display ad.

G. & S. RHIMES ORGANIC GROWERS
HILL VIEW, CHURCH LANE, WEST MEON, PETERSFIELD GU32 1JB
Tel: 01730 829208 Contact: Mr G. Rhimes
Soil Association licence no. G2039.
Vegetables, potatoes and soft fruit in season (summer and autumn).

SCOLTOCKS HEALTH FOODS

1 MARKET PLACE, RINGWOOD BH24 1AN
Tel: 01425 473787 Contact: Yvonne Tilley
Member of National Association of Health
Stores, member of Institute of Health Food
Retailing. Dietary foods, vegetarian
specialist. Organic fresh seasonal
vegetables.

SUNNYFIELDS ORGANIC

JACOBS GUTTER LANE, TOTTON,
SOUTHAMPTON SO40 9FX
Tel: 023 80 871408 Fax: 023 80 871146
Contact: Ian Nelson
Email: infor@sunnyfields.co.uk
Soil Association registered (symbol no.
B655) fruit and vegetable growers. Farm
shop open 7 days. Home delivery to Hants,
Dorset and W/S London. 2,500 + products,
box scheme.

TIME FOR CHANGE LTD

167 FAWCETT RD., SOUTHSEA PO4 0DH
Tel: 02392 818786
Retail shop with 100% natural products
run by vegan workers co-operative.
Wholefoods, household goods, cosmetics,
radical books and mags, aromatherapy
oils, recycled cards, toiletries, fresh pastries
and bread, t-shirts, herbs and spices.

TURF CROFT ORGANIC HERBS

TURF CROFT COTTAGE, BURLEY,
RINGWOOD BH24 4DF
Tel & Fax: 01425 403502
Contact: Simon Weir
Wide range of fresh cut culinary herbs for
wholesale. Soil Association symbol, BDAA
member.

UPTON READHEADS ORGANIC POULTRY

UPTON HOUSE FARM, WONSTON,
WINCHESTER SO21 3LR
Tel: 01962 760219 Fax: 01962 761419
Contact: Robin Readhead
Supply all organic meats in own
refrigerated transport around M25 (to 10
miles), M3 (to 10 miles), M4 (to Swindon).
OF&G certified (no. UK2 F05065). Other
delivery within 10 miles of M3, M4, M23,
M25, M27.

WYCHWOOD WATERLILY FARM

FARNHAM RD., ODIHAM,
HOOK RG29 1HS
Tel: 01256 702800 Fax: 01256 701001
Contact: Ann or Clare Henley
Email: cnhenley@aol.com
Waterlilies & water plants—a small family
business. Odiham Waterlily collection on
site owned by Clair Henley. All plants pond
ready—new 'Waterwych' that keeps water
clear and pure. Catalogue available.

This analysis means that, due to the way money is put into circulation, we have an economic system that needs to grow or inflate constantly. This is a major cause of our system's continuous and insatiable need for economic growth, a need that must be satisfied regardless of whether the growth is proving beneficial. If ever growth fails to materialize, and inflation does not occur, the money supply will contract and the economy will move into recession. Politicians naturally do not want inflations and recessions occurring during their periods in office, so they work very closely with the business community to ensure that growth takes place. This is despite the damage that continual expansion is doing, both to human society and the natural world.

Richard Douthwaite, *The Ecology of Money* (1999)

HEREFORDSHIRE

A BUNDANCE PRODUCE
GLENTHORPE, LITTLE BIRCH,
HEREFORD HR2 8BD
Tel: 01981 540181 Contact: Tim Headley
Bio-dynamic/organic growers of vegetable
crops, specialising in salads. Box scheme in
Herefordshire.

ARCHWOOD GREENHOUSES
ROBINSWOOD, GOODRICH HR9 6HT
Tel: 01600 890125 Contact: Mr J. Seal
Compost systems. Robust pressure-
preserved timber 2ft, 3ft or 4ft square bins.
Single, double or triple systems.
Removeable front boards. No post holes to
dig.

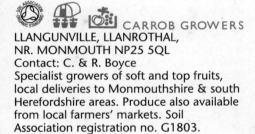 CARROB GROWERS
LLANGUNVILLE, LLANROTHAL,
NR. MONMOUTH NP25 5QL
Contact: C. & R. Boyce
Specialist growers of soft and top fruits,
local deliveries to Monmouthshire & south
Herefordshire areas. Produce also available
from local farmers' markets. Soil
Association registration no. G1803.

 DUNKERTONS
CIDER COMPANY & CIDER HOUSE
RESTAURANT
LUNTLEY, PEMBRIDGE,
NR. LEOMINSTER HR6 9ED
Tel: 01544 388653 Fax: 01544 388654
Restaurant 01544 388161
Contact: Ivor Dunkerton
Strong, tasty, still and sparkling ciders and
perries from traditional varieties of fruit.
Bottled and draught. Soil Association no.
P528. Restaurant uses organic ingredients
where possible.

FODDER
26-27 CHURCH ST., HEREFORD HR1 2LR
Tel: 01432 358171 Fax: 01432 277861
Contact: Jonathan Seddon-Harvey
Fodder stocks an extensive range of
organic fruit and vegetables, breads, dairy
produce, wholefoods and wines.

 GEORGE'S
25 HIGH ST., KINGTON HR5 3AX
Tel: 01544 231400
Contact: Amanda Mackenzie
A licensed wholefood shop stocking a wide
range of good foods which include many
organic products. Supplements and
remedies are available and we are pleased
to order any item which may not be in
stock.

GREEN ACRES ORGANIC PRODUCE
GREEN ACRES FARM SHOP, DINMORE,
HEREFORD HR4 8ED
Tel: 01568 797045 Contact: S. Jenkins
Soil Association no. J14M (member since
1982). All seasonal organic veg and fruit,
and additive-free and free range meats.
Organic Turkeys at Christmas. Local
deliveries.

STEVE & SUE HALL
HANLEY MEADOWS, HOPLEYS GREEN,
ALMELEY HR3 6QX
Tel: 01544 340689
Contact: Steve or Sue Hall
Bio-dynamic holding producing mainly
protected crops under cold glass. Winter
salads, tomatoes, beans, peppers etc. Also
small Shorthorn suckler herd and two acres
top fruit.

HARDWICKE ORGANICS
HARDWICKE HILL, WINSLOW,
BROMYARD HR7 4SX
Tel: 01885 483364 Fax: 01885 488483
Contact: Caroline Lingham
Organic grower at Hardwick Hill, Bromyard
(Soil Association reg. no. G2141).
Retail at 80 THE HOMEND, LEDBURY HR8
4AB. Tel: 01531 633058. Soil Assn no. P4467.

HAY WHOLEFOODS AND DELICATESSEN
LION ST., HAY-ON-WYE HR3 5AA
Tel: 01497 820708
Contact: Marion & Mandy (Partners)
Small but comprehensive wholefood shop
with wide range of organic goods including
wine, cheese, vegetables and basic
groceries. Good delicatessen with organic
choice where possible. Box scheme.

KINGSTREET FARMHOUSE BED AND BREAKFAST
KINGSTREET FARMHOUSE, EWYAS
HAROLD, HEREFORD HR2 0HB
Tel: 01981 240208
Contact: Emma Harrington
Bed and breakfast offering organic and
local produce. Period furnishings. Quiet
location and lovely views.

LEDBURY WHOLEFOODS
82 THE HOMEND, LEDBURY HR8 1BX
Tel: 01531 632889 Contact: Sheila Burns
Wholefoods and healthfoods. Many organic
lines plus veg collecting point. 70+ herbs
and spices, 12+ coffee bean varieties. If you
don't see it, please ask, we'll try and get it.

MEADOWLAND MEATS
MODEL FARM, HILDERSLEY,
ROSS-ON-WYE HR9 7NN
Tel: 01989 562208 Fax: 01989 769724
Contact: Patrick McIlroy
Retail and doorstep delivery of organic and
free range produce. Members of Soil
Association, reg. no. P1791.

   J.R.MEE

SPRINGFIELD FARM, STEENSBRIDGE, LEOMINSTER HR6 0LU
Tel: 01568 760270 Fax: 01568 760418
Contact: R. Mee
Farmers and packers of high grade table
birds (chickens and turkeys) for sale to
wholesalers and retailers—also at our Farm
Gate.

NITTY GRITTY WHOLEFOODS
24 WEST ST., LEOMINSTER HR6 8ES
Tel: 01568 611600
Contact: Pamela Horsley
Wholefood herbal remedies, local produce,
free range eggs, traditional herbs & plants,
fruit trees, organic bread daily, organic
cakes.

OAT CUISINE
47 BROAD ST., ROSS-ON-WYE HR9 7DY
Tel: 01989 566271
Contact: Trevor Rogers (Owner)
A thriving shop, and bistro-type eat in and
take-away business with a wonderfully
friendly atmosphere in the very heart of
Ross-on-Wye. Some organic produce.

THE ORGANIC MARKETING COMPANY LTD
LEIGHTON COURT, LOWER EGGLETON,
LEDBURY HR8 2UN
Tel: 01531 640819 Fax: 01531 640818
Email: mail@organicmarketing.co.uk
Website: www.organicmarketing.co.uk
Contact: Kathryn Goldthorpe
Nationwide wholesale supplier of
organically grown vegetables, fruit and
other produce. Many crops are planned
with our own co-operative growers to
meet specific customer requirements. Soil
Association reg. no. P1999.

NORGROW
INTERNATIONAL LIMITED

FOOD INGREDIENTS FOR ALL SEASONS

**WORKING DIRECTLY WITH GROWERS AND PROCESSORS
SUPPLYING THE INDUSTRY WITH QUALITY PRODUCTS
LICENCED BY THE SOIL ASSOCIATION**

- FRUIT AND VEGETABLES
- PEAS, BEANS & PULSES
- HERBS & SPICES
- ESSENTIAL OILS

- SEEDS, GRAINS & LENTILS
- NUTS
- RICES
- SUGARS

SPECIALIST ITEMS INCLUDING:

SOUP MIXES ~ PASTA SHAPES ~ HONEYS ~ TEAS ~ COFFEES
RETAIL PACKED PRODUCTS DIRECT FROM ORIGIN

MORE THAN JUST SUPPLY

PROJECT PARTNERING AND MANAGEMENT
SUPPLY CHAIN AUDITING AND CERTIFICATION

FULL COMPANY DETAILS ON OUR WEB SITE
OR CALL FOR AN INFORMATION PACK

NORGROW INTERNATIONAL LIMITED
GRANGE FARM LODGE, LEVERINGTON COMMON
WISBECH, CAMBRIDGESHIRE, PE13 5JG

TELEPHONE +44-1945-410810 FAX +44-1945-410850
E-MAIL sales@norgrow.com WEB SITE http://www.norgrow.com

Know your food...

Which biblical figure sold his birthright for a "pottage of lentils"?
Which part of fig is used as a mild laxative?
How much polyunsaturated oil do sesame seeds contain?

the Organic Adventure

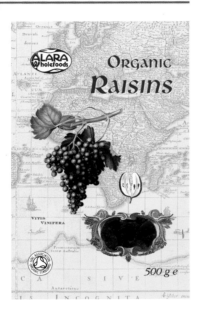

Almonds
Brazil nuts
Cashew nuts
hazel nuts
Walnuts
Apricots
figs
Prunes
Raisins
Sultanas
Sesame seeds
Sunflower seeds
Red lentils
Cous cous

Travel with Alara to the four corners of the Earth and discover:

high quality organic products carefully sourced directly from around the world offered at the excellent prices you have been waiting for,

Innovative, elegant, eye catching designs with the 'Know your food...' quiz on every packet,

the farm that the products come from traced on the web site,

the origin, history of domestication of the plants, in-depth nutritional analysis and health promoting properties, recipes and many interesting facts on the web site

www.alara.co.uk

organics direct ™

food as nature intended.....
fresh produce, dairy,
bread & groceries
from the farm to your door
at the best prices

winner of the soil association's organic
box scheme of the year award 1999
(company operated category)

open every day!
nationwide delivery!

call now for your free brochure

020 7729 2828

or order online @
www.organicsdirect.co.uk

be kind to yourself
and the planet,
eat organic!

Some things change...

The organic food industry is constantly evolving - and this striking new design from Infinity Foods illustrates the point beautifully. Fresh and vibrant, it captures both the natural elements which inspired our beginnings in 1970 and the pioneering spirit which drives us today.

...others never will.

As a workers co-operative, we understand the value of lasting relationships. So you can count on us to be as committed to your business as we are to ours.

- Friendly and efficient service
- Soil Association registered [P1465]
- National distribution
- UK's widest choice of products
- Sourcing of ingredients
- Import and Export facility
- Promotion of 'fair trade' goods

For further information and a catalogue call Infinity Foods on

01273 424060

INFINITY FOODS CO-OPERATIVE LTD
Franklin Rd, Portslade, East Sussex, BN41 1AF
TEL:01273 424 060 FAX:01273 417 739
www.infinityfoods.co.uk

Grow organic, buy organic, eat organic - and now *save* organic

Save now to support high quality organic enterprises - from farmers and growers to distributors and retailers.

The **Organic Saver** Account from Triodos Bank gives you easy access, security and a competitive interest rate. And your savings are targeted for investment in organic farms and businesses. So while you earn a healthy return, you're helping to ensure there's plenty of organic choice. Call **0500 008 720** for details.

Triodos ⊛ Bank
financing organic food and farming

Triodos Bank partner

Triodos Bank, Brunel House, 11 The Promenade, Bristol BS8 3NN
Tel: 0500 008 720, Fax: 0117 973 9303, Email: mail@triodos.co.uk www.triodos.co.uk

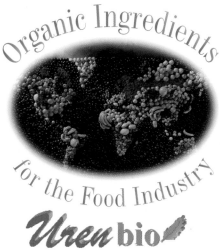

Would you like to know more about organic food?

Soil Association

The Soil Association is the driving force behind the organic movement. Our core mission has always been based on these interconnections: healthy soil, healthy food and healthy people.

Over the past five years we have successfully:

- Achieved change in food and farming systems through lobbying and policy work.

- Campaigned for sustainable agriculture and environmental protection.

- Set the standards of production for organic foods. Our symbol of trust and quality can be found on over 70% of the UK's organic produce.

- Supported farmers and growers, encouraging and helping them to go organic.

- Promoted and informed so that people everywhere can have the opportunity to buy and eat organic food be it from a box scheme, a local market, a corner shop or a supermarket.

Find out more about what we do and how you can be involved. Go to

www.soilassociation.org

Soil Association

Soil Association, Freepost (BS4456), Bristol BS1 6ZY

T 0117 929 0661   **F** 0117 925 2504   **E** info@soilassociation.org

charity no 206862

SimplyOrg@nic
Food Company Ltd

SimplyOrganic Food Company is a nationwide organic supermarket dedicated to providing customers with the most extensive organic range in the United Kingdom, including fresh fruit & vegetables, meat & fish, groceries, wines & beers and baby care.

Order by telephone, fax or internet and we will deliver your organic shopping before midday on the day of your choice – Tuesday to Saturday.

To receive your free catalogue call us today, visit us on our interactive website www.simplyorganic.net or simply return the coupon below. It couldn't be simpler.

0845 1000 444

www.simplyorganic.net   **info@simplyorganic.net**

SimplyOrganic Food Company
The Natural Choice
The UK's largest home delivery organic supermarket

- ✂ - - -

Please send me a FREE copy of the SimplyOrganic Food Company catalogue.   ref OD2000

Mr / Mrs / Miss / Ms (please print)

Address _____   Postcode _____

Telephone No. _____   Signature _____

We may make our mailing list available to carefully chosen companies whose products or services may interest you. Please tick this box if you do not wish to receive such offers.   ☐

To receive your free catalogue, return to: SimplyOrganic Food Company, FREEPOST, Units A62-A64, New Covent Garden Market, London SW8 5YY or telephone 0845 1000 444, or email info@simplyorganic.net

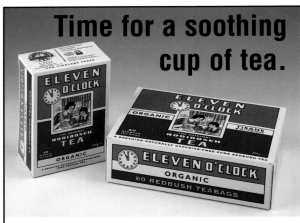

organic coffee, tea & herb teas

select your coffee sample pack...

When you try to buy organic coffee and tea in the shops - or wholesale from your catering supplier - there is often little choice. Also, coffee is best freshly roasted and stored in the fridge. It can be months old when you get it.

We are one of the few independent merchants to hold an organic certificate for coffee roasting and tea blending. We have perhaps the widest range in the UK, with seven origins of coffee on various roasts; various grades of Darjeeling and Assam teas; and many herb teas. Many of our coffees are both organic and fairly traded and our prices are fair too. For trade customers we can pack to order, even creating your own labels if required. Retail customers can visit our Notting Hill or Spitalfields outlets in London, check us on www.coffee.uk.com or send sae for price list. Better still, for £6, why not design your own 500gm coffee sample pack. Tick the box below for two different types of coffee and a full price list.

grind: ... fine (paper filter, electric espresso) ... medium fine (general, stove top espresso) ... medium ... (percolator, cafetière) ... whole beans
roast: ... medium/mild   (creamy and mild) ... medium/strong (stronger and thinner) ... continental (burnt, for cappucino etc)

your details: name...address............................
....code........................
phone..(optional in case we need to clarify your order)

the tea and coffee plant Now send a cheque for £6 to 'the tea and coffee plant' 170 Portobello Rd, London, W11 2EB. Allow 14 days for delivery. Only 1 pack per address.
www.coffee.uk.com tel: 0207 221 8137

Express Espresso

Wholesale suppliers of freshly roasted organic coffee delivered to your door.*

*Phone for details and a free price list.
tel: 020 7586 6461 or 07979 801825
email: expressespresso@hotmail.com

COMPASSION IN WORLD FARMING
...is the UK's leading farm animal welfare organisation.

Last year, CIWF helped to achieve two major farm animal victories. On Jan 1 it became illegal in the UK for pregnant sows to be chained to the floor or kept in narrow stalls. On June 15 the EU Ministers voted to ban the battery cage.

In the new millennium, CIWF continues to campaign on many issues:

- Millions of animals, donkeys, horses, lambs, cows and pigs are transported across long distances often without food, rest or water

- Sows are kept in tethers and stalls in many countries across the EU

- Dairy cows are milked to capacity, often suffering from lameness and mastitis

- Broiler chickens are kept in cramped windowless sheds, forced to grow at twice their natural rate

- Animals are genetically engineered to alter their genetic make-up to make them grow faster, bigger or leaner

By joining CIWF you could help up us to win an end to these cruel factory farming systems. To become a supporter costs just £21 a year or £1.75 a month. To become a life supporter costs £1000. Students, the unemployed and senior citizens can join for just £10 a year.

To join by credit card or to request a special joining pack, please call Kerry Cutting on 01730 264 208. Alternatively, please e-mail Kerry@ciwf.co.uk. Enquiries about advertising in Agscene, our quarterly magazine, are also very welcome. Our freepost address is Kerry Cutting, AQM, FREEPOST (GI/2198), Petersfield, Hants GU32 3BR.

Website: www.ciwf.co.uk Registered Office: Charles House, 5A Charles Street, Petersfield, Hants GU32 3EH Reg. No. 2998256 England

THE ORGANIC BABY & TODDLER COOKBOOK

Daphne Lambert and Tanyia Maxted-Frost

The Organic Baby & Toddler Cookbook is a comprehensive but easy-to-follow nutrition guide for babies from weaning to toddlerhood (four to six months to three years old). *The Organic Baby & Toddler Cookbook* recommends a seasonal, mainly raw wholefood organic diet, emphasising raw food in spring and summer and lightly cooked in autumn and winter. It advises on how to achieve optimum health for babies and toddlers.

It includes the basic principles of good nutrition for mother and baby, information on why to eat organic (the positives and negatives in summary, with some statistics/facts thrown in for good measure), seasonal meal planners, recipes for meals and juices, tips on how to adapt the meals into the family routine, the ideal lunchbox, and more.

Tanyia Maxted-Frost is author of *The Organic Baby Book* (see below); **Daphne Lambert** is organic chef/nutritionist of the Penrhos School of Food and Health. She runs a regular Mother & Baby course at her certified organic restaurant/school in Herefordshire. Daphne also has a regular column on growing your own organic food in *Healthy Eating* magazine, and has featured in several national magazines with her recipes, including *BBC Vegetarian*. **Green Books 128pp ISBN 1 870098 86 2 £6.95 paperback** May 2000

THE ORGANIC BABY BOOK
How to plan and raise a healthy child
Tanyia Maxted-Frost

This is the first popular guide to the benefits of an organic and GM-free wholefood diet for conceiving and raising a healthy child, and the first to review all organic products now available for your baby, for pregnant and breastfeeding mothers, and for young families. *The Organic Baby Book* shows that it is now possible to eat, drink and buy nearly everything needed for mother and baby organically: fresh organic wholefoods • organic cotton reusable nappies (from seven companies) • readymade babyfoods (over 11 brands) • cot blankets • bras and nursing pads • baby clothing • bodycare (over 30 brands) • food supplements • bedding • and more.

Over 600 organic and environmentally-friendly products, companies, relevant organisations, annual events and useful resources are reviewed. The book also features: the experiences of parents who have gone organic and reaped the rewards • how to 'green' your house for your baby • and the vaccination versus healthy immune system debate.

Tanyia Maxted-Frost has been heavily involved in the UK organic food scene since 1996. She writes for several consumer and trade titles on organic food and health issues. **Green Books 160pp 234 x 156mm ISBN 1 870098 79 X £7.95 paperback**

You can buy these books at green retailers and high street bookshops. New stockists are always welcome.

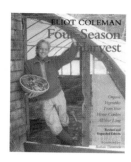

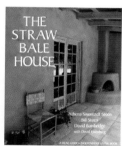
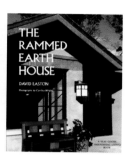
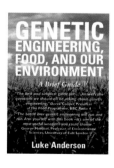

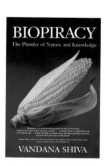

Fountains Dairy announce a full range of *organic* pure natural cheeses

Fountains organic traditional English cheeses are handmade in open vats using traditional time honoured methods to original recipes.

There are no artificial ingredients and preservatives.

The Soil Association approves the factory and cheeses.

THE ORGANIC RANGE:

Cheddar (mild, medium and mature)

Red Leicester (velvety, smooth, nutty flavour)

Double Gloucester (smooth full flavoured, the colour of honey)

White Cheshire (white, piquant, mellow with a flaky crumbly texture)

Wensleydale Original (made with 100% Wensleydale milk, lightly pressed smooth textured cheese, a clean fresh, full flavour)

Background to Fountains Dairy

Fountains Dairy is located in an old Wensleydale Village and has been producing traditional Wensleydale cheese for over 100 years. Wensleydale cheese was first introduced to England by Cistercian monks who settled locally at Jervaulx Abbey not far from where the present creamery is sited today.

Fountains produce many forms of the six major British territorial varieties and have captured gold medals in many major national and international shows.

Is Organic Cheese Healthier?

Organic cheese is produced from guaranteed organic milk. The grass on which the cows graze is spared the application of synthetic insecticides, herbicides, fungicides and fertilisers and is farmed by a system of production that mirrors the natural laws of nature and emphasises the interdependency of all life.

Our cheeses are suitable for vegetarians and are GM free.

**Fountains Dairy Products Ltd.,
Kirkby Malzeard, Lower Wensleydale,
Nr. Ripon, North Yorkshire HG4 3QD
Tel: 01765 658212 Fax: 01765 658732**

ORGANIC OPTIONS

15A BROAD ST., LEOMINSTER HR6 8BT
Tel: 01568 612154 Contact: Chris Gunson
Email: gunson@gn.apc.org
Specialist organic shop with everything
you need: meat and fish, dairy, bakery,
fruit & vegetables, frozen meals, dairy and
dairy-free ices, wine and beer, Neal's Yard
toiletries. Ecover with refills, organic
clothing.

   PENRHOS COURT

HOTEL & RESTAURANT
KINGTON HR5 3LH
Tel: 01544 230720 Fax: 01544 230754
Contact: Martin Griffiths
Email: enquiries@penrhos.co.uk
Website: www.penrhos.co.uk
Short health breaks. Hotel with organic
restaurant on the border of Herefordshire
and Wales. See display ad.

   PENRHOS SCHOOL

OF FOOD & HEALTH
KINGTON HR5 3LH
Tel: 01544 230720 Fax: 01544 230754
Contact: Martin Griffiths
Email: daphne@penrhos.co.uk
Website: www.penrhos.co.uk
Chef/nutritionist runs courses on food and
health. Soil Association registered (no.
E2051). Green Cuisine 2000, eco/organic
events. See display ad.

   PROSPECT ORGANIC GROWERS

PROSPECT COTTAGE, BARTESTREE,
HEREFORD HR1 4BY
Tel: 01432 851164
Contact: Christine Edwards
Email:
christine@prospectorganics.freeserve.co.uk
Soil Association no. G517. Producer of
organic vegetables—own farm shop. We
sell veg, fruit, dairy, eggs, meat and bread,
also wholefoods. Green Growers member.

    PAUL RICHARDS HERBAL SUPPLIES

THE FIELD, EARDISLEY HR3 6NA
Tel & Fax: 01544 327360
Email: jopc@ereal.net
Contact: Paul Richards
Certified organic products made with
herbs grown in our Herefordshire herb
farm. Fresh echinacea and hypericum
tinctures; calendula, hypericum and
comfrey oils and ointments. Contract
medicinal herb growers and tincture
suppliers.

    THE SEPTEMBER ORGANIC DAIRY

NEWHOUSE FARM, ALMELEY,
NR. KINGTON HR3 6LJ
Tel & Fax: 01544 327561
Contact: Adam Glyn-Jones
Email: september@ereal.net
Website: www.september.ereal.net
We produce a range of 100% organic ice
creams, accredited by the Soil Association
and manufactured on our own organic
dairy farm in Herefordshire using milk,
eggs and cream produced on the farm.

  SUNNYBANK VINE NURSERY

THE OLD TROUT INN, DULAS HR2 0HL
Tel: 01981 240 256
Contact: B.R. Edwards (Owner)
Specialist grape vine producer, largest
selection in the UK. Dessert and wine
grapes, both for outdoors and under glass.
Mail order only.

  SURVIVAL FOODS

UNIT 2, COBNASH RD.,
KINGSLAND HR6 9RW
Tel & Fax: 01568 708344
Contact: M. Poulton (Partner)
Wholefood wholesaler and cash and carry.
Large organic range, pre-packs or bulk
quantities.

KAREN TIBBETTS
HENCLOSE ORGANIC FARM PRODUCE,
LITTLE DEWCHURCH, HEREFORD HR2 6PP
Tel: 01432 840826 Contact: Karen Tibbetts
Soil Association symbol standard meat:
lamb, kid, pork, sausages and bacon. Also
goat's milk plus seasonal vegetables and
soft fruit.

UPPER BRIDGE ENTERPRISES
UPPER BRIDGE COURT,
BRILLEY HR3 6HG
Tel & Fax: 01497 831267
Contact: Roger Withnell
Email: ube@lineone.net
Organically reared Tamworth pork,
Hebridean lamb, Aberdeen Angus beef,
Brecon Buff geese.

H. WESTON & SONS LTD
THE BOUNDS, MUCH MARCLE,
LEDBURY HR8 2NQ
Tel: 01531 660233 Fax: 01531 660 619
Contact: Roger Jackson
Email: tradition@westons-cider.co.uk
Website: westons-cider.co.uk
Soil Association organic standard certified
no. 2092/91. Producer of 'strong organic
cider', the only cider to have won the *You*
magazine and Soil Association's organic
food awards Best Alcoholic Product.
Producer of a unique organic spritzer
(alcohol 1%). Nationwide delivery. See
display ad.

 **WIGGLY WIGGLERS**
LOWER BLAKEMERE FARM,
BLAKEMERE HR2 9PX
Tel: 01981 500391 Fax: 01981 500108
Contact: Heather Gorringe
Email: wiggly@wigglywigglers.co.uk
Website: wigglywigglers.co.uk
Earthworms and associated products
including Can o' Worms for recycling
kitchen waste into worm casts and liquid
feed. Small and large scale. Free home
guide available. Members of the
Composting Association.

   **WILLEY WINKLE**
PURE WOOL BEDDING
MANUFACTURERS
OFFA HOUSE, OFFA ST.,
HEREFORD HR1 2LH
Tel: 01432 268018
Contact: Jeff Wilkes (Owner)
We manufacture pure wool organic cot,
crib and moses mattresses. Also adult
bedding. The wool we use comes from
Highgrove Estate.

 WYEDEAN WHOLEFOODS
4 GLOUCESTER ROAD,
ROSS ON WYE HR9 5BU
Tel & Fax: 01989 562340
One-stop organic shopping with over 700
organic lines. Dairy and eggs, meat and
poultry, bread, fruit, vegetables and
commodity lines.

The modern world has favoured centralising, dependency-creating, unecological technologies. In the conventional production-orientated economy, whether business-centred or state-centred, it has rarely occurred to governments—and scientists, technologists and engineers—to develop technologies designed to help people become more self-reliant; and because producers have been able to externalise their environmental costs, the market has provided little incentive to develop resource-conserving, non-polluting technologies.

James Robertson, *Transforming Economic Life* (1998)

HERTFORDSHIRE

    BROUGHTON

PASTURES ORGANIC FRUIT WINES
THE OLD BREWERY, 24 HIGH STREET.,
TRING HP23 5AH
Tel:01442 823993 Contact: Brian Reid
Email: organicfruitwine@aol.com
The UK's premier producer of Organic Fruit
Wines. Flavours include Blackcurrant,
Elderberry, Ginger and Mead. Highly
Commended in the 1997 and 1998
Organic Food Awards. Soil Association no.
P1652.

EASTWOODS OF BERKHAMSTED
15 GRAVEL PATH, BERKHAMSTED HP4 2EF
Tel: 01442 865012 Fax: 01442 875203
Contact: Joe Collier
Soil Association 1998 award for Best Small
Butcher's Shop in UK. Two organic food
awards 1997 (bacon and sausages), Q
member, Soil Association reg. no. R1858.
Organic Food Awards Specialist Shop of
the Year 1999.

COOKS DELIGHT
360-4 HIGH STREET,
BERKHAMSTED HP4 1HU
Tel: 01442 863584 Fax: 01442 863702
Contact: Rex Tyler
Email: cooksd@globalnet.co.uk
Website: www.cooksdelight.co.uk.
Soil Association registered processor. 100%
organic food and wine shop. Mail order by
courier anywhere. Ethically sourced Bio-
dynamic produce (our speciality); also
organic cotton clothes.

ENVIRONMENTALLY SOUND LTD,
ORGANIC KOSHER FOODS
VERITAS HOUSE, 47 FALKLAND ROAD,
HIGH BARNET EN5 4LQ
Tel: Enqs 020 8441 1983 / Sales: 0800 458
K.O.S.H.E.R (0800458 678437) Fax: enqs
020 8441 5484, Sales 0800 980 6198
Contact: Leon Pein
Email: environmentally.sound@virgin. net
Website: www.organickosher.co.uk or
http://business.virgin.net/
environmentallysound
Organically sourced Kosher, halal and
conventional foods: chicken, lamb, beef,
duck, turkey, goose, eggs, veal, venison
and convenience foods and cooked
products, plus organically sourced kosher
salmon (absolutely delicious). National and
international delivery.

COUNTRY ORGANICS
UNIT 14, HODDESDON INDUSTRIAL
CENTRE, 15 PINDAR RD.,
HODDESDON EN11 0DD
Tel: 01992 447000 Fax: 01992 449000
Contact: Judith Collison/Sharon Davis
Email:
countryorganics@netscapeonline.co.uk
Import/export of organic pasta, olive oil
and pretzels. Also supplying food
ingredients for manufacturers. Large range
of other organic products available on
request.

FAIRHAVEN WHOLEFOODS LTD
27 JUBILEE TRADE CENTRE,
OFF JUBILEE RD., OFF BALDOCK RD.,
LETCHWORTH SG6 1SP
Tel: 01462 675300 Fax: 01462 483008
Contact: Robin Sternberg (Director)
Customers welcome 9-5 Monday to
Saturday, easy parking. We also deliver
weekly all over Hertfordshire, Bedfordshire,
Buckinghamshire and Cambridgeshire.
Organic wholefoods as well as fresh
produce.

DOWN TO EARTH
7 AMWELL END, WARE SG12 9HP
Tel: 01920 463358
Wholefood shop and café open 8 a.m. to
5.30 p.m. Mon to Fri, 9 a.m. to 5.30 p.m.
Sat. Organic fruit and vegetables.

FIELDFARE ORGANICS
OAKCROFT, DUDSWELL LANE,
BERKHAMSTED HP4 3TQ
Tel: 01442 877363 Fax: 01442 879950
Contact: Ray Calow (Partner)
Email: office@fieldfare-organics.com
Website: fieldfare-organics.com
Upmarket box scheme providing
customers with choice from a wide range
of organic fruit and vegetables, bread,
dairy, meat and wholefoods. Soil
Association symbol no. P1870, OF&G
members and founder members of
Organic Retail Guild, est. 1993.

FULL OF BEANS
2 CHURCH ST.,
SAWBRIDGEWORTH CM21 9AB
Tel: 01279 762002 Contact: Trula Wheeler
Wholefood shop with a wide range of
organic fruit and veg and special dietary
supplements.

HARMONY
53 HIGH STREET, TRING HP23 5AG
Tel: 01442 822 311 Contact: Susan Gould
We sell most products except fresh fruit
and vegetables.

HATFIELD HOUSE
HATFIELD AL9 5NF
Tel: 01707 260228 Fax: 01707 275719
Contact: Mrs E. Dean
Organic vegetable and ornamental gardens
(62 acres). The gardens of Hatfield are open
to the public 25th March to 24th September
2000. Soil Association registered.

CLARE JAMES
13A HEMPSTEAD RD.,
KINGS LANGLEY WD4 8BJ
Tel: 01923 263195
Contact: Bridget Johnstone
Health food shop selling a large range of
organic foods (excluding fresh vegetables,
meat and poultry), from dried herbs to
rice, including bread, nuts, fruit, eggs, and
flours etc.

MILL GREEN MILL
MILL GREEN, HATFIELD AL9 5PD
Tel: 01707 271362 Fax: 01707 272511
Local history museum and working
watermill. Stoneground wholemeal flour
milled in the traditional way at a restored
18th century watermill open to the public.
Soil Association reg. no. P1470.

M.S.B. MASTER SOIL BUILDERS
UNIT 3, BINGHAMS PARK FARM,
POTTEN END HILL, WATEREND,
HEMEL HEMPSTEAD HP1 3BN
Tel: 01442 216203 Fax: 01442 268640
Contact: J. Warren
Email: mastersoil@aol.com
Website: www.mastersoil.co.uk
Suppliers of organic fertilisers and organic
body care products: shampoos, body
creams, moisturisers, cleansing.

THE ORGANIC WHOLEFOOD NETWORK
33 ALEXANDRA ROAD,
WATFORD WD1 3QX
Tel: 01923 490526 Fax: 01923 490659
Contact: Barry Couldridge
Ring for details—delivery to local collection
points (approximately 3 miles radius of
Watford). Fruit and vegetables (seasonal).
Delivery areas covered AL1-10, HA2-8,
HP1-27, SG1-18, SL1-9 and WD1-7.

WESTMILL FOODS LTD
10 DANE STREET,
BISHOPS STORTFORD CM23 3XZ
Tel: 01279 658473 Fax: 01279 657723
Contact: David Reay
Allinson wholemeal organic flours for
bread baking and self-raising organic
wholemeal for cakes and biscuits.

KENT

J.J. BARKER LTD
HOOK PLACE FARM, SOUTHFLEET,
GRAVESEND DA13 9NH
Tel: 01474 833555 Fax: 01474 834364
Contact: Lawrence Frohn
Email: sales@jjbarker.co.uk
UK based grower and importer, packer and
distributor of organic produce—mainly
salads and legumes primarily for the UK
multiples. Soil Association reg. no. P2380.

BENENDEN VINEYARD
BROOM HILL FARM, DINGLEDEN,
BENENDEN TN17 4JT
Tel: 01580 240976
Contact: Keith Francis (Owner/Grower)
Wine grapes, cider apples.

A.G. BROCKMAN & CO
PERRY COURT FARM, GARLINGE GREEN,
CANTERBURY CT4 5RU
Tel & Fax: 01227 738449
Contact: Patrick Brockman
Oldest organic farm in Kent, producing
beef, vegetables, cereals and stone ground
flour to Demeter (Bio-dynamic) standards
(UK6 102). Available through the farm
shop, box scheme and local farmers'
markets, and from other retailers and
wholesalers in South and South East
England.

BURSCOMBE CLIFF FARM
EGERTON, ASHFORD TN775BB
Tel & Fax: 01233 756468
Contact: Ben or Hilary Jones
Soil Association symbol (no. G683) for
beef, lamb and pigs and small-scale fruit—
a new enterprise. Selling through natural
farms, butchers Hawkhurst and direct
through farmers' markets and from farm
gate. Member of WWOOF.

CANTERBURY WHOLEFOODS
10 THE BOROUGH, CANTERBURY CT1 2DR
Tel: 01227 464623 Fax: 01227 764838
Email:
info@canterburywholefoods.freeserve.co.uk
Website: www.canterburywholefoods.com
Stockists of over 3000 wholefood lines
(retail and wholesale) with huge organic
range of fruit and veg, wines and beers,
breads etc, also many non-foods and
remedies. Free delivery service; price list
available. Members of National Association
of Health Stores and Soil Association
registered (no. R1676).

CAPRICORN ORGANICS
40 RYDAL DRIVE, BEXLEYHEATH DA7 5EE
Tel: 020 8306 2786 Contact: Alison Wise
Email:
alison@capricornorganics.fsnet.co.uk
Website: www.capricorn.freewire.co.uk
Fresh organic fruit and veg (mostly from the
UK) delivered to your door. Individual orders
and seasonal boxes. We cover London SE
postcodes and the borough of Bexley.

DABBS PLACE ORGANIC FARM
COBHAM, GRAVESEND DA13 9BL
Tel: 01474 814333 Fax: 01474 814333
Contact: Robert Fermor
Email: sferm@globalnet.co.uk
Organic grower, fruit and vegetable box
scheme, delivery service. Soil Association
Symbol no. F16S. Delivery areas: DA13,
DA11, DA12, DA3, TN13, TN15, ME19,
ME18, ME20, ME1, ME2, ME4, ME5, ME7,
ME8, ME14, ME15, ME17.

DEFENDERS LTD
OCCUPATION RD., WYE,
ASHFORD TN25 5EN
Tel: 01233 813121 Fax: 01233 813633
www.defenders.co.uk
Defenders supplies a comprehensive range
of biological controls and integrated control
products to gardeners by mail order.

ELMSTONE FARM

ELMSTONE LANE,
GRAFTY GREEN ME17 2AJ
Tel: 01622 858970 Fax: 01622 858434
Contact: Julian Vyner
Email: julian@elmstone.freeserve.co.uk
Apples and pears. Soil Association
registered (no. G1156).

 ESPECIALLY HEALTH

119 HIGH ST., SEVENOAKS TN13 1UP
Tel: 01732 741181 Fax: 01732 740719
Contact: Mrs Wendy Kent (Proprietor)
Organic vegetables and wholefoods,
vitamins, minerals, natural remedies,
aromatic oils and other products to help
you enjoy good health. Allergy testing and
vitamin/mineral analysis, extensive product
and dietary information.

  GALA COFFEE & TEA LIMITED

MILL HOUSE, RIVERSIDE WAY,
DARTFORD DA1 5BS
Tel: 01322 272411 Fax: 01322 278600
Contact: Louise Lloyd-Rossi
Email: gala@gala-coffee-tea.co.uk
Gala is a unique company focused on the
special requirements of both retailers and
food service companies producing coffee
and tea under private label.

  GRANARY HERBS

THE GRANARY, MILGATE PARK,
ASHFORD RD., BEARSTED ME14 4NN
Tel: 01622 737314 Fax: 01622 739781
Contact: Christine Brown (Proprietor)
Mail order only (no callers). Soil Association
member. Tinctures, fluid extracts and creams
made from fresh organic home grown herbs.

  PETER HALL & SONS LTD

TARGET FARM, MARDEN TN12 9AT
Tel: 01622 831376 Fax: 01622 831654
Contact: Peter Hall
Email: peter.hall@farming.co.uk
Soil Association member G769. Grower of
organic hops (used in Wychwood Corngrue
Beer, Fullers Honeydew and Caledonian
Golden Promise), grower of organic apples
and pears.

**HENRY DOUBLEDAY
RESEARCH ASSOCIATION (HDRA)**
YALDING ORGANIC GARDENS, BENOVER
RD., YALDING, NR. MAIDSTONE ME18
Tel & Fax: 01622 814650
Opened in 1995, Yalding demonstrates a
'Green History of Gardening'. See main
entry under Warwickshire, or under
Associations.

   IVY HOUSE FARM

IVY HOUSE, SANDHILLS, ASH,
NR. CANTERBURY CT3 2NG
Tel: 01304 812437 Contact: M. Ward
Our farm, registered with the Soil
Association, produces a range of
organically grown vegetables for wholesale
and retail. Our farm shop also sells
organically grown produce from other
certified producers.

LUDDESDOWN ORGANIC FARMS LTD
COURT LODGE, LUDDESDOWN,
NR. COBHAM DA13 0XE
Tel: 01474 813376 Fax: 01474 812048
Contact: Gerry Minister (Farm manager)
We are a 850 acre farm producing cereals,
peas, beans, red clover for seed,
vegetables, beef, forage and thatching
straw, all to the standards laid down by the
Soil Association and UKROFS. We retail as
much as possible from the farm (including
a vegetable box delivery scheme and
home produced beef) as well as
wholesaling. Soil Association no. S38S.

PETER MACEY

PARKHOUSE FARM, RECTORY LANE,
CHART SUTTON, MAIDSTONE ME17 3RD
Tel: 01622 843229
Organic fruit farm (Soil Association reg. no.
G1455). Dessert and cooking apples, plums,
pears, sold on the tree or some ready
picked. Old fashioned varieties. Ring in
advance. Also self-catering cottage for rent.

MACK MULTIPLES DIVISION

TRANSEESA ROAD,
PADDOCK WOOD TN12 6UT
Tel: 01892 835577 Fax: 01892 838249
Contact: Dr Alan Legge
Email:
elliot.mantle@multiples.mwmack.co.uk
Importers and ripeners of organic bananas
and organic coconuts. Minimum order 25
cartons. Distribution in England and Wales.
Soil Association reg. no. P2304.

MAIDSTONE HEALTH FOODS

28 ROYAL STAR ARCADE,
MAIDSTONE ME14 1JN
Tel: 01622 691179 Fax: 01622 851339
Contact: Valerie Veal (Partner)
We stock an increasing range of organic
goods.

MICHAELS WHOLEFOODS

UNIT 5, NORTHDOWN INDUSTRIAL PARK
ST. PETERS, BROADSTAIRS CT10 3JP
Tel: 01843 604601/2 Fax: 01843 604603
Contact: Michael Pile
Email:
info@michaels-wholefoods.busclub.net
Wholesaler, distributor and packer of dry
foods and branded lines. Manufacturer of
sweet snack mixes and mueslis. Operating
south of a rough line between
Peterborough and Bristol. Organic Farmers
& Growers certification no. UKP021027.

NATURAL LIFE

66 GROSVENOR RD.,
TUNBRIDGE WELLS TN1 2AS
Tel: 01892 543834 Contact: Mrs Hawey
Small family business with friendly service.
Food, vegetarian supplements and
aromatherapy oils. Will deliver to elderly
and disabled.

NEAL'S YARD REMEDIES

THE GLADES SHOPPING CENTRE,
BROMLEY BR1 1DD
Tel & Fax: 020 8313 9898
Contact: Emma Moscow
Natural health products including herbal,
homeopathic and flower remedies,
aromatherapy oils, vitamins, minerals,
books, natural cosmetics and toiletries. All
staff are highly trained to help customers
find the appropriate remedy.

NORTH DOWNS DAIRY CO LTD

GROVE DAIRY FARM, BOBBING HILL,
SITTINGBOURNE ME9 8NY
Tel: 01795 844444 Fax: 01795 844029
Contact: Alastair Jackson
Email: sales@northhdownsdairy.co.uk
North Downs Dairy produces and packs a
range of organic cheese under the Pilgrim's
Choice brand. Most of the cheese is
traditionally hand made on the farm, and
all are Soil Association approved.
Nationwide coverage.

ORGANIC HEALTH (CANTERBURY)

UNIT 22, inside SCATS COUNTRY STORE,
MAYNARD ROAD, WINCHEAP TRADING
ESTATE, CANTERBURY CT1 3RH
Tel & Fax: 01227 472774
Contact: Jackie Garfit
Award winning, Soil Association licensed
(no. R2592) specialist retailer of one of the
widest ranges of organic and special diet
foods in the country. Incredible range of
organic fruit and veg, meat, fish, bread etc.
Opening times Tues-Weds 9 a.m. to 5 p.m.

RAINHAM HEALTH FOOD CENTRE
28 THE PRECINCT, RAINHAM ME8 7HW
Tel: 01634 362267 Fax: 01634 262853
Contact: S.L. Stock (Partner)
Wide selection of organic foods available, excluding fruit and vegetables. Organic hazels, almonds and walnuts in shells. Especially recommended is our delicious wheat-free muesli containing 11 organic ingredients.

THE REAL ICE COMPANY
LODGE RD., STAPLEHURST TN12 0QY
Tel: 01580 892200 Fax: 01580 893414
Contact: David Alfille
Email: david@realice.whd.net
Manufacturer of private label organic ice cream for major retailers and food servicers.

REGENT HEALTH
12 ALBERT ROAD, BELVEDERE DA17 5LT
Tel: 01322 446244
Contact: Derek Rogers (Owner)
Good and increasing range of organic foods: fresh, chilled, frozen, cereals, bread, pasta, eggs, fruit, nuts and much more.

RIPPLE FARM ORGANICS
CRUNDALE, CANTERBURY TN25 5EQ
Tel: 01227 730898
Soil Association producer, licenced for vegetables, fruit and herbs. Delivery area: East Kent.

SUPER NATURAL LTD
BORE PLACE, CHIDDINGSTONE, EDENBRIDGE TN8 7AR
Tel: 01732 463255 Fax: 01732 740264
Contact: Caroline Dunmall
(Fundraising & Marketing Administrator)
Email: carolined@commonwork.org
Website: www.commonwork.org
Soil Association approved organic composts, mulch and soil conditioner, liquid plant food made from own cow manure. Available at garden centres and branches of Homebase and Robert Dyas.

TERRE DE SEMENCES
RIPPLE FARM, CRUNDALE, NR. CANTERBURY CT4 7EB
Tel: 01227 731815 / 0966 448379
Fax: 01227 767187 Contact: Chris Baur
Email: info@terredesemences.com
Website: www.terredesemences.com
Supplier of organically/Bio-dynamically grown vegetable and flower seeds. 1400 varieties. Largest source of organically grown seed in England. Superb catalogue available for £2.50 + £1.50 p+p.

THAMES ORGANIC PRODUCE LTD
SHEERNESS PRODUCE TERMINAL, SPADE LANE, SITTINGBOURNE ME9 7TT
Tel: 01634 269200 Fax: 01634 269269
Contact: Pepe Morant
Email: p.morant@teresauk.co.uk
Website: www.kentnet.co.uk/thamesuk
Specialists in Spanish organic produce, prepacking and sourcing products, from the basics to exotics. Soil Association reg. no. P2654.

WINGHAM COUNTRY MARKET
SHATTERLING, CANTERBURY CT3 1JW
Tel & Fax: 01227 720567 Contact: Andrew
We sell an extensive range of organic produce at our farm shop, including fresh vegetables grown on our Soil Association registered (no. G977) farm.

The transfer of herbicide resistance to wild, weedy relatives of crops threatens to create 'superweeds' that are resistant to herbicides and hence uncontrollable. As a strategy for Monsanto to sell more Round-Up, and Ciba Geigy to sell more Basta, genetically engineered herbicide-resistant crops make sense. Yet this strategy runs counter to a policy of sustainable agriculture, since it undermines the very possibility of weed control.

Vandana Shiva, *Biopiracy* (1998)

LANCASHIRE

   CHORLEY HEALTH FOOD
18 NEW MARKET ST., CHORLEY PR7 1DB
Tel: 01257 276146
Contact: Mr J. Clark (Owner)
Adjacent to main car park, taxi rank and bus station. We stock a good range of organic foods, drinks and supplements, and are always happy to supply any non-stock line either over the counter or by mail order.

    LIBBY FLINTOFF
BROOK HOUSE FARM, TARNACRE LANE, ST. MICHAEL'S ON WYRE, PRESTON PR3 0TB
Tel & Fax: 01995 679728
Contact: Libby Flintoff
Email: libby.flintoff@ukgateway.net
Two acres of protected cropping and fields. Vegetables grown to Soil Association standards (reg. no. G1898). Produce supplies local box scheme.

HEAD DYKE LANE, PILLING,
PRESTON PR3 6SJ
Tel: 01253 790541 Fax: 01253 790541
Fold House Farm produces a range of vegetables for wholesale markets in conjunction with a beef suckler enterprise. Soil Association reg. no. G2176.

A. & D. GIELTY
LYNCROFT FARM, BUTCHERS LANE, AUGHTON GREEN, ORMSKIRK L39 6SY
Tel: 01695 421712 Fax: 01695 422117
Contact: Alf Gielty
Email: office@aanddgielty.co.uk
Website: www.aanddgielty.co.uk
Organic vegetables, potatoes and salads available year round. Large orders delivered in bulk or pre-pack. Organic inputs also supplied. Box scheme in operation, and farm shop open Thursday 3 p.m. - 7 p.m. Organic eggs also available

   GROWING WITH NATURE
BRADSHAW LANE NURSERY, PILLING, NR. PRESTON PR3 6AX
Tel & Fax: 01253 790046
Contact: Alan Schofield
Marketing locally produced vegetables from four organic producers. Delivery service throughout Lancashire. Soil Association reg. no. RS44N.

HARWOOD PRIDE LTD
UNIT G2, RIVERSIDE INDUSTRIAL ESTATE, RISHTON, NR. BLACKBURN BB1 4NF
Tel: 01252 548747 Fax: 01252 373291
Manufacturer of organic crisps.

  THE HERB STALL
FERROCRETE FARM, ARKHOLME, CARNFORTH LA6 1AU
Tel: 01524 221965
Contact: Jo Fowler (Partner)
A small holding and farm shop whre herbs and vegetables are grown, preserves made, and fruit and other produce available. Also Church Streeet market on Wednesdays and Saturdays.

GUY LEHMANN SFI LTD
GLENFIELD HOUSE, GLENFIELD PARK, PHILIPS RD., BLACKBURN BB1 5PF
Tel: 01254 682479 Fax: 01254 682492
Contact: Mark Lehmann
Email: sales@guylehman.com
Website: www.guylehmann.com
Specialists in supply of organic bulk dry mustard ingredients. Bulk organic wine, spirit and speciality vinegar. Organic sunflower, millet, linseed, caraway, pumpkin. All products Soil Association certified. Will deliver to all UK and Europe (minimum delivery: dry goods 25kg, liquids 1000ltrs).

Lancashire

 MIDDLE WOOD TRUST
MIDDLE WOOD, ROEBURNDALE WEST,
LANCASTER LA2 8QX
Tel: 015242 22214
Contact: Rod Everett or Michael (Manager)
Email: middlewood@lancs.ac.uk Website:
www.marketsite.co.uk/middlewd/index
Forest garden, courses and organic
conversion advisory service, permaculture
design. Middle Wood Trust is a charity
promoting sustainable development and
permaculture. Demonstration forest
garden and organic garden in constuction.

NORMAN OLVERSON LTD
KERSHAW'S FARM, SMITHY LANE,
SCARISBRICK, ORMSKIRK L40 8HN
Tel: 01704 840392 Fax: 01704 841096
Contact: Brian Olverson
Email: enquiries@redvelvet.co.uk
Website: www.redvelvet.co.uk
Farmers, pre-packers and beetroot
processors. Soil Association reg. no. P2631.

ONLY NATURAL
64 STANDISHGATE, WIGAN WN1 1UW
Tel: 01942 236239
Contact: Mrs B. Arrowsmith
Health food shop stocking a large selection
of organic products; teas, juices, pasta,
cereals, rice cakes etc. Orders taken for
organic vegetables.

ORGANIC ALTERNATIVES
CLAPHAM NURSERY, CLAPHAM,
LANCASTER LA2 8ER
Tel: 015242 51739 & 01729 824333
Contact: Laura English
Protected greenhouse crops for bag/home
delivery scheme. Organic eggs, table
poultry, beef, lamb and organic groceries.
One-stop organic shop in Settle Market
Place. Soil Association nos. P5562, G4295.

 F.I.P. & C.F. ROBINSON
MIDDLE HIGHFIELD, HALTON,
LANCASTER LA2 6PQ
Tel: 01524 811020 Fax: 01524 811020
Contact: Catherine Robinson
Producer of dairy products.

SINGLE STEP CO-OPERATIVE LTD
78A PENNY ST., LANCASTER LA1 1XN
Tel: 01524 63021
Contact: Julie Lawrence (Co-op worker)
We sell a wide range of vegetarian and
vegan foods with a large number of
organic lines including fruit, vegetables,
bread and pre-packed foods.

TASTE CONNECTION
76 BRIDGE ST., RAMSBOTTOM,
BURY BL0 9AG
Tel: 01706 822175 Fax: 01706 822941
Contact: Iseult or Adrian Richards
Email: tasteconnections@aol.com
Website: www.tasteconnection.com
Speciality and organic food shop (two
storey). First floor is almost entirely
organic: veg, meats, dairy, general grocery.
Basement has deli counter with huge
cheese selection. Speciality: olive oils from
around the world.

WHALE TAIL CAFÉ
78A PENNY ST., LANCASTER LA1 1XN
Tel: 01524 845133
Contact: Tricia Rawlinson
Spacious and friendly café offering home
made veggie and vegan food, including
organic snacks and on Fridays an organic
main meal option.

LEICESTERSHIRE AND RUTLAND

CHEVELSWARDE ORGANIC GROWERS
CHEVEL HOUSE, THE BELT, SOUTH
KILWORTH, LUTTERWORTH LE17 6DX
Tel: 01858 575309
Contact: John & Ruth Daltry
Email: john@chevel.freeserve.co.uk
Farm shop open during daylight hours for
local sales. Boxes delivered to depots in
Leicester, Rugby, Market Harborough and
Lutterworth. Soil Association no. D03M.
Also wine grower.

CURRANT AFFAIRS
9A LOSEBY LANE, LEICESTER LE1 5DR
Tel: 0116 251 0887 Contact: Kevin Taylor
Website: www.currantaffairs.co.uk
Currant Affairs is a natural food store
selling a wide range of organic produce.
We also have an on-site bakery producing
freshly prepared takeaway.

GOODNESS FOODS
18 SILVER ST., LEICESTER LE1 5ET
Tel: 0116 262 4859 Contact: Mr A. Carter
Email: goodness@chosen1.fsnet.co.uk
Health food/wholefood retailer.

GREAT CLAYBROOKE FLOUR
HALL HOUSE, HALL LANE, ULLESTHORPE,
LUTTERWORTH LE17 5DD
Tel: 01455 202443 Fax: 01455 202553
Contact: David Mountford
Email: claybrook.mill@pipemedia.co.uk
Producer of traditional stoneground flours
and cereal products. Registered with Soil
Association no. P1578. National mail order
service for organic flours, cereals, grains,
flakes, nuts, seeds and yeasts.

GROWING CONCERN
HOME FARM, WOODHOUSE LANE,
NANPANTAN, LOUGHBOROUGH LE11 3YG
Tel & Fax: 01509 239228 Contact: M. Bell
Redevelopment since winning Organic
Food Award includes visitors' rare breed
centre, on farm bakery-restaurant, ready
made meals. Also mail order.

HUNGARY LANE FARM
SUTTON BONNINGTON,
LOUGHBOROUGH LE12 5NB
Tel: 01509 673897
Contact: Jo & Sue Bradley (Partners)
Bio-dynamic produce, Demeter symbol—
shop open Saturdays from end August to
end February. Fresh vegetables, beef, lamb,
chicken, freezer packs.

ORGANIC LIVESTOCK
MARKETING CO-OPERATIVE (O.L.M.C.)
CARPENTERS HOUSE,
TUR LANGTON LE8 0PJ
Tel: 01858 545564 Fax: 01858 545100
Contact: Mrs M. Weston (Administrator)
We supply organic carcasses (beef, lamb
and pork) wholesale to abattoirs, butchers
and other retailers. We also arrange sales of
store cattle and lambs for members.

OSBASTON KITCHEN GARDEN
OSBASTON HALL, OSBASTON,
NR. NUNEATON CV13 0DR
Tel: 01455 440811 Contact: Flick Rohde
Walled kitchen garden growing vegetables,
fruit and herbs, available in limited
quantities on open days and at local
farmers' markets. Soil Association Organic
Certification GCS001/G1523.
Demonstration of garden-scale organic
methods.

PASTA CONCILIO

UNIT 4-5 ROYAL WAY, OFF BELTON ROAD
WEST, LOUGHBOROUGH LE12 6XB
Tel: 01509 212 373 Fax: 01509 265 512
Contact: Brian Poulson
Email: franco@pastaconcilio.fsnet.co.uk
Produce high quality filled pasta and
ravioli, cannelloni, tortelloni, gnocchi, full
HACCP systems regarding all production.
Soil Association no. P4149. National
delivery.

PAUL'S

66-68 SNOW HILL,
MELTON MOWBRAY LE13 1PD
Tel: 01664 560572 Fax: 01664 410345
Contact: Paul Jones (Director)
We manufacture a range of fresh organic
foods and supply a wide variety of fresh
organic produce, grown locally and
imported. Soil Association reg. no. P738.

RUTLAND ORGANICS (HERBAL MEDICINES) LTD

TOWN PARK FARM, BROOKE LE15 8DG
Fax: 01572 770808 Contact: P N Chenery
Website: www.rutlandorganics.co.uk
Soil Association approved fresh organic
medicinal tinctures.

SEEDS OF CHANGE

FREEBY LANE,
WALTHAM ON THE WOLDS LE14 4RS
Tel: 0800 9520000 Contact: Lynn Simpson
Website: www.seedsofchange.com
Seeds of Change offer accessible day to
day products, all 100% certified organic.
The range includes pasta sauces, dried
pasta, soups and tomato ketchup.

N. & S. STAINES

BAMBURY FARM, PEATLING MAGNA,
LEICESTER LE8 3QU
Tel: 0116 247 8907 Fax: 0116 247 8907
Contact: Sue Staines
Email: sue@bamburyfarm.freeserve.co.uk
Mixed organic farm (Soil Association reg.
no. P/G1104) growing vegetables and
producing lamb, pork, beef and eggs for
local deliveries.

STOUGHTON LODGE ORGANIC FARM

STOUGHTON LANE, STOUGHTON,
LEICESTER LE2 2FH
Tel: 0116 271 4278 Fax: 0116 272 0640
Contact: Mr Leake
Wholesale producer of cereals, pulses and
potatoes.

WHISSENDINE WINDMILL

MELTON ROAD, WHISSENDINE LE15 7EU
Tel: 01664 474172
Contact: Nigel Moon (Owner)
Organic Farmers and Growers registered
(P080027 UK2). Flour produced in 19th
century windmill on millstones. Flour,
oatmeal, ryemeal, barley. All cereals stone
ground.

MICHAEL F. WOOD

51 HARTOPP RD., LEICESTER LE2 1WG
Tel: 0116 270 5194
Contact: R.J. Wood (Partner)
Retail butcher selling beef, lamb, pork and
chickens; also bread and flour. Soil
Association reg. no. R1979.

As a beginning composter, you may wonder if your compost bin will attract flies.
Small fruit flies are often attracted to food scraps placed near the very top of a pile.
Do not 'dump and run' when adding food scraps. Instead, bury the scraps 6–12"
below the surface, or cover them with leaves, straw, composting materials or garden
soil. When there is no easy-to-eat food for flies, they fly away.

John Roulac, *Backyard Composting* (1999)

LINCOLNSHIRE

  ALL ORGANIC

17 STAMFORD WALK, STAMFORD PE9 2JE
Tel: 01780 756766 Fax: 01780 470252
Contact: Andrew and Tanja Bone
Email: allorganicshop@aol.com
Retail shop selling a full range of only
organic groceries including wines, beers and
spirits. Local produce from Spa Farm,
Apethorpe, and specialising in Demeter
produce where possible.

BARKSTON HEATH MUSHROOMS

HEATH LANE, BARKSTON HEATH,
GRANTHAM NG32 2DE
Tel: 01400 230845 Fax: 01400 230901
Contact: Malcolm Hensby
Growing organic mushrooms. Soil
Association reg. no. H20M.

 BLYTON ORGANICS

CHURCH LANE, BLYTON,
GAINSBOROUGH DN21 3JZ
Contact: William Coggon
Seasonal box scheme offering mixed
vegetables, salad, soft fruit and top fruit.
Soil Association licences G2118, P5066.
Delivery to Lincoln city (DN21).

BRIDGE FARM ORGANIC FOODS

BRIDGE FARM, SNITTERBY CARR,
GAINSBOROUGH DN21 4UU
Tel: 01673 818272 Fax: 01673 818477
Contact: Patty Phillips
Soil Association reg. no. G2283. Producers
of goat's cheese, eggs and organic
vegetables. Customers join our
conservation group and benefit from open
farm days, regular newsletters,
involvement in conservation tasks.

  CHEERS NURSERIES

ELEVEN ACRE LANE, KIRTON,
BOSTON PE20 1LS
Tel: 01205 724258 Fax: 01205 724259
Contact: Henry Cheer
Raise organic vegetable transplants.

COTTAGE ORGANICS

THE COTTAGE, MADVILLE LANE,
STICKNEY, BOSTON PE22 8DW
Tel: 01205 480602 Contact: Mr D Chick
Soil Association registered (no. G1403).
Producer of soft fruit and veg.

 EDEN FARMS

OLD BOLINGBROKE, SPILSBY PE23 4EY
Tel & Fax: 01790 763582
Contact: Marjorie Stein (Partner)
Email: edenfarmsorganic@compuserve.com
Website: www.edenfarmsorganic.fsnet.co.uk
Eden Farms has been growing organic
vegetables for 18 years, and is a 70-acre
farm selling vegetables to supermarkets,
wholesalers and box schemes in
Nottingham and Lincoln.

ENZAFRUIT WORLDWIDE LTD

WEST MARSH RD., SPALDING PE11 2BB
Tel: 01775 717000 Fax: 01775 717001
Contact: Nick Rickett
Email: nick.rickett@enzafruit-worldwide.co.uk
Website: www.enzafruit-worldwide.co.uk
Major fruit importer servicing all of the
main major multiple retailers; specialist in
fruit ripening. Year-round supply of apples,
pears, kiwi, mango and avocado. Soil
Association registered since August 1977
(no. P2137).

THE FIVE-SAILED WINDMILL

EAST STREET, ALFORD LN13 9EQ
Tel: 01507 462136
Contact: Geoff Dees (Proprietor)
Email: enquiries@fivesailed.co.uk
Working windmill producing range of
stoneground organic flours and cereals of
high nutritional value and flavour. Mill and
shop open all year, also stockists and home
delivery. Soil Association certified no.
P2063. Deliver nationally.

GLEADELL BANKS (AGRICULTURE) LTD
LINDSEY HOUSE, HEMSWELL CLIFF,
GAINSBOROUGH DN2 5TH
Tel: 01427 421223 Fax: 01427 421230
Contact: Brian Wilburn (Grain Trader)
Organic grain marketing specialists. Soil
Association no. P596. Organic marketing
company committed to serving and
promoting organic farming since 1986.
Market specialists for all types and grades
of certified organic cereals and pulses. See
display ad.

HOLBEACH WHOLEFOODS
32 HIGH ST., HOLBEACH,
SPALDING PE12 7DY
Tel: 01406 422149 Contact: D.R. West
Email: d.west@easynet.co.uk
Natural food store—loose wholefoods,
vegetarian and vegan foods, natural
healthcare, organic bread, fruit and veg to
order. Bulk discounts. Owners vegan,
ethical business.

KEEP YOURSELF RIGHT
4 RAVENDALE STREET,
SCUNTHORPE DN15 6NE
Tel: 01724 854236 Fax: 01724 280804
Contact: Mrs Mary Moss
Health food shop. Good selection of
organic products throughout the store.

LOUTH WHOLEFOOD CO-OP
7-9 EASTGATE, LOUTH LN11 9NB
Tel: 01507 602411 Contact: J. Hough
Wholefood shop stocking wide range of
organic foods including bread, dairy
products, fruit and vegetables, wines, beers,
dried fruit, nuts, jams, chocolate, ice creams,
biscuits, flours, patés, teas and essential oils.

MAUD FOSTER MILL
WILLOUGHBY RD., BOSTON PE21 9EG
Tel: 01205 352188
Contact: James Waterfield
The tallest working windmill in Britain
producing stoneground organic flours to
Soil Association symbol standard for the
wholesale and retail trade.

S.M. MCARD (SEEDS)
39 WEST RD, POINTON,
SLEAFORD NG34 0NA
Tel & Fax: 01529 240765
Contact: Susan McArd (Manager)
Mail order supplier of vegetable, herb and
flower seed including unusual vegetables.
Farm seed available in small quantities.

MOUNT PLEASANT WINDMILL
KIRTON-IN-LINDSEY DN21 4NH
Tel: 01652 640177 Contact: Patrick White
Four-sailed windmill, restored 1991.
Producing a range of Soil Association (no.
P1497) organic stoneground flours solely
by windpower. Mill, flour sales, tea room,
open Friday to Sunday all year. Organic
bakery open Saturdays & Sundays all year.

THE NATURAL REMEDY
WAREHOUSE
4 BROADGATE HOUSE, WESTLODE ST.,
SPALDING PE11 2AF
Tel: 01775 724994 Fax: 01775 761104
Contact: H. Girdlestone
We stock organic vegetables and fruit to
order, plus bread and pre-packs of cereals
and teas. Special orders catered for.

NEWFARM ORGANICS
J.F. & J. EDWARDS & SONS, SOULBY LANE,
WRANGLE, BOSTON PE22 9BT
Tel: 01205 870500 Fax: 01205 871001
Contact: Jane Edwards
Email: newfarmorganics@zoom.co.uk
webiste: www.newfarmorganics.co.uk
We produce beef, cabbage, cauliflower,
broccoli, potatoes, cereals and pulses. OF&
G registered (no. UK2 31UKF120010). We
supply to the wholesale market and to
various box schemes.

OERLEMANS FOODS UK LTD
THE OLD GRANARY, MANOR FARM,
AYLESBY, GRIMSBY DN37 7AW
Tel: 01472 750115 Fax: 01472 877848
Contact: John Burnett
Email: info@oerlemans.co.uk
Website: www.oerlemans.co.uk
Organic frozen vegetables, fruit and oven chips in retail and industrial packaging. Grown in Holland and Germany and frozen under SKAL accreditation. Licensed by the Soil Association as an importer.

B.M.SADD
BIRCHWOOD FARM, DRAWDYKE,
SUTTON ST. JAMES, SPALDING PE12 0HP
Tel: 01945 440 388
Email: gaa@dialstart.net
Producer of quality organic produce, specialising in vegetables. Boxes containing our own and bought-in produce available for collection. Member of the Soil Association (no. S34M).

WILLIAM SINCLAIR HORTICULTURE LTD
FIRTH RD., LINCOLN LN6 7AH
Tel: 01522 537561 Fax: 01522 513609
Email: info@william-sinclair.co.uk
Manufacturers of compost, lawn care, fertilisers, bark and mulches.

SPICE OF LIFE
4 BURGHLEY CENTRE, BOURNE PE10 9EG
Tel: 01778 394735 Fax: 01406 362939
Contact: D.R. West (Owner)
Email: d.west@easynet.co.uk
Retailer of natural foods and healthcare, bulk loose wholefoods, new world music, Ecover refill centre, organic fruit and bread, mail order, bulk discounts, vegan society discounts.

STRAWBERRY FIELDS
SCARBOROUGH BANK, BOSTON,
STICKFORD PE22 8DR
Tel & Fax: 01205 480490
Contact: Pam Bowers
Email:
Pam@strawberryfields75.freeserve.co.uk
Producing strawberries and an extensive range horticultural of crops, including lettuce, celery, herbs and the more unusual types of vegetables. Mostly sold in wholesale quantities. Soil Association reg. no. B40M.

UNIVEG
10 MANOR ROAD, KITRON,
BOSTON PE20 1PL
Tel: 01205 722374 Fax: 01205 723047
Contact: Sarah Clark or Anna Young
Email: sales@univeg.co.uk
An extensive range of vegetables and salads from the UK and overseas providing supermarkets, processors, veg prep and ready meal manufacturers with year round continuity of supply.

WILSFORD ORGANICS
11 MAIN ST., WILSFORD,
GRANTHAM NG32 3NS
Tel: 01400 230224
Soil Association licensed G1708. Local veg sales, and for wholesale. Eggs sold locally. Please phone to order.

WOODLANDS FARM
KIRTON HOUSE, KIRTON,
NR. BOSTON PE20 1JD
Tel: 01205 722491 Fax: 01205 722905
Contact: Andrew Dennis
Growing organic vegetables for wholesale, Local and direct sales. Box scheme home delivery service. Organic Bronze Turkeys available Christmas and Easter. Soil Association reg. no. G2224. Deliveries to LN11 and PE20.

 CHRISTOPHER'S
DELICATESSEN & FINE ORGANIC
FOODS LTD
103 LARRISTON ROAD, VICTORIA PARK,
LONDON E9 7HJ
Tel: 020 8986 2466 Fax: 020 8986 5668
Contact: Christopher Powney
Email: christohperdeli@easicom.com
Wide range of meats, cheeses and pasta,
organic and GM-free. Also delivery service
free within 2 miles.

   CLEAN BEAN TOFU
37E PRINCELET ST., LONDON E1 5LP
Tel: 020 7247 8349
Contact: Neil McLennan
We produce fresh organic tofu, using
traditional techniques, which is sold at our
stall at Spitalfields Organic Market and
through selected London retailers. Soil
Association no. P2200.

FRESH & WILD
196 OLD STREET, LONDON EC1V 9FR
Tel: 020 7250 1708
Customer Careline: 0800 9175 175
Email: shop@freshandwild.com
Website: www.freshandwild.com
Organic store with deli. Fresh food, healthy
choices, friendly people.

FUERST DAY LAWSON LTD
DEVON HOUSE, 58-60 ST. KATHERINE'S
WAY, LONDON E1 9LB
Tel: 020 7488 0777 Fax: 020 7702 3200
Contact: Frank Horan
Email: seeds@fdl.co.uk
Seeds, pulses, honey, fruit juices, essential
oils suppliers and processors of all dry
commodities in a Soil Association
approved facility.

NAPIER BROWN & CO LTD
1 ST. KATHARINE'S WAY, LONDON E1W 1XB
Tel: 020 7335 2500 Fax: 020 7335 2502
Contact: C. Seargent
Email: sales@napierbrown.co.uk
Website: www.napierbrown.co.uk
Napier Brown are the largest independent
sugar distributor in the UK. We offer a wide
range of organic sugars and syrups in both
industrial and retail packs from factories
approved by the Soil Association. We
deliver nationally.

    OLD
SPITALFIELDS ORGANIC MARKET
65 BRUSHFIELD ST., LONDON E1 6AA
Tel: 01279 444663 Contact: Jenny Usher
Sundays 10-5. Registered producers and
traders selling fruit and veg, breads, meat,
dairy, wholefoods, wine, tofu, juice bar etc.
London's largest organic market, near
Liverpool Street Station.

THE ORGANIC DELIVERY COMPANY
7 WILLOW ST., LONDON EC2A 4BH
Tel: 020 7739 8181 Fax: 020 7613 5800
Contact: John Barrow
Email: info@organicdelivery.co.uk
Website: www.organicdelivery.co.uk
Organic food of the highest quality
delivered to your door in the evening
throughout London. Highly commended
in the Soil Association awards and
registered with them.

ORGANICS DIRECT
7 WILLOW ST., LONDON EC2A 4BH
Tel: 020 7729 2828 Fax: 020 7613 5800
Contact: John Barrow
Email: info@organicsdirect.co.uk
Website: www.organicsdirect.co.uk
Food as nature intended from the farm to
your door right across the UK mainland.
Vegetarian organic groceries. Organic Box
Scheme of the Year 1999. Soil Assoociation
registered. See display ad.

PAUSE
11 NEW INN YARD, LONDON EC2A 3EY
Tel: 020 7729 1341
Contact: Iain Hickinbottom
Website: www.thehoxtoncollective.co.uk
We are a totally organic juice bar and
café/gallery offering breakfast, lunch and
delivery to local businesses. On Sundays
we have live music, and are available for
parties and openings. Mon-Fri 8.00 a.m. to
6.00 p.m. Sundays 12.00 till late.

PEACHES HEALTH FOODS
143 HIGH STREET, WANSTEAD,
LONDON E11 2RL
Tel & Fax: 020 8530 3617
Contact: Sue Win
Health store with organic wine, vegan and
vegetarian pastas, tofu, teas, drinks,
cheese, breads, jams, nuts, seeds and dried
fruits. All organic if available, try us and
see.

RUSH POTATOES LTD
1 HARBOUR EXCHANGE SQUARE,
LONDON E14 9GE
Tel: 020 7363 7887 Fax: 020 7363 7870
Contact: Murray Hogge
Email: sales@rushpotatoes.co.uk
Website: www.rushpotatoes.co.uk
Soil Association P2109. We specialise in the
production of out-of-season organic
potatoes for import to the UK. Direct
deliveries, or preparation and distribution
from our Boston warehouse.

Above all rivers thy river hath renown,
Whose beryl streamès, pleasant and preclare,
Under thy lusty wallès runneth down;
Where many a swan doth swim with wingès fair,
Where many a barge doth sail, and row with oar,
Where many a ship doth rest with top-royal.
O town of townès, patron and not compare,
London, thou art the flower of Cities all.

William Dunbar, from 'To the City of London',
in *The River's Voice: An Anthology of Poetry* (1999)

Key

 Producers

 Wholesalers

 Import/Export

 Retailers

 Mail Order

 Restaurants

 Day Visits/B&B

 Farm Gate Sales

 Box Schemes/ Delivery Service

 Garden/Farm Sundries

 Manufacturers & Processors

LONDON NORTH

ALARA WHOLEFOODS LTD
110-112 LAMLEY ST., LONDON NW1 0PF
Tel: 020 7387 9303 Fax: 020 7388 6077
Contact: Alex Smith
Email: alexsmith@alara.co.uk
Website: www.alara.co.uk
Alara are specialist manufacturers and packers of organic products including muesli, nuts, dried fruits and cereals. Soil Association certified P1301. See display ad.

ALTERNATIVES HEALTH STORE
1369 HIGH RD:, WHETSTONE,
LONDON N20 9LN
Tel: 020 8445 2675
Contact: Mrs H. Thankey (Manager)
Organic and special diet foods, frozen and chilled. Books, aromatherapy oils, herbal and homeopathic remedies, vitamins and supplements. Clinic for alternative treatments.

BAKOVEN LTD
BUILDING E, THE CHOCOLATE FACTORY,
WESTERN ROAD, LONDON N22 6UH
Tel: 020 8889 7159 Fax: 020 8889 2428
Contact: M. Hampton
Bakers of organic rye bread. Soil Association reg. no. P2628.

THE BEER SHOP
8 PITFIELD STREET, LONDON, N1 6EY
Tel: 020 7739 3701 Contact: M. Kemp
Sales of organic beer, lager, cider and wine, wholesale and retail.

BUMBLEBEE
30-33 BRECKNOCK RD., LONDON N7 0DD
Tel & Fax: 020 7607 1936
Contact: Gillian Haslop
Email: bumblebee@virgin.net
Website: www.bumblebee.co.uk
A wide range of organic and vegetarian foods, specialising in organic wines and cheeses, olive oils and mediterranean foods, gluten and wheat-free products. Delivery to postcode areas EC1, EC2, N1-N6, N19, NW1, NW3, NW5, W1, WC2 and other areas.

THE CELTIC BAKERS
230B THE BROADWAY, WEST HENDON,
LONDON NW9 7ED
Tel & Fax: 020 8202 2586
Contact: Syd Aston (Proprietor)
A dedicated organic bakery specialising in most aspects of bread production including 100% ryes and sourdough methods. Soil Association reg. no. P2009, Demeter 267.

COMMUNITY FOODS LTD
BRENT TERRACE, LONDON NW2 1LT
Tel: 020 8450 9419/9411 Fax: 020 8208 1551/1803 Contact: Colin Winter
Email: info@communityfoods.co.uk
Website: www.communityfoods.co.uk
Soil Association no. P1422. We are an importer and distributor of a large range of natural products including several hundred organic lines. Bulk dried fruit, nuts, pulses etc., plus brands like Clipper, Sanchi, Crazy Jack, Nature's Path, Piramide, Eunature, Emile Noel, Monki, Shady Maple, Barnhouse and many more.

What is new in the public health debate is the emphasis on the less visible aspect of our social arrangements, such as relative poverty, powerlessness, and loss of community, which are now known to be important to health.

Robin Stott, *The Ecology of Health* (2000)

THE DUKE OF CAMBRIDGE
30 ST. PETERS STREET
ISLINGTON, LONDON N1 8JT
Tel: 020 7359 1877
Fax: 020 7359 5877
Contact: Esther Boulton or Geetie Singh
Email:eb@singhboulton.demon.co.uk
Website: www.singhboulton.co.uk
Organic gastro-pub (Soil Assn. certified)
with menu changing twice daily. Regional
European style. Prices range from £4 for
starter to £12 for main meal (£6 lunch
available during the week). Children's
meals, plus organic baby food. 40 wines,
and interesting selection of organic beers.

EXPRESS ESPRESSO
4 CROSSFIELD RD., LONDON NW3 4NS
Tel: 020 7586 6461 Contact: John Hedges
Email: expressespresso@hotmail.co.uk
Express Espresso supplies freshly roasted
organic coffee to the restaurant trade. All
coffee is certified organic from the Tea and
Coffee Plant at Old Spitalfields Market.
Free delivery throughout London.

FRESH & WILD
49 PARKWAY, CAMDEN TOWN,
LONDON NW1 7PN
Tel: 020 7428 7575
Customer careline: 0800 9175 175
Email: shop@freshandwild.com
Website: www.freshandwild.com
Organic store with deli and juice bar, open
seven days a week. Fresh food, healthy
choices, friendly people. Joint winner
Organic Shop of the Year Award 1999.

GREEN BABY CO LTD
345 UPPER STREET, ISLINGTON,
LONDON N1 0PD
Tel: 020 7226 4345 Fax: 020 7226 9244
Contact: Eluned Rogers
Email: greenbabyco.@hotmail.com
Website: www.greenbabyco.com
A mail order service for planet-friendly
parents. Green Baby sells organic clothing
and toys, washable nappies, gel-free
disposables and natural toiletries for all the
family.

HAELAN CENTRE
41 THE BROADWAY, CROUCH END,
LONDON N8 8DT
Tel: 020 8340 4258 Fax: 020 8292 2232
Contact: Nino Booth (Owner)
One of Britain's original wholefood stores,
offering a complete range of vegetarian
and vegan organic food, including an
on-site complementary health clinic.

THE HAMPSTEAD TEA & COFFEE COMPANY
PO BOX 2448, LONDON NW11 7DR
Tel: 020 8731 9833 Fax: 020 8458 3947
Contact: Kiran Tawadey
Email: info@hampsteadtea.com
Website: www.hampsteadtea.com
Organic Food Award winners 98 & 99 for
our high quality range of Bio-dynamic and
fair trade teas. Certified by BDAA. Products
at health food stores and by mail order.

JFB LTD
21 BERNARD ROAD, LONDON N15 4PE.
Tel & Fax: 020 8808 2007
Contact: Mr Inder Johar
Email: isjohar@aol.co.uk
Exclusively organic bakers since 1981,
supplying all of London with fresh daily
organic bread. Full range of sourdough
and yeasted breads. Fully certified by the
Soil Association.

JUST ORGANIC
113 WILBERFORCE RD., LONDON N4 2SP
Tel & Fax: 020 7704 2566
Contact: Dee & Mike Adams
We deliver weekly boxes of organic
vegetables and fruit to homes in north,
east and west London, as well as the West
End. Choice of £10 or £15 box with free
delivery. Soil Association reg. no. P2042.

NATURAL HEALTH

339 BALLARDS LANE, N. FINCHLEY,
LONDON N12 8LT
Tel & Fax: 020 8445 4397
Contact: D. Thankey
Organic foods, frozen fresh foods,
vitamins, supplements, herbal and
homeopathic remedies, aromatherapy
products, cruelty-free cosmetics, slimming
and body building products, books,
magazines etc. Clinic for complementary
and alternative therapies.

 NEAL'S YARD REMEDIES

68 CHALK FARM RD., CAMDEN,
LONDON NW1 8AN
Tel: 020 7284 2039
Neal's Yard Remedies manufactures and
sells natural cosmetics in addition to
stocking an extensive range of herbs,
essential oils, homeopathic remedies and
reference material.

 THE ORGANIC CAFÉ

23-25 LONSDALE ROAD,
LONDON NW6 6RA
Tel: 020 7372 1232 Fax: 020 7625 6472
Contact: Nick Herbert
Soil Association registered for four years;
Time Out Food Awards finalist. We serve
organic vegetarian and meat dishes.

ORGANIC CAFÉ SHOPS

54 SALISBURY ROAD, LONDON NW6 6RA
Tel: 020 7372 1232 Contact: Carol
Email: nick@organic.café.co.uk
Website: www.organic.café.co.uk
The shops provide ready to eat food & deli
food.

 ORGANIC DAYS

UNIT 118, CRUSADER INDUSTRIAL ESTATE,
167 HERMITAGE RD., LONDON N4 1LZ
Tel: 020 8802 1088 Fax: 020 8802 3862
Contact: Adrian Lauchlan
Email: info@organicdays.co.uk
Website: www.organicdays.co.uk
We supply organic chocolates, sweets, jams,
teas, biscuit and cake mixes along with a
range of dried products such as beans, rices,
muesli, nuts, fruit via our website.

 ORGANICO

63 HIGH STREET, LONDON N8 7QB
Tel: 020 83400401 Fax: 020 83400402
Contact: C. Redfern
Email: info@organico.co.uk
Website: www.organico.co.uk
Import and distribution of authentic high
quality produce, supplying the specialist
organic and wholefood trade. Wines,
juices, pasta, sauces, babyfoods, bakery,
tofu—organic quality guaranteed.

  SAUCE ORGANIC DINER

214 CAMDEN HIGH STREET,
LONDON NW1 8QR
Tel: 020 7482 0777
Contact: Karen or Ross Doherty
Email: dining@sauce.prestel.co.uk
Website:www.sauce-organicdining.co.uk
Organic diner catering for all ages and
tastes, ranging from simple burgers to
whole plates of organic food. Kid's menu
and take-away. Fully licensed: cocktails,
organic beers and wines, and a juice bar.

 GEORGE SKOULIKAS LTD

UNIT 5, 998 NORTH CIRCULAR RD.,
COLES GREEN RD., LONDON NW2 7JR
Tel: 020 8452 8465 Fax: 020 8452 8273
Contact: Colin Morrison (Sales Director)
Importers and distributors of organic olive
oil, olives, lemon juice, sun-dried
tomatoes, tahini, sesame bars, halva and
ready to eat polenta. Soil Association reg.
no. P1174.

Monocultures are an essential component of globalization, which is premised on homogenization and the destruction of diversity. Global control of raw materials and markets makes monocultures necessary.

This war against diversity is not entirely new. Diversity has been threatened whenever it has been seen as an obstacle. Violence and war are rooted in treating diversity as a threat, a perversion, a source of disorder. Globalization transforms diversity into a disease and deficiency because it cannot be brought under centralized control.

Homogenization and monocultures introduce violence at many levels. Monocultures are always associated with political violence—the use of coercion, control, and centralization. Without centralized control and coercive force, this world filled with the richness of diversity cannot be transformed into homogeneous structures, and the monocultures cannot be maintained. Self-organized and decentralized communities and ecosystems give rise to diversity. Globalization gives rise to coercively controlled monocultures.

Monocultures are also associated with ecological violence—a declaration of war against nature's diverse species. This violence not only pushes species toward extinction, but controls and maintains monocultures themselves. Monocultures are non-sustainable and vulnerable to ecological breakdown. Uniformity implies that a disturbance to one part of a system is translated into a disturbance to other parts. Instead of being contained, ecological destabilization tends to be amplified. Sustainability is ecologically linked to diversity, which offers the self-regulation and multiplicity of interactions that can heal ecological disturbance to any part of a system.

Vandana Shiva, *Biopiracy* (1998)

LONDON SOUTH

ABEL & COLE
8-13 MGI ESTATE, MILKWOOD ROAD,
LONDON SE24 0FJ
Tel: 0800 376 4040 Fax: 020 7737 7785
Contact: Emma Hardie
emain: telesales@abel-cole.co.uk
Website: www.abel-cole.co.uk
Abel & Cole offer an imaginative seasonal
selection of organically grown fresh
produce, delivered to your home direct
from our network of organic growers.
Complete with weekly recipe cards, we
GUARANTEE your tailored box to be the
best quality and value for money in
London!! Soil Association no. P2043.

ALTER ECO ORGANICS
51 HARTISMERE ROAD, LONDON SW6 7UE
Tel: 020 7385 3009/020 7381 5388
Contact: Steve Christopher
Email: schris3767@aol.com
Directly linked with the award-winning
Scragoak Organic Farm, offering a free
delivery service of farm fresh seasonal
organic produce in the London area.
Delicious boxes from only £6.00.

BALDWINS HEALTH FOOD CENTRE
171 WALWORTH RD., LONDON SE17 1RW
Tel: 020 7701 4892 Fax: 020 7252 6264
A general health food store stocking a
range of organic brands including Evernat
and Whole Earth, in addition to a selected
range of herbs and aromatherapy oils.

DANDELION
120 NORTHCOTT RD.,
LONDON SW11 6QU
Tel: 0171 350 0902
Contact: Hilel Friedman
Wide range of organic fresh and dried
foods including take-away foods, vitamins,
supplements etc.

ECO CLOTHWORKS
PO BOX 16109, LONDON SE23 3WA
Tel: 020 8299 1619 Fax: 020 8299 6997
Contact: Linda Row
Email: clothworks@hotmail.com
Website: www.clothworks.co.uk
Clothworks' aim is to promote the use of
eco textiles and provide information about
ethical issues surrounding clothing.
Children's organic bedding and clothing
and organic nappies are available by mail
order. Also a range of clothes for women.

FARM-A-ROUND LTD
OFFICE B136 - B143, NEW COVENT
GARDEN MARKET, NINE ELMS LANE,
LONDON SW8 5PA
Tel: 0207 627 8066 Fax: 0207 627 4698
Contact: Isobel Davies
Email: info@farmaround.co.uk
Website: www.farmaround.co.uk
Home deliveries of fresh fruit and
vegetables to Greater London area from
£6.50. Also boxes of processed fruit and
vegetables for wholesale.

FOOD BRANDS GROUP LTD
9-10 CALICO HOUSE, PLANTATION
WHARF, BATTERSEA, LONDON SW11 3TN
Tel: 020 7978 5300 Fax: 020 7924 2732
Contact: Alex Hannon
Email: a.hannon@fbg.co.uk
Food Brands Group imports organic juice,
beer, cider, wine and coffee from a number
of countries throughout the world, for
distribution through major multiple
retailers and specialist organic shops in the
UK. Soil Association registered (no. P2230).

GREEN & BLACK'S
2 VALENTINE PLACE, LONDON SE1 8QH
Tel: 020 7633 5900 Fax: 020 7633 5901
Email: enquiries@wholeearthfoods.co.uk
Website: www.wholeearthfoods.co.uk
Green & Black's make award winning,
quality organic chocolate combining the
highest environmental and ethical
standards. Their delicious range of organic
chocolate products includes chocolate
bars, hot chocolate, cocoa, ice creams,
chocolate covered almonds and chocolate
hazelnut spread. Certified by the Soil
Association and available nationwide at
supermarkets, good health food stores and
delicatessens.

 GREEN SHOOTS
4 SAXON CENTRE, WINDSOR AVENUE,
LONDON SW19 3RR
Tel & Fax: 01483 203179
Mobile: 0793 047 0072
We specialise in high quality weekly home
deliveries in SW, W and NW London areas,
with a wide range of fresh produce and
organic food and drinks. We also distribute
Bio-dynamic wheatgrass.

GREENWICH ORGANIC FOODS
86 ROYAL HILL, GREENWICH,
LONDON SE10 8RT
Tel: 020 8488 6764
Contact: Catherine Russell
Email: info@greenwichorganic.co.uk
Website: www.greenwichorganic.co.uk
We have the largest range in South-East
London. We sell everything from bread and
dairy to ice cream. We have an emphasis
on fresh fruit and vegetables, and stock all
wholefoods. Delivery service available.

 INNER CITY ORGANICS
3 EVANDALE RD., BRIXTON,
LONDON SW9 7JJ
Tel: 020 7733 4899 (24hr)
Contact: Ronnie Smith (Owner)
Unique service offering specific orders over
the phone, minimum £12. Sunday night for
Monday evening delivery, by 2 p.m. Friday
for Friday night delivery. Collection possible.

 **NATURALLY THE ORGANIC
CONVENIENT STORE LTD**
899-901 FULHAM RD., FULHAM,
LONDON SW6
Contact: Jonathan
Natural organic food store selling complete
range of organic products including meats,
fish, bread and dairy, fruit and vegetables
and green groceries.

 NEAL'S YARD REMEDIES
HEAD OFFICE: 26-34 INGATE PLACE,
BATTERSEA, LONDON SW8 3NS
Tel: 020 7498 1686 Fax: 020 7498 2505
Email: mail@nealsyardremedies.com
CUSTOMER SERVICES
Tel: 020 7627 1949
Email: cservices@nealsyardremedies.com
Neal's Yard Remedies manufactures and
sells natural cosmetics in addition to
stocking an extensive range of herbs,
essential oils, homeopathic remedies and
reference material.

 NEAL'S YARD REMEDIES
CHELSEA FARMERS MARKET, SYDNEY ST.,
LONDON SW3 6NR
Tel: 020 7351 6380
Neal's Yard Remedies manufactures and
retails natural cosmetics in addition to
stocking an extensive range of herbs,
essential oils, homeopathic remedies and
reference material.

ORGANIC TRADE LTD
PREMIER HOUSE, 325 STREATHAM HIGH
ROAD, STREATHAM, LONDON SW16 3NT
Tel: 020 8679 8226 Fax: 020 8679 8823
Contact: Craig Whitelaw
Email: info@organictrade.co.uk
Website: www.organictrade.co.uk
Import wholesalers of all organic edible
nuts, dried fruits, pulses, seeds and cereals.
Delivery to all of UK.

THE ORGANIC WHOLESALE COMPANY
8-13 MAHATMA GHANDI INDUSTRIAL ESTATE, MILKWOOD ROAD, LONDON SE24 0FJ
Tel: 020 7798 8988 Fax: 020 7737 7785
Email: trade@organicwholesale.co.uk
Website: www.organicwholesale.co.uk
Wholesale of high quality fresh organic produce at sensible prices delivered throughout the UK. With a professional customer service team and fully guaranteed quality control, this Soil Association registered company would welcome enquiries from any enterprise seeking high quality fresh organic produce, whether pre-packed or loose.

ORGANIQ FOOD STORE
607 GARRATT LANE, EARLSFIELD, LONDON SW18 4SU
Tel: 020 8947 1087 Fax: 020 8947 6490
Contact: Gillian Jakeway
Established organic food store and free home delivery service. Stocks exclusively organic food and drink and eco-cleaners. Everything available for delivery in SW London, including meat and frozen produce. Delivery areas covered include: SW18, SW19, SW17, SW11, SW12, SW4 and SW6.

PROVENDER
103 DARTMOUTH RD., FOREST HILL, LONDON SE23 3HT
Tel: 020 8699 4046
We sell organic wholefoods, organic fresh produce, organic dairy produce. We bake organic bread on the premises as well as cakes, pastries, savouries, pizza, scones and more, using some organic ingredients. Also an alternative health centre.

QUEENS HEALTH FOOD SHOP
64 GLOUCESTER RD., LONDON SW7 4QT
Tel: 020 7584 4815 Fax: 020 8204 9520
Contact: Miss Shah
Email: sanjita-shah@hotmail.com
An independent health store running for 16 years, specialising in children's care, anti-ageing, Bach flower remedies, hair nutrients, sex life, building up the immune system and body building.

RAVENSBOURNE WINE
UNIT 6.0.2. BELL HOUSE, 49 GREENWICH HIGH RD., LONDON SE10 8JL
Tel & Fax: 020 8692 9655
Contact: Terry Short (Director)
Specialist bespoke drinks service. Wines, minerals, beers from around the world. Supply for parties, promotions, receptions, exhibitions, conferences, boardrooms, weddings. Corporate gift packing.

THE REALLY HEALTHY COMPANY LTD
PO BOX 4390, LONDON SW15 6YQ
Tel: 020 8780 5200 Fax: 020 8780 5199
Contact: Andrew
Soil Association licence no. P2531.
Greenfoods—organic Klamath blue green algae.

J.SAINSBURY PLC
STAMFORD HOUSE, STAMFORD ST., LONDON SE1 9LL
Tel: 020 7695 6000 Fax: 020 7695 7811
Contact: Robert Duxbury
Email: rjd@tao.sainsburys.co.uk
Website: www.j-sainsburys.co.uk
Food retailer with one of the widest ranges of organic food in the country.

Key

 Producers

 Wholesalers

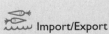 Import/Export

 Retailers

 Mail Order

 Restaurants

 Day Visits/B&B

 Farm Gate Sales

 Box Schemes/ Delivery Service

 Garden/Farm Sundries

 Manufacturers & Processors

SIMPLY ORGANIC FOOD COMPANY LTD
UNIT A62-A64, NEW COVENT GARDEN MARKET, LONDON SW8 5EE
Tel: 0845 1000 444 Fax: 020 7622 4447
Contact: Simon Grant
Email: info@simplyorganic.net
Website: www.simplyorganic.net
The UK's largest home delivery organic supermarket. Nationwide daily delivery of 1200 organic products including fruit and vegetables, beers and infant care.
Delivered to your home or office on a day of your choice. See display ad.

TODAY'S LIVING
92 CLAPHAM HIGH ST., LONDON SW4 7UL
Tel: 020 7622 1772 Contact: H. Soor
We sell health foods: wholefoods, baby foods, frozen and chilled foods etc., plus supplements, herbal remedies, homeopathic remedies and body building products.

WELL BEAN
9 OLD DOVER RD., BLACKHEATH, LONDON SE3 7BT
Tel: 020 8858 6854
Contact: Derek Rogers (Owner)
Wholefood health shop with large stocks of organic foods and access to deliveries of organic vegetables and fruit. Nutritional advice, homeopath, chiropodist, reflexologist, allergy testing, aromatherapy etc.

WELL BEING
19 SYDENHAM RD., LONDON SE26 5EX
Tel: 020 8659 2003
Contact: Mr Melvyn Stevens (Proprietor)
We sell a large range of organic fruit and vegetables, cereals, pulses, breakfast cereals, chilled and frozen produce, sauces, etc. in a retail environment.

   WHOLE EARTH FOODS LTD
2 VALENTINE PLACE, LONDON SE1 8QHH
Tel: 020 7633 5900 Fax: 020 7633 5901
Email: enquiries@wholeearthfoods.co.uk
Website: www.wholeearthfoods.co.uk
Since 1976 Whole Earth Foods have led and guided the movement to organic food. We offer a wide range of organic products: peanut butters, spreads, breakfast cereals, canned goods, children's breakfast cereals and soft drinks. Soil Association reg. no. P1117. Available nationally in major supermarkets and good health food stores. See display ad.

 WINDMILL ORGANICS LTD
66 MEADOW CLOSE, LONDON SW20 9JD
Tel: 020 8395 9749 Fax: 020 8286 4732
Contact: Noel McDonald
Windmill supply only organic products. Yoghurts, cheese, tofu products and ambient grocery lines (1500 products). Brands include: Biona, Allos, Rapunzel, Voelkel. National coverage.

LONDON WEST

 AINSWORTHS
HOMEOPATHIC PHARMACY
38 NEW CAVENDISH ST.,
LONDON W1M 7LH
Tel: 020 7935 5330 Fax: 020 7486 4313
Contact: Tony Pinkus
Email: ainshom@msn.com
Website: www.ainsworths.com
Homeopathic remedies for cattle, sheep,
pigs, horses and humans. Lectures with the
Soil Association to teach farmers how to
use homeopathy as an aid to conversion.

  ALARA
58-60 MARCHMONT STREET,
LONDON WC1N 1AB
Tel: 020 7837 1172 Fax: 020 7833 8089
Contact: Xavier Kara
All organic products. Vitamins, beauty,
fresh veg, fruit and dairy.

BUSHWACKER WHOLEFOODS
132 KING STREET, HAMMERSMITH,
LONDON W6 1QU
Tel: 020 8748 2061
Contact: Chris Shipton (Partner)
Everything you would expect in a good
wholefood shop, with the emphasis on
organically grown products including fresh
fruit and vegetables, free range eggs and
baby foods. We veto genetically modified
foods. We pack down organic foods. Soil
Association no. R1566. (We have been Soil
Association members since the early 80s).

 BUXTON FOODS LTD
12 HARLEY ST., LONDON W1N 1AA
Tel: 020 7637 5505 Fax: 020 7436 0979
Contact: Elizabeth Buxton
Email: e.buxton@stamp-collection.co.uk
Website: www.stamp-collection.co.uk
We produce the stamp collection range of
award winning organic, wheat-free, dairy-
free products including flour, chocolates,
pasta, bread, sauces, and sheep cheeses.
Soil Association reg. no. P1975.

 CLEARSPRING LTD
19A, ACTON PARK ESTATE,
LONDON W3 7QE.
Tel: 020 8749 1781 Fax: 020 8811 8893
Contact: Sam Katz
Email: info@clearsprings.co.uk
Website: www.clearsprings.co.uk
Clearspring's three kitchens contain own
brand and other manufacturer's
unprocessed, pure natural food products,
available direct and nationwide through
natural food and health stores,
delicatessens, and supermarkets. The
Organic Kitchen includes fruit sweetened
iced teas, 100% fruit jams and purées,
pasta, cold-pressed culinary oils and pure
seaweed food capsules. The Dietetic
kitchen has non-dairy wheat-free, sugar-
free, and low-sodium foods including
brands like Rice Dream milk, Imagine
puddings, and Seagreens Table Condiment.
The Authentic Japanese Kitchen offers the
widest range of traditionally made
macrobiotic Japanese foods in Europe.

 FRESH & WILD
210 WESTBOURNE GROVE,
LONDON W11 2RH
Tel: 020 7229 1063
Customer careline: 0800 9175 175
Email: shop@freshandwild.com
Website: www.freshandwild.com
Organic store with deli and juice bar. Fresh
food, healthy choices, friendly people.

 THE FRESH FOOD CO
326 PORTOBELLO RD.,
LONDON W10 5RU
Tel: 020 8969 0351 Fax: 020 8964 8050
Contact: Jo Young
Email: organics@freshfood.co.uk
Website: www.freshfood.co.uk
The UK's original and biggest secure
organic online supermarket. The Fresh
Food Company sells more than 4,500
organic and wild-harvested foods and
drinks, and non-toxicity household
necessities by phone, fax, email and
through the internet.

C. LIDGATE

110 HOLLAND PARK AVENUE,
LONDON W11 4UA.
Tel: 0171 727 8243 Fax: 0171 229 7160
Contact: David Lidgate (Director)
Organic beef and lamb from Highgrove,
home of HRH Prince Charles. Deliveries to
city and West London daily. Eros award for
Top Twenty London food shops, National
Pie Championships in 1993 & 1996,
Utrecht European Championship Gold
Medal awards 1998, *Tatler* magazine Best
UK Butchers 1998/99.

MILLER OF KENSINGTON

14 STRATFORD ROAD, KENSINGTON,
LONDON W8 6QD
Tel: 020 7937 1777
Contact: Mohamed El Banna
The only organic butcher in Kensington,
selling meat and poultry. Soil Association
and Demeter registered.

NEAL'S YARD BAKERY LTD

6 NEAL'S YARD, LONDON WC2H 9DP
Tel: 020 7836 5199 Fax: 020 7379 1544
Contact: John Loffler
Bakers of a wide range of organic breads,
cakes and pastries. Everything is baked on
the premises, with an extensive variety of
vegetarian savouries and sweets to take
away and to eat in upstairs café. Soil
Association registered.

NEAL'S YARD REMEDIES

15 NEAL'S YARD, COVENT GARDEN
LONDON WC2H 9DP
Tel: 020 7379 7222
Neal's Yard Remedies manufactures and
retails natural cosmetics in addition to
stocking an extensive range of herbs,
essential oils, homeopathic remedies and
reference material.

NEAL'S YARD REMEDIES

9 ELGIN CRESCENT LONDON W11 2JA
Tel: 020 7727 3998
Neal's Yard Remedies manufactures and
retails natural cosmetics in addition to
stocking an extensive range of herbs,
essential oils, homeopathic remedies and
reference material.

ORGANIC CAFÉ SHOPS

269 PORTOBELLO ROAD, LONDON W11
Tel: 020 7372 1232 Contact: Carol Charlton
Email: nick@organic.café.co.uk
Website: www.organic.café.co.uk
The shops provide ready to eat food and
deli food.

ORGANIC CAFÉ SHOPS

102 GOLBORNE ROAD, LONDON W10
Tel: 020 7372 1232 Contact: Carol Charlton
Email: nick@organic.café.co.uk
Website: www.organic.café.co.uk
The shops provide ready to eat food and
deli food.

PLANET ORGANIC

42 WESTBOURNE GROVE,
LONDON W2 5SH
Tel: 020 7221 7171 Fax: 020 7221 1923
Contact: Renée J. Elliott
Email: planetorganic.com
We deliver by bicycle within a three mile
radius around the shop.

PORTOBELLO WHOLEFOODS

266 PORTOBELLO ROAD,
LONDON W10 5SY
Tel: 020 8968 9133 Fax 020 8960 1840
Contact: Kate Dafter
Portobello Wholefoods stocks an ever-
increasing range of healthfood products,
including natural remedies, vitamins and
minerals, organic produce and gluten-free.
Regular special offers and friendly service
provides everything you need in a
healthfood shop—and more . . . Open 7
days a week.

REALFOOD
14 CLIFTON RD., LITTLE VENICE,
LONDON W9 1SS
Tel: 020 7266 1162 Fax: 020 7266 1550
Email: joy.realfood@aol.com
Started by Kevin Gould as a retailer in
1991, our group now includes a traiteur, a
café called Love, and consultancy. Large
organic range including fruit and veg.

 SAM-I-AM
4 SHARON ROAD, CHISWICK,
LONDON W4 4PD
Tel: 020 8995 9204
Website: www.nappies.net
Sam-I-Am! cotton nappies and accessories
at the environmentally friendly alternative
to disposables. Our new 100% organic
cotton nappy is produced in the UK.

THE TEA & COFFEE PLANT
170 PORTOBELLO ROAD,
LONDON W11 2EB
Tel: 020 7221 8137 Contact: Ian Henshall
Email: coffee@pro-net.co.uk
Website: www.coffee.uk.com
We despatch freshly roasted organic coffee
throughout the UK. Members of OF&G
(cert. no. 11UKP070055). We also supply
for trade coffee and organic tea and tea
bags. See display ad.

**THOROGOODS
(ORGANIC MEAT) SPECIALISTS**
113 NORTHFIELDS AVE, EALING,
LONDON W13 9QR
Tel: 020 8567 0339
Contact: Paul Thorogood (Owner)
Small private family business run personally
by Mr Thorogood, who oversees buying of
meat and processing of all mail orders.
Established 38 years selling quality meat.
Good selection of home made sausages
using quality organic pork. Organic bacon
and home cooked ham. Open Tuesday to
Saturday 8 a.m. to 5 p.m. See display ad.

**VERONICA'S BRITISH
HISTORIC RESTAURANT**
3 HEREFORD ROAD, BAYSWATER,
LONDON W2 4AB
Tel: 020 7229 5079 Fax: 020 7229 1210
Contact: Veronica Shaw (Owner)
Award-winning restaurant specialising in
re-creation of mediaeval to 21st Century
British food and offering outside catering
facilities.

WHOLEFOOD LTD
24 PADDINGTON ST.,
LONDON W1M 4DR
Tel: 020 7935 3924
Contact: M. Barham (Co. Secretary)
Organic fruit and vegetables, wines,
groceries, packed meats. Also a good
range of vitamins and other supplements.
Also books and magazines.

> Through intellectual property rights an attempt is made to take away what belongs
> to nature, to farmers and to women, and to term this invasion 'improvement' and
> 'progress'. Violence and plunder as instruments of wealth creation are essential to
> the colonization of nature and of our bodies through the new technologies. Those
> who are exploited become the criminals, those who exploit require protection. The
> North must be protected from the South so that it can continue its uninterrupted
> theft of the Third World's genetic diversity. The seed wars, trade wars, patent
> protection, and intellectual property rights in the GATT are claims to ownership
> through separation and fragmentation. If the regime of rights being demanded by
> the United States is implemented, the transfer of funds from poor to rich countries
> will exacerbate the Third World crisis 10 times over.
>
> Vandana Shiva, *Biopiracy* (1998)

CHORLTON WHOLEFOODS
64 BEECH RD., CHORLTON-CUM-HARDY,
MANCHESTER M21 9EG
Tel: 0161 881 6399
Contact: George Reynolds (Owner)
Complete range including fruit and veg,
dairy produce and dried goods. Free
delivery service within 10 miles (min order).

R.M. CORNMELL
459 HALLIWELL RD., BOLTON BL1 8DE
Tel: 01204 846844
Contact: R.M. Cornmell (Owner)
Member of National Federation of Meats
and Food Trades—logo in shop. Organic
food specialist: bread, cheese, meats,
bacon, ham, sausage and wholefoods. At
Altrincham Market on Thursdays.

HEALTH & VEGETARIAN STORE
33 OLD CHURCH STREET, NEWTON
HEATH, MANCHESTER M40 2JN
Tel: 0161 683 4456 Contact: Pamela Fynan
Organic bread, vegetables, food
supplement, help and advice regarding
anything I sell. Friendly atmosphere. Local
deliveries.

HOME FARM DELIVERIES
STUDIO 19, IMEX BUSINESS PARK,
HAMILTON RD., MANCHESTER M13 0PD
Tel: 0161 224 8884 Fax: 0161 224 8826
Contact: Mike Shaw
Email: home.farm@tvc.org.utc
Website: www.homefarm.co.uk
Organic food delivered to your door. Soil
Association registered R3042.

LIMITED RESOURCES
53 OLD BIRLEY ST., HULME,
MANCHESTER M15 5RF
Tel: 0161 226 4777 Fax: 0161 226 3777
Contact: John Piprani
Email: office@limitedresources.co.uk
Website: www.limitedresources.co.uk
Fresh organic foods with free home
delivery to central & south Manchester.
Trading 11 years, workers co-op, range of
400 organic and green products inc. fruit
and veg, dairy, bakery, wines, vinegars,
cleaning products. Soil Association
registered.

MOSSLEY ORGANIC AND FINE FOODS
11-13 ARUNDEL STREET, MOSSLEY,
MANCHESTER OL5 0NY
Tel: 01457 837743 / 837542
Fax: 01457 837743
Contact: Pauline Proctor Email:
organics@mossleyfoods.freeserve.co.uk
Huge range of natural food, many organic.
Fresh, quality organic fruit and vegetables
always available. Chilled, frozen, dairy
produce. Many organic wines and beers.
Specialist, individual friendly service. Soil
Association member.

NEAL'S YARD REMEDIES
UNIT 1, ST. JAMES'S SQUARE, JOHN
DALTON STREET, MANCHESTER M2 6DS
Tel: 0161 835 1713 Contact: Sue Yarnell
Neal's Yard Remedies manufactures and
retails natural cosmetics in addition to
stocking an extensive range of herbs,
essential oils, homeopathic remedies and
reference material.

Experiments are also showing that the potential exists for genes which code for
antibiotic resistance (or any other genes) to be transferred to bacteria and other
microorganisms from GE crops growing in the field.

Luke Anderson, *Genetic Engineering, Food, and Our Environment* (1999)

ON THE EIGHTH DAY
CO-OPERATIVE LIMITED
111 OXFORD ROAD, ALLSAINTS,
MANCHESTER M1 7DU
Tel & Fax: 0161 273 4878
Contact: Tim Gausden (Co-op member)
Email: 8th-day@eighthy.demon.co.uk
Website: www.eighthy.demon.co.uk
Since 1970 we have run Manchester's only
vegetarian wholefood shop and café. We
stock a vast range of organic products
including grains, pulses and flours. Where
possible we stock organic over
conventional products.

 ORGANIX WHOLEFOODS LTD
UNIT 6, SEVENDALE HOUSE, 7 DALE ST.,
MANCHESTER M1 1JA
Tel & Fax: 0161 228 0220
Contact: John Callaghan
One-stop natural foodstore and
complementary health clinic. Extensive
range of organic food, wines, fair traded
products. A green oasis in the heart of the
city: ring or write for our brochure.

 ST. ANNES WINE STORES
3 ST. ANNES RD.,
CHORLTON-CUM-HARDY M21 2TQ
Tel: 0161 881 3901 Contact: D.Scott
A retail off licence selling a wide range of
organic wine, plus some organic beer.

  UNICORN GROCERY
89 ALBANY RD., CHORLTON,
MANCHESTER M21 0BN
Tel: 0161 861 0010 Fax: 0161 861 7675
Contact: Kellie Bubble
Email: office@unicorn-grocery.co.uk
Website: www.unicorn-grocery.co.uk
We are a large, friendly wholesome
foodstore specialising in fresh and organic
produce. Over 900 good value lines.
Fresh–Organic–Fair. Soil Association
membership GCS018/R2957.

A shift of taxation away from employment and incomes and on to energy use and pollution will encourage local production for local consumption by raising the costs of centralised energy-intensive processes and long distance transport. Removing subsidies and regulations that favour non-local production and non-local provision of services will do the same. By reducing land prices, site-value taxation will make land and housing more affordable for local people.

James Robertson, *Transforming Economic Life* (1998)

Key

 Producers
 Wholesalers
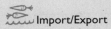 Import/Export

 Retailers
 Mail Order
 Restaurants
 Day Visits/B&B

 Farm Gate Sales
 Box Schemes/ Delivery Service
 Garden/Farm Sundries
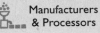 Manufacturers & Processors

MERSEYSIDE

  ABBOTTS
VEGETABLE & HERB GARDEN
45 GLENAVON RD., PRENTON,
BIRKENHEAD, WIRRAL L43 0RB
Tel: 0151 608 4566
Contact: Simon H. Dyson (Owner)
Soil Association member 2150. Vegetable
box scheme, supplier to village stores,
hotels and restaurants. Local produce
freshly harvested and delivered weekly.

THE BILLINGTON FOOD GROUP LTD
CUNARD BUILDING, LIVERPOOL L3 1EL
Tel: 0151 236 2265 Fax: 0151 236 2493
Contact: Edward Billington (Industrial
Sales), Simon Haywood (Retail Sales),
Caroline Hemming (Export Sales)
Email: bfg@billingtons.co.uk
Website: www.billingtons.co.uk
Billingtons supplies a range of organic cane
sugars to retail and manufacturing sectors,
both within UK and worlwide. All products
are certified by the Soil Association.

KOMBUCHA HEALTH LTD
UNIT A3B, NEW BRUNSWICK BUSINESS
PARK, BRUNSWICK WAY, LIVERPOOL L3 4BD
Tel: 0151 709 0008 Fax: 0151 709 0008
Contact: Arthur Wilson
Manufacture biologically active fermented
tea drink, Kombucha 1, using a natural
process. Finest organic ingredients to the
highest standards of quality. 100% organic.
Soil Association certified (no. P2657).
Delivery to all major healthfood
wholesalers—mail order service.

 ONLY NATURAL
48 WESTFIELD ST., ST. HELENS WA10 1QF
Tel: 01744 759797
Contact: Mrs B. Arrowsmith
Healthfood shop stocking a range of
organic foods, but not fresh fruit and veg.

 ORGANIC DIRECT
3 BANCROFT CLOSE, LIVERPOOL L25 0LS
Tel & Fax: 0151 298 2468 Contact: Ruth
We offer over 30 varieties of organic fruit
and vegetables. We also have organic
bread and a range of organic wholefoods.
Free home deliveries within Merseyside
and Wirral areas.

   WINDMILL
WHOLEFOOD CO-OP
337 SMITHDOWN RD., LIVERPOOL L15 3JJ
Tel: 0151 734 1919 Contact: Kerry
Email: windmill@windmill.abelgratis.co.uk
Website: www.merseyworld.com/windmill
Wide range of vegetarian and vegan
organic wholefoods, fruit, vegetables,
wines and beers. Ethical bodycare and
cleaning products. Magazines and books.
Soil Association licensed (no. GCS018/
R1736). Deliveries to L1-L8, L11-L18, L20-
L23.

If we wish to move from our present 'disease service' to a true 'health service'. . . we
need policy initiatives which promote both health and health care. This is no more
than a return to traditional medical systems, in which the delivery of health and
health care are so closely entwined as to be indistinguishable. The reality of our
present health system is far from this.

Robin Stott, *The Ecology of Health* (2000)

MIDDLESEX

 BIG OZ INDUSTRIES LTD
PO BOX 48, TWICKENHAM TW1 2UF
Tel: 020 8893 9366 Fax: 020 8894 3297
Contact: Anne Lotter
Email: anne@bigoz.co.uk
Website: www.bigoz.co.uk
Big Oz imports a range of organic
breakfast cereals from Australia. All our
grains are certified by the Biological
Farmers of Australia in compliance with
EEC reg. no. 2092/91. See display ad.

 COUNTRYSIDE
WHOLEFOODS LTD
19 FORTY HILL, ENFIELD EN2 9HT
Tel: 020 8363 2933 Fax: 020 8342 0580
We run a mail order delivery service from
our shop and warehouses, which stock a
wide range of wholefoods, both organic
and non-organic, fresh fruit and vegetables
(not by mail order) and associated green
and recycled products.

 GAIA WHOLEFOODS
123 ST. MARGARET'S RD.,
TWICKENHAM TW1 2LH
Tel: 020 8 892 2262
Contact: David Kennington
Hours: Mon-Fri 9.30-7 p.m., Sat 9.30-5 p.m.
Fresh vegetables and fruit, dried fruit, nuts,
grains, convenience foods, bread, eggs,
dairy produce, flours, seeds, grains, flakes,
juices, take-away, biscuits and baby foods.
Soil Association Symbol no. R1562.

GLOCREST LTD
STUDIO 6, BENTINCK COURT,
BENTINCK RD., WEST DRAYTON UB7 7RQ
Tel & Fax: 020 8789 0755
Contact: Kate Symons
Email: sales@glocrest.com
Website: www.glocrest.com
UK-based company supplying wholesale
and retail trade with comprehensive range
of Italian organic grocery products and
organic wine. We also sell direct to the
public through our e-commerce website
and mail order. All products certified in
accordance with EU regulations.

ORGANIKA—
THE ORGANIC STORE
8 STAINES RD., TWICKENHAM TW2 5AH
Tel: 020 8 893 3310 Fax: 020 8 404 1129
Contact: Robert Owen (Director)
Email: organika@compuserve.com
Website: www.organika.co.uk
Exclusively organic produce with nearly
2000 lines, including wine, beer, meat,
poultry, baby food, fresh fruit and
vegetables, cooking oils, chocolate, pasta,
nuts, rice, dairy produce, tea and coffee.
Home delivery service. Nationwide delivery
via website.

Most people think that there's only one type of money because one type is all they've
ever known. They know about foreign currencies, but they see these, quite correctly,
as essentially the same sort of money as they use in their own countries. . . . there are,
potentially at least, many different types of money, and each type can affect the
economy, human society and the natural environment in a different way.

Richard Douthwaite, *The Ecology of Money* (1999)

NORFOLK

  ADAS TERRINGTON

TERRINGTON ST. CLEMENT,
KINGS LYNN PE34 4PW
Tel: 01553 828621 Fax: 01553 827229
Contact: Dr Bill Cormack
(Research Team Manager)
Email: bill.cormack@adas.co.uk
Website: www.adas.co.uk
Producer of organic potatoes, vegetables,
cereals and pulses to UKROFS standard.
Research into stockless arable organic
rotations, organic pig production, organic
production of sugar beet and energy use
farming systems.

THE ARK RESTAURANT

THE STREET, ERPINGHAM NR11 7QB
Tel: 01263 761535
Contact: Mike Kidd (Proprietor)
Restaurant with accommodation, growing
organic vegetables and herbs, using local
meat and fish, organic wherever possible.
Everything home produced.

 ARTHUR'S WHOLEFOODS

3A WELLINGTON RD., DEREHAM NR19 2BP
Tel: 01362 697750
Contact: Tony & Jasmine Park
Organic fresh fruit, vegetables and organic
products. Full range of wholefoods,
fairtrade, free range eggs, recycled paper
products, biodegradeable cleaning
products, comrehensive refill service (e.g.
Ecover, honey, vinegar, shampoo and
coffee).

THE BOOJA BOOJA COMPANY

HALL FARM, BUNGAY RD.,
HEMPNALL NR15 2LJ
Tel: 01508 499049 Fax: 01508 498770
Contact: Colin Mace
Britain's first manufacturer of organic
chocolates. Dairy-free (certified by Vegan
Society), gluten-free delicious chocolates.
Soil Association no. P4181.

BRITISH WILD FLOWER PLANTS

BURLINGHAM GARDENS, 31 MAIN RD.,
NORTH BURLINGHAM NR13 4TA
Tel: 01603 716615
Contact: Linda Laxton (Proprietor)
Wild flower plants grown from native
British stock using peat-free compost and
Soil Association approved inputs. No
insecticides used on products for wildlife
gardening. Catalogue available annually.

   CRONE'S

FAIRVIEW, FERSFIELD RD.,
KENNINGHALL NR16 2DP
Tel: 01379 687687 Fax: 01379 688323
Contact: Robert & Jane Crone
Award winning producer of a range of
single variety organic apple juices and
blended juices, and producer of a range of
ciders, all organic to Soil Association
standard (reg. no. P1587). Farm gate sales
by appointment only. See display ad.

DEVONSHIRE FOODS

UNITS 1B & 1C, SOVEREIGN WAY,
TRAFALGAR INDUSTRIAL ESTATE,
DOWNHAM MARKET PE38 9SW
Tel: 01366 382260 Fax: 01366 385590
Large range of pre-packed organic foods
and branded goods.

  DIANE'S PANTRY

8 MARKET PLACE, REEPHAM,
NORWICH NR10 4JJ
Tel: 01603 871075
Contact: Diane Turner (Owner)
Wholefood, healthfoods, supplements and
small bakery with coffee shop attached.
Organic bread baked to order.

  GREEN CITY CENTRAL

42-46 BETHEL ST., NORWICH NR2 1NR
Tel: 01603 631007 Contact: Tigger
The shop acts as a contact point for local
veg box scheme and is stockist of a wide
range of organic and GMO-free foods.

ANNE & KEITH HOOD
THE STABLES, GRESHAM,
NORWICH NR11 8AD
Tel: 01263 577468 Contact: A. or K. Hood
Soil Assn. symbol no. G1112. Organic veg,
fruit and dairy produce, box scheme, or
from the door. Six acre holding. N.B. No
honey at present. Occasional organic beef.

PATRICK KEMP
EVERGREEN FARM, CHURCH LANE,
GRESSENHALL, DEREHAM NR19 2QQ
Tel: 01362 860190 Contact: Patrick Kemp
Soil Association no. G1111. Seasonal fruit
and vegetables grown on farm, eggs,
sometimes poultry.

KETTLE FOODS
BARNARD RD., BOWTHORPE,
NORWICH NR5 9JB
Tel: 01603 744788 Fax: 01603 740375
Contact: Pippa Rowntree
Website: www.kettlefoods.co.uk
Kettle Foods make Kettle Organics—the
first gourmet, hand cooked organic potato
chips available in major retailers. .

LETHERINGSETT WATER MILL
RIVERSIDE RD., LETHERINGSETT,
HOLT NR25 7YD
Tel: 01263 713153
Contact: Mr Mike Thurlow
Water Mill (1798) restored to working
order producing organic 100%
wholewheat flour. Demeter BDAA member
(no. 262). Working demonstrations when
we make flour (varies between winter and
summer). Mail order sales; deliveries to
NR25 & all Norfolk.

MANGREEN TRUST
MANGREEN, SWARDESTON,
NORWICH NR14 8DD
Tel: 01508 570444 Fax: 01508 578899
Contact: Adrian Holmes
Email: trust@mangreen.u-net.com
Website: www.personal.u-net.com/
~mangreen/mangreen
We farm 1 1/2 acres of vegetables and fruit
to Soil Association standards (cert. no.
D10E). Retail outlet supplies fresh produce,
both local and imported, complemented
by general grocery items.

THE NATURAL FOODSTORE
NORFOLK HOUSE YARD,
ST. NICHOLAS ST., DISS IP22 3LB
Tel: 01379 651832
Contact: S.G. Cullen (Partner)
Our aim is to provide good quality
wholefoods at affordable prices. We are
entirely vegetarian with plenty of choice
for vegans and those on special diets. We
provide an increasing range of organically
grown produce and use minimal
packaging in recyclable materials.

NATURAL SURROUNDINGS
BAYFIELD ESTATE, HOLT, NR25 7JN
Tel: 01263 711091
Contact: Peter Loosley (Owner)
Centre for wildlife gardening and
conservation wildflower nursery: 10 acre
site open to the public.

NEAL'S YARD REMEDIES
26 LOWER GOAT LANE, NORWICH NR2 1EL
Tel: 01603 766681
Neal's Yard Remedies manufactures and
retails natural cosmetics in addition to
stocking an extensive range of herbs,
essential oils, homeopathic remedies and
reference material.

Today, millions of people are making soil in their gardens via composting. Perhaps
the single most powerful thing we can do as stewards of the planet is to care for the
small patches of land surrounding our houses.

John Roulac, *Backyard Composting* (1999)

ORGANICS-ON-LINE LTD
PARK HOUSE, GUNTHORPE HALL,
MELTON CONSTABLE NR24 2PA
Tel: 01263 861991 Fax: 01263 860964
Contact: Annette Ward (MD)
Email: annette.ward@organics-on-line.com
Website: www.organics-on-line.com
Business to business internet trading site.
Organics-on-line offers the world's largest
range of organic products in a one-stop-
shop internet site. The site acts as a means
of facilitating trade direct from the
producer to the buyer and is targeting
business to business trade in organics. See
display ad.

 RAINBOW WHOLEFOODS
WAREHOUSE, 21 WHITE LODGE ESTATE,
HALL RD., NORWICH NR4 6DG
Tel: 01603 630484 Fax: 01603 664066
Contact: Richard Austin (M.D.)
Email: rainbow@paston.co.uk
Rainbow Wholefoods actively support the
growth in popularity of organic produce
by listing an extensive range from wines,
beers, pulses, fruit, vegetables in jars,
chocolate, cakes and breads, cheeses and
even Japanese noodles!
SHOP, 16 DOVE ST., NORWICH NR2 1DE
Tel & Fax: 01603 625560
Contact: Richard Austin (M.D.)
Registered with the Soil Association, we are
a friendly shop with a massive range of
organic foods from pasta to chocolate,
wines, and fruit and vegetables.

 ST. BENEDICTS FOOD STORE
43 ST. BENEDICTS STREET,
NORWICH NR2 4PG
Tel: 01603 623309
Contact: Mr R.D. Pike (Owner)
Retailer and wholesaler of organic produce
to the public and the catering trade.

  J. S AVORY EGGS
HIGHFIELD FARM, GREAT RYBURGH,
FAKENHAM NR21 7AL
Tel: 01328 829249 Fax: 01328 829422
Contact: Elizabeth Savory
Email: jegshighfield@net.co.uk Website for
B&B: www.broadland.com/highfield
J. Savory Eggs laying flock, converting June
2000 (Soil Association no. G2947).
Speciality egg production. Mrs E. Savory,
farmhouse B&B, member FHB, Four
Diamonds ETB.

 SESAME WHOLEFOOD DELIVERIES
11 MATLOCK ROAD, NORWICH NR1 1TL
Tel: 01603 433908
Contact: Nigel Robinson
We deliver wholefoods in Norfolk and
Suffolk and by mail order throughout the
UK. Our range is largely organic and
includes bulk packs. We sell wholefoods,
environmentally friendly cleaning
products, vegetables and bread.

Biodiversity erosion starts a chain reaction. The disappearance of one species is related to the extinction of innumerable other species with which it is interrelated through food webs and food chains. The crisis of biodiversity, however, is not just a crisis of the disappearance of species, which serve as industrial raw material and have the potential of spinning dollars for corporate enterprises. It is, more basically, a crisis that threatens the life support systems and livelihoods of millions of people in Third World countries.

Vandana Shiva, *Biopiracy* (1998)

 STUBBINGS
MARKET PLACE,
BURNHAM MARKET PE31 8HF
Tel: 01328 738337 Fax: 01328 730668
Contact: Mike Stubbings
Fruit, vegetables, speciality groceries, some
wholefoods and organics.

 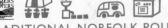
TRADITIONAL NORFOLK POULTRY
GARAGE FARM, HARGHAM RD.,
SHROPHAM NR17 1DS
Tel: 01953 498434 Fax: 01953 498962
Contact: Mark Gorton
Email: og@tnp.co.uk
We are producers and processors of
organic chicken and turkeys all year round.
We are members of Organic Farmers and
Growers no. 31UKF120071.

THE TREEHOUSE RESTAURANT
14-16 DOVE ST., NORWICH NR2 1DE
Tel: 01263 713320
Wholefood vegetarian & vegan meals
cooked fresh on the day. Gluten and sugar-
free items also available. Scrumptious cakes
and desserts, take-away meals.

The 20th-century capitalist/socialist struggle has revolved around who shall control the 'commanding heights' of the economy—big finance, or big government. The challenge of the 21st-century is to evolve an economic system which cannot be 'commanded' by any interest group, but is designed to secure economic freedom, self-reliance and democracy for all.

James Robertson, *Transforming Economic Life* (1998)

As it is not possible to insert a new gene with any accuracy, the gene transfer may also disrupt the tightly controlled network of DNA in an organism. Current understanding of the way in which genes are regulated is extremely limited, and any change to the DNA of an organism at any point may well have knock-on effects that are impossible to predict or control. The new gene could, for example, alter chemical reactions within the cell or disturb cell functions. This could lead to instability, the creation of new toxins or allergens, and changes in nutritional value.

Luke Anderson, *Genetic Engineering, Food, and Our Environment* (1999)

Key

 Producers

 Wholesalers

 Import/Export

 Retailers

 Mail Order

 Restaurants

 Day Visits/B&B

 Farm Gate Sales

 Box Schemes/ Delivery Service

 Garden/Farm Sundries

Manufacturers & Processors

NORTHAMPTONSHIRE

DAILY BREAD CO-OPERATIVE LTD
THE OLD LAUNDRY, BEDFORD RD.,
NORTHAMPTON NN4 7AD
Tel: 01604 621531 Fax: 01604 603725
Contact: John Clarke
Email: northampton@dailybread.co.uk
Website: www.dailybread.co.uk
Soil Association member (P4448) We retail
and wholesale wholefoods, with an
increasing range of organic flours, grains,
nuts, fruits, etc. Also organic milk, bread,
fruit and veg, yoghurts and cheeses.

FERTIPLUS GARDEN PRODUCTS
NORTH LODGE, ORLINGBURY RD.,
ISHAM, KETTERING NN14 1HW
Tel & Fax: 01536 722424
Contact: James Holton
Email: jim@fertiplus.co.uk
Website: www.fertiplus.co.uk
Manufacturers, packagers and distributors
of organic horticultural fertilisers, including
FertiFowl pelleted poultry manure. See
display ad.

GOODNESS FOODS
SOUTH MARCH, DAVENTRY NN11 4PH
Tel: 01327 706611 Fax: 01327 300436
Contact: Lesley Cutts
Email: lesley.cutts@goodness.co.uk
Website: www.goodness.co.uk
Members of the Soil Association (no.
P1636). We distribute and package many
organic foods, and manufacture organic
low fat flapjacks and organic muesli. Also
contract packing of organic products.

> We need a transition to an alternative
> economic paradigm that does not
> reduce all value to market prices and
> all human activity to commerce.
>
> Vandana Shiva, *Biopiracy* (1998)

GRANOVITA UK LTD
5 STANTON CLOSE, FINEDON ROAD IND.
ESTATE, WELLINGBOROUGH NN8 4HN
Tel: 01933 273717 Fax: 01933 273729
Email: gvita@globalnet.co.uk
GranoVita UK manufactures a wide range of
vegetarian products, many of which are
organic. Our range includes the following
organic products; breakfast cereals, sauces,
soya drinks, patés, desserts—and a great
deal more. Our organic certifying bodies are:
QC&I, Organic Farmers & Growers (UK2),
and the Soil Assn (UK5). See display ad.

 LEAFCYCLES
24 ST MICHAELS AVENUE,
NORTHAMPTON NN1 4JQ
Tel: 01604 628956
Contact: Jenny Vaughan Email:
leafcycles@digworkers.freeserve.co.uk
Soil Association reg. no. P2173. Fruit and
vegetable boxes can be collected from us
(near town centre) or Daily Bread.
Deliveries during daytime, and evening to
Abington only. Delivery areas: NN1, NN2,
NN3, NN4, NN5, NN7, NN8 & NN16.

 MARTLET NATURAL FOODS
MEADOW CLOSE, ISE VALLEY,
WELLINGBOROUGH NN8 4BH
Tel: 01933 442022 Fax: 01933 440815
Producers and suppliers of retail and bulk
organic products. Preserves, chutneys,
cider and wine vinegars, honey, molasses,
malt, sugar syrups, mincemeat, sauces.
Also seaweed extract, biostimulants and
fertilisers. Soil Association approved.

SUPERIOR INTERNATIONAL LTD
HALDENS PARKWAY, THRAPSTON NN14 4QS
Tel: 01832 733777 Fax: 01832 735200
Contact: Gary Mason
Email: organics@superior-int.co.uk
Superior International are wholly owned by
Greery International. We import, pack and
distribute organic fresh produce. Specialist
areas are fruit (top and stone, citrus and
grapes) and salads.

NORTHUMBERLAND

THE BARN BAKERY

LEE MOOR FARM, RENNINGTON,
ALNWICK NE66 3RL
Tel: 01665 577155 Fax: 01665 577155
Contact: Kathryn Potts
Email: the-barn-bakery@beeb.net
Freshly baked organic bread and rolls which
taste delicious because they are made with
skill and care in the traditional way. Also
organic tea cakes, scones, spice buns,
flapjacks and pizzas. Soil Association reg. no.
P4320. Delivery areas covered include
Northumbria, Tyneside & Edinburgh.

THE GOOD LIFE SHOP

50 HIGH ST., WOOLER NE71 6BG
Tel & Fax: 01668 281700
Email: timsharp@compaserve.com
Contact: Tim & Diana Sharp
Organic produce includes: pasta flour,
cheese, coffee, tea, cereals, seeds, rice and
biscuits. Other organic products on
request, as available.

THE GREEN SHOP

54 BRIDGE ST.,
BERWICK UPON TWEED TD15 1AQ
Tel & Fax: 01289 330897
Contact: Ross Boston
Selling organic products was a founding
principle of the shop. Seeds, clothes,
toiletries, chilled and pre-packed foods,
chocolates, alcohol, fresh breads, milk,
meat, fruit and veg link. 600+ certified
organic products. Delivery to 30 miles.

MARKET SHOP

48 BRIDGE ST.,
BERWICK-UPON-TWEED TD15 1AQ
Tel & Fax: 01289 307749
Contact: Derek & Julie Jones (proprietors)
Wholefood shop. Range of organic dry
goods, cheese, soy milk, paté etc. for
personal shoppers.

NORTH EAST ORGANIC GROWERS

WEST SLEEKBURN FARM, BOMARSUND,
BEDLINGTON NE22 7AD
Tel: 01670 821070
Contact: Bryony Stimpson
Email: neog@care4free.net Website:
www.made-in-northumberland.co.uk
Bags of fresh organic veg, fruit, herbs,
delivered to a network of 'link groups'
around Northumberland, Tyne & Wear
and into Co. Durham. Soil Association
registered for growing and packing
(GC5015/P1779), and BOF members.

ORGANIC NATURAL FOODS LTD

HIGHTHORN FARM, ELLINGTON,
MORPETH NE61 5JP
Tel & Fax: 01670 862 966 / 0191 414 0269
Contact: Rob, Lal or Steve
Email: lal@organica.ic24.co.uk
We are a workers' co-op running a box
scheme throughout the North-East. Full
range of fruit, vegetables, bread and
wholefoods. Wholesale and home delivery
service.

Many experts now agree that we ignore at our children's peril the importance of
creating healthy sperm and eggs, a pollution-free womb, and sufficient health bank
of all the nutrients needed for a rapidly developing embryo and foetus. . . . If both
parents are in optimum health when they conceive, their offspring are likely to be
as well.

Tanyia Maxted-Frost, *The Organic Baby Book* (1999)

NOTTINGHAMSHIRE

INSKIPS ORGANICS
16 MAIN STREET, EAST BRIDGFORD,
NOTTINGHAM NG13 8PA
Tel: 01949 21057 or 01949 20289
Fax: 01927 21057
Contact: Charles or Jennifer Holt
Email: inskipsorg@aol.com
Organic fruit, veg, breads and dairy produce, frozen foods and groceries on sale at our village shop, from a variety of suppliers. Own Soil Association registered smallholding producing excess for additional sales.

THE NATURAL FOOD CO
37 MANSFIELD RD.,
NOTTINGHAM NG1 3FB
Tel: 0115 955 9914 Contact: R. Haresh
We are a well stocked wholefoods shop, organic lines expanding all the time: cereals, honeys, pulses, grains, condiments, teas, coffee, fruit and veg, chocolate, baby foods etc.

 P.J. ONIONS
SHELTON LODGE, NR. NEWARK NG23 5JJ
Tel: 0194 985 0268 Fax: 0194 985 0714
Contact: Peter Onions
Organic poultry producer and processor. Board member of Organic Farmers and Growers.

 OUT OF THIS WORLD
VILLA ST., BEESTON,
NOTTINGHAM NG9 2NY
Tel: 0115 943 1311 Contact: Nigel Clifton
Small chain of ethical and organic supermarkets in Newcastle upn Tyne, Nottingham and Cheltenham (also organic café). Selling over 4000 products, most food products certified organic, plus fairly traded crafts, recycled paper and bodycare products etc. Consumer co-op with over 17,500 members.

The United States has accused the Third World of piracy. The estimates for royalties lost are $202 million per year for agricultural chemicals and $2.5 billion annually for pharmaceuticals. In a 1986 U.S. Department of Commerce survey, U.S. companies claimed they lost $23.8 billion yearly due to inadequate or ineffective protection of intellectual property. Yet, as the team at the Rural Advancement Foundation International in Canada has shown, if the contributions of Third World peasants and tribespeople are taken into account, the roles are dramatically reversed: the United States would owe Third World countries $302 million in agriculture royalties and $5.1 billion for pharmaceuticals. In other words, in these two biological industry sectors alone, the United States should owe $2.7 billion to the Third World. It is to prevent these debts from being taken into account that it becomes essential to set up the creation boundary through the regulation of intellectual property rights; without it, the colonization of the regenerative processes of life renewal is impossible. Yet if this, too, is allowed to happen in the name of patent protection, innovation and progress, life itself will have been colonized.

Vandana Shiva, *Biopiracy* (1998)

THE PANTRY
76 CAROLGATE, RETFORD DN22 6EF
Tel: 01777 708124 Contact: Hazel Cope
Mainly organic grocery items: flour, honey, oats, muesli, organic wines, cheeses.

PHOENIX ORGANICS
SPRINGS COTTAGE,
SUTTON CUM GRANBY NG13 9QA
Tel & Fax: 01949 850021
Contact: Corinne
Box scheme, fruit, veg, eggs, bread, baby food, milk-free/gluten-free diets, cleaning products.

ROOTS NATURAL FOODS
526 MANSFIELD RD., SHERWOOD,
NOTTINGHAM NG5 2FR
Tel: 0115 960 9014 Fax: 0115 912 0132
Contact: Richard Yerrell
Pure vegetarian, organic retailer, box scheme and delivery service. Discounts on bulk purchases.

ROSEMARY'S HEALTH FOODS
6 LINCOLN ST., NOTTINGHAM NG1 3DJ
Tel: 0115 950 5072
Contact: Kim Edwards (Manager)
Health foods and wholefoods retailer.

 DI SHOULS
BARN FARM COTTAGE, KNEETON ROAD,
EAST BRIDGFORD NG13 8PJ
Tel: 01949 20196 Contact: Mrs Di Shouls
A prize winning B&B serving organic food. Overlooking the Trent Valley, £17.50 per person per night. Organic (short stay) holidays up to 6 people. Organic farmhouse dinners. Organic foods now available at 'Inskips' in village, located on Main Street, East Bridgford. They can be contacted on 01949 21057 (ask for Jenny or Charles). Soil Association member.

TRINITY FARM / AWSWORTH NURSERY
AWSWORTH LANE, COSSALL NG16 2RZ
Tel: 0115 944 2545
Educational day visits, Organic Farmers and Growers certified.

VITRITION LTD
MAIN ST., LANEHAM,
RETFORD DN22 0NA
Tel: 01777 228741/228848
Fax: 01777 228737 Contact: Paul Forster
Email: optivite@compuserve.co.uk
Website: www.optivite.co.uk
Full species range of organic animal feeds including compounds, balances, concentrates and supplements; custom mixers, nationwide delivery service. Vitrition formulate and manufacture organic compounds and minerals for farm livestock to Organic Farmers and Growers and Soil Association criteria.

Key

 Producers   Wholesalers   Import/Export

 Retailers   Mail Order   Restaurants   Day Visits/B&B

 Farm Gate Sales   Box Schemes/ Delivery Service   Garden/Farm Sundries   Manufacturers & Processors

OXFORDSHIRE

  BRITISH BAKELS
GRANVILLE WAY, off LAUNTON RD.,
BICESTER OX6 0JT
Tel: 01869 247098 Fax: 01869 242979
Contact: P.J. Hemson
Email: phemsonBB@bakels.com
Website: www.Bakels.com
Soil Association reg. no. P2725.
Manufacturers of organic cake mixes,
scone mixes, muffin mixes, bread
improvers, crumb softeners and baking
powders. All UK.

BROOK COTTAGE FARM
BROOK COTTAGE FARM,
CHARNEY BASSETT, WANTAGE OX12 0EN
Tel: 01236 868492
Contact: Dianne Godfrey
Soil Association no. G806. Fruit, veg, beef,
eggs and fodder (small bales of wrapped
haylage and hay) at Saturday farm shop.
'Kissing Bridge Vegetables' local organic
box scheme no. P806.

CORNER FARM
OAKLEY ROAD, HORTON CUM STUDLEY,
OXFORD OX33 1BJ
Tel: 01865 358933 Fax: 01865358 806
Contact: Mrs S. Ayers
Organic farm and shop. Soil Association
member. Fruit, vegetables, meat, fish,
wholefoods. Delivery within the Oxford area.

COTSWOLD SPECIALITY FOODS LTD
AVENUE 3, STATION LANE,
WITNEY OX8 6JB
Tel: 01993 703294 Fax: 01993 774227
Contact: L. Keys
Email: laurie@cotswoldhoney.demon.co.uk
Website: www.cotswoldhoney.demon.co.uk
Processor and bottler of organic honey for
retail and industrial use. Soil Association
members.

  EASTBROOK FARM
ORGANIC MEATS
50 HIGH ST., SHRIVENHAM SN6 8AA
Tel: 01793 782211
Contact: Graham Burrows
Eastbrook Farm Organic Meats supplies a
full range of fresh organic meat, bacon,
cured ham and sausages. We guarantee the
highest levels of animal welfare, with all our
livestock being reared on chemical-free
pastures. Soil Association symbol no. P535.

M. FELLER SON & DAUGHTER
54/55 COVERED MARKET,
OXFORD OX1 3DY
Tel: 01865 251164 Fax: 01865 200553
Email: mfeller@mfeller. co.uk
Website: www.mfeller.co.uk
Family-run organic butcher shop in the
traditional 200 year old Oxford covered
market. Soil Association member no.
P4455. Free delivery service available in the
Oxford area: OX1, OX2, OX3 & OX4.

FINE LADY BAKERIES LTD
SOUTHAM ROAD, BANBURY OX16 7RR
Tel: 01295 227600 Fax: 01295 271430
Contact: A.W. Moutter
Email: info@finelady.co.uk
Fine Lady Bakeries Ltd produce a range of
organic bread and rolls for both the retail
and sandwich making industries. Soil
Association licence no. P1543.

FRUGAL FOOD
17 WEST SAINT HELEN STREET,
ABINGDON OX14 5BL
Tel: 01235 522239
Contact: Val Stoner (Proprietor)
Specialist grocer; wholefoods, cheese,
wine, cleaning products, supplements,
remedies. Friendly, knowledgeable staff.

GLUTTONS DELICATESSEN
110 WALTON STREET, OXFORD OX2 6AJ
Tel: 01865 553748
Contact: Adrian Tennissen
Excellent and imaginative deli. Large range
of home made foods, organic wines,
cheeses, yoghurts and other produce.
Helpful and knowledgeable staff.

SERENA HOWARD
21 MARKET PLACE,
CHIPPING NORTON OX7 5NA
Tel & Fax: 01608 642973
Contact: Serena Howard (Owner)
Box scheme for veg and fruit (individual
requirements taken into consideration)
plus eggs, bread and dairy produce. Soil
Association registered no. R1816.

IVY COTTAGE B&B
SULGRAVE ROAD, CULWORTH,
BANBURY OX17 2AP
Tel: 01295 768131
Contact: Mrs J. McKenzie (Proprietor)
Cosy B&B in attractive village. Organic
produce, free range eggs, sheep, cats.
Many attractions nearby. B&B from £20
per head per night. Holiday flat for 2-3 also
available from £200 per week.

JORDANS
8 UPPER HIGH ST., THAME OX9 3ER
Tel: 01844 212056 Fax: 01844 260220
Contact: Peter Jordan
Email: jordans@fsbusiness.co.uk
Website: www.thame.net
Comprehensive fresh food delicatessen,
meat, wine, grocery etc. with an increasing
organic range.

F.W.P. MATTHEWS LTD
STATION RD.,
SHIPTON UNDER WYCHWOOD,
CHIPPING NORTON OX7 6BH
Tel: 01993 830342 Fax: 01993 831615
Contact: Paul Matthews
Email: sales@fwpmatthews.co.uk
Website: www.fwpmatthews.co.uk
Soil Association licence no. P1521. A family
firm producing a range of white and
wholemeal flours as well as whole grain
and wheatfeed. All volumes catered for—
1.5kg to 25 tonnes. Nationwide coverage.

MEAT MATTERS
2 BLANDYS FARM COTTAGE,
LETCOMBE REGIS, WANTAGE OX12 9LJ
Tel: 0800 067426 Fax: 01235 772526
Contact: Diane Glass
Meat Matters delivers fresh organic
poultry, eggs, fish, fruit, vegetables and
groceries to over 3000 customers
throughout the UK. Delivery is free within
M25 area, in Oxfordshire, Berkshire, south
Bucks and south Hertfordshire, with a small
charge elsewhere. Please telephone for
information and price list. See display ad.

MUTCHMEATS LTD
NEWCLOSE LANE, WITNEY OX8 7GX
Tel: 01993 772972 Fax: 01993 776239
Contact: G. Biddington
Private kill facility.

NATURES HARVEST
4A CHURCH LANE, BANBURY OX16 8LR
Tel: 01295 253208
Contact: A. Boother (Partner)
Health food shop, member of Soil
Association (no. R2268). Pack all own fruit,
pulses, nuts etc. on premises. Prices very
competitive.

Looking down on the Earth from space at night, astronauts see an illuminated
planet—vast city clusters lit up by millions of light bulbs as well as the flares of oil
wells and refineries. . . .

Herbert Girardet, *Creating Sustainable Cities* (1999)

NEAL'S YARD REMEDIES
5 GOLDEN CROSS, CORNMARKET STREET, OXFORD OX1 3EU
Tel: 01865 245436
Neal's Yard Remedies manufactures and retails natural cosmetics in addition to stocking an extensive range of herbs, essential oils, homeopathic remedies and reference material.

   THE OLD DAIRY
PATH HILL FARM,
WHITCHURCH ON THAMES,
READING RG8 7RE
Tel & Fax: 0118 984 2392
Contact: Elizabeth Rose
Email: theolddairy@freeuk.com
Own produced organic beef, lamb, pork, poultry, vegetables and fruit all produced on Hardwick Estate. Also available: farmhouse cheeses, eggs, dairy products and bread. Ring for details of weekly order scheme and collection times. Soil Association reg. no. PRO7M.

 ROWSE HONEY LTD
MORETON AVENUE,
WALLINGFORD OX10 9DE
Tel: 01491 827400 Fax: 01491 827434
Contact: Mr Stuart Bailey (MD)
Email: rowse.honey@rowsehoney.co.uk
Website:www.rowsehoney.co.uk
Importer and processor of organic honey from Argentina, New Zealand, Australia, Mexico and Turkey. Also importer and processor of organic pure Canadian maple syrup. Soil Association no. P2357. See display ad.

  SARSDEN PARTNERSHIP
WALLED GARDEN, SARSDEN ESTATE,
CHIPPING NORTON OX7 6PW
Tel: 01608 659670 Fax: 01608 659670
Contact: Ms. H.W. Scott
Email: Helen-Sarsden@talk21.com
Soil Association members (no. G2986). Certified organic July 2000 on a four acre holding—additional seven acres in conversion, organic in 2002. Producing field scale vegetables and salad crops.

   M.S AUNDERS
STEP FARM, LECHLADE ROAD,
FARINGDON SN7 8BH
Tel: 01367 240558 Fax: 01367 244324
Soil Association no. S335. Sell organic lamb, beef and pork. Jointed and frozen. opening times by arrangement.

   TOLHURST ORGANIC PRODUCE
WEST LODGE, HARDWICK,
WHITCHURCH-ON-THAMES,
PANGBOURNE, READING RG8 7RA
Tel: 0189 843428/841304
Fax: 0189 843428 Contact: Iain Tolhurst
Email: tolhurstorganic@yahoo.com Website: www.yell.co.uk/sites/tolhurst-organic
Soil Association G515. Organic growers since 1976. Box scheme deliveries to Reading and Oxford.

  UHURU WHOLEFOODS
48 COWLEY ROAD, OXFORD OX4 1HZ
Tel: 01865 248249
Contact: Ms Annette Mnqxitama
Supplier of wide range of organic and non-organic wholefoods. Organic dairy and non-dairy produce, organic beers, ciders and organic vegan and vegetarian wines. Pick up point for organic veg box scheme.

Composting *reduces* your generation of rubbish. After you reduce its volume, you can *reuse* the compost in your garden. Then, the compost *recycles* nutrients back into soil and plant life. That's why the Government considers composting to be recycling. Increased plant growth helps to *restore* the health and beauty of our neighbourhoods.

John Roulac, *Backyard Composting* (1999)

SHROPSHIRE

 R.D. ANDERSON
ELLESMERE ROAD ORGANIC NURSERY,
COCKSHUTT, ELLESMERE, SY12 0JH
Tel: 01939 270270
Contact: R.D. Anderson (Owner)
We are an organic nursery producing fruit,
salad and vegetables for sale direct to the
public.

  BROAD BEAN
60 BROAD STREET, LUDLOW SY8 1NH
Tel: 01584 874239
Contact: Cy & Stanley Jones (proprietors)
Retailers of organic wines, dairy produce, meat,
wholefoods & fine foods, plus essential oils,
vitamins, supplements, relaxation tapes, Brita
water filters and cartridges. Collection point
for local vegetable box scheme.

COWHALL ORGANIC PRODUCE
Soil Association producer no. G4116: beef,
sheep and organic potatoes. More
vegetables in future. Outlet at Myriad
Organics (see below).

EARTHWORM CO-OP LTD
WHEATSTONE, LEINTWARDINE, SY7 0LH
Tel: 01547 540461 Contact: Hil Mason
Suppliers of willow for basket making,
hurdles etc; venue for low cost hire for
camps, courses, meetings. Demonstration
wetland system and organic/veganic
gardens. WWOOF host farm.

   FOOD FOR THOUGHT
THE ORGANIC FOOD CENTRE,
4 THE SQUARE, MUCH WENLOCK TF13 6LX
Tel: 01952 728038 Fax: 01952 728573
Contact: Alastair
Soil Association no. R2086. Specialist
organic food store: local delivery service,
extensive range of organic, additive-free
and fair traded foods plus bodycare,
supplements, remedies and household
goods.

FORDHALL ORGANIC FARM
TURNHILL LANE, MARKET DRAYTON TF9 3PS
Tel: 01630 638255 Contact: A. Hollins
Supplies R.M. Cornmell in Bolton. There
have never been any chemicals used on
the farm for over 80 years.

GET REAL ORGANIC FOODS
SHOTTON FARM, HARMER HILL,
SHREWSBURY SY4 3DN
Tel & Fax: 01939 210925
Contact: S. Beckett
Email: info@get-real.co.uk
Website: www.get-real.co.uk
Produce organic frozen pies: meat,
vegetarian and vegan. Also organic frozen
desserts and cakes, plus Christmas
puddings/cake and mince pies. Soil Assn.
approved and vegetarian symbol. We sell
to health food shops and Waitrose:
national distribution. See display ad.

The use of 'substantial equivalence' as a basis for risk assessment is seriously flawed,
and cannot be depended on as a criterion for food safety. It focuses on risks that can
be anticipated on the basis of known characteristics, but ignores unintended effects
that may arise. Genetically engineered food may, for example, contain unexpected
new molecules that could be toxic or cause allergic reactions. A product could not
only be 'substantially equivalent', but even be identical with its traditionally
produced counterpart in all respects bar the presence of a single harmful compund.

Luke Anderson, *Genetic Engineering, Food, and Our Environment* (1999)

JOHN AND JACKIE GUNTON

GREEN GORSE WOOD,
WHITCHURCH RD., PREES SY13 3JZ
Contact: John & Jackie Gunton
We grow a wide range of vegetables
organically. We sell only our own fresh
produce from our stall at Whitchurch
(Shropshire) Market on Friday mornings
throughout the year.

HARVEST WHOLEFOODS

LYDHAM, BISHOPS CASTLE SY9 5HB
Tel: 01588 638990 Fax: 01588 630298
Contact: Sue Jones (Proprietor)
Complete range of organic products
including wholefoods, fresh fruit and
vegetables, bread, frozen, chilled, herbs
and spices, household and bodycare,
vegetable and herb seeds and garden
products, etc. Open 9-5.30 Mon-Sat.

HONEYSUCKLE WHOLEFOOD CO-OPERATIVE LTD

53 CHURCH ST., OSWESTRY SY11 2SZ
Tel: 01691 653125
Contact: Chas, Liz, Suzy, Jilly
Traditional wholefood shop, established
1978, specialising in organic foods and
fresh organic fruit and vegetables. Soil
Association licence nos. GCS051, P5639.

HOPE ORGANIC PRODUCE

HOPE HOUSE, SANDY LANE, STOKE
HEATH, MARKET DRAYTON TF9 2LG
Tel: 01630 638348 Contact: Pete Bartram
Email: pgb@aol.com
Wide range of potted herb plants and
some cut herbs. Limited range of tunnel
and outdoor crops—cherry toms, peppers,
cucumbers, aubergines, French beans,
garlic courgettes, etc. Visitors welcome but
best to phone late evening before.

HOPESAY GLEBE FARM

HOPESAY, CRAVEN ARMS SY7 8HD
Tel: 01588 660737 Fax: 01588 660737
Contact: Phil & Nicky Moore
Email: hopesay.organics@barclays.net
Family run organic holding (since 1996)
producing vegetables, eggs, lleyn pedigree
sheep and English honey. We supply
restaurants, local shops, a box scheme and
produce markets. B&B organic breakfast in
tranquil Area of Outstanding Natural Beauty.

IAN AND RUTH MASON

FIVE ACRES, FORD, SHREWSBURY SY5 9LL
Tel: 01743 850832 Contact: Ruth Mason
Growers and retailers of apples, plums and
soft fruits and free range egg producers.
Soil Association no. G1457.

MYRIAD ORGANICS

22 CORVE ST., LUDLOW SY8 1DA
Tel: 01584 872665 Fax: 01584 879356
Contact: Jane Straker
Complete range of organic food and drink.
New delicatessen counter with take-out
snacks. Much of our produce is local, some
from our own market garden. Soil
Association registered.

ORCHARD HERBS

SOWBATH FARM, SHAWBURY,
SHREWSBURY SY4 4ES
Tel: 01939 250064 Fax: 01939 250064
Contact: Mike Griffiths
Fresh and dried medicinal and culinary
herbs. Soil Association member no. G2187.

ORGANIC BY ORDER

BENTLEY HOUSE, CLUNGUNFORD,
CRAVEN ARMS SY7 0PN
Tel: 01588 660747 Fax: 01588 660126
Contact: G. Lambert
Soil Association nos. P1916/G1915.
Organic vegetable and fruit box scheme
covering Shropshire, north Herefordshire
and Powys (part), offering standard boxes
and an 'order your own' service.

ORGANIC MATTERS

LEIGH MANOR, MINSTERLEY SY5 0EX
Fax: 01743 891929 Contact: D. Stacey
Email: d.stacey@dial.pipex.com
Website: www.organicmatters.co.uk.
Founded by 6 organic dairy farmers.

PIMHILL FARM

HARMER HILL, SHREWSBURY SY4 3DY
Tel: 01939 290342 or 290075 shop.
Fax: 01939 291156 Contact: Ginny Mayall
Email: info@pimhillorganic.co.uk
Website: www. pimhillorganic.co.uk
Mixed farm, organic for 51 years. Farm
shop and café sell organic and local quality
products. Chef on site supplies a range of
home baking. Open every day. Educational
visits for school children. Soil Association
nos. M16M, P1600. See display ad.

THE SHROPSHIRE SPICE COMPANY
UNIT 10, THE GREEN INDUSTRIAL ESTATE,
CLUN SY7 8LG
Tel: 01588 640100 Fax: 01588 640900
Email: office@shropshire-spice.co.uk
Established in 1976, the company
developed a well known stuffing mix
range, which now includes 4 organic
varieties. Soil Association accredited.

WILD THYME WHOLEFOODS
1/ 2 CASTLEGATES, SHREWSBURY SY1 2AQ
Tel: 01743 364559 Contact: Olly
A wide range of organic and natural
products including fresh fruit and
vegetables, nuts, pulses, snacks, beverages,
bodycare, household, local crafts and
complementary medicines.

For many millions of people the late 20th-century world economic system is
violent and destructive, unfree and disorderly. We must transform it into a 21st-
century system designed and able to meet the needs of people and the Earth,
including their needs for freedom and peace and order.

James Robertson, *Transforming Economic Life* (1998)

While we're officially warned during pregnancy about drugs, alcohol, cigarette
smoking, and even toxoplasmosis (which can cross the placenta and harm your
baby), pesticide residues and other serious byproducts of intensive farming in our
food don't even rate a mention. Surely we should be encouraged by the
government, and by leading organisations such as the National Childbirth Trust, to
go organic so that we avoid these dangers?

Tanyia Maxted-Frost, *The Organic Baby Book* (1999)

Key

 Producers

 Wholesalers

 Import/Export

 Retailers

 Mail Order

 Restaurants

 Day Visits/B&B

 Farm Gate Sales

 Box Schemes/ Delivery Service

 Garden/Farm Sundries

 Manufacturers & Processors

SOMERSET

ALVIS BROS LTD
LYE CROSS FARM, REDHILL, BRISTOL BS40 5RH
Tel: 01934 864600 Fax: 01934 862213
Contact: Ann Wait
Lye Cross organic Cheddar, Double
Gloucester, Red Leicester, Blue Stilton—
available nationwide. Suitable for vegetarians.
Soil Association approved (reg. no. P1542).

ARCADIA ORGANICS
THE COTTAGE, CLAVERHAM COURT,
LOWER CLAVERHAM, BRISTOL BS49 4PZ
Tel: 01934 876886 Contact: Rosie Knifton
Soil Association Symbol holder no. G1866.
20 acre organic holding producing
vegetables for our local box scheme, which
delivers in North Somerset.

AVALON VINEYARD
THE DROVE, EAST PENNARD,
SHEPTON MALLET BA4 6UA
Tel: 01749 860393 Contact: Hugh Tripp
Soil Association registered grower and
producer of organic English white wine,
traditional Somerset cider, a range of fruit
wines and mead. Visitors welcome:
vineyard walk and free tasting.

BOWERINGS ANIMAL FEEDS LTD
THE DOCKS, BRIDGWATER TA6 3EX
Tel: 01278 458191 Fax: 01278 445159
Contact: Andrew Armstrong
Email: armstrong.andrew@virgin.net
Manufacturers of organic feeds for all farm
animals; suppliers of other farm inputs. Soil
Assn licence no. P2246. Nationwide
coverage. See display ad.

CERES NATURAL & ORGANIC FOODS
9-11 PRINCES STREET, YEOVIL BA20 1EN
Tel: 01935 428791 Fax: 01935 426862
Organic and natural foods retailers. Soil
Association accredited (no. R1560).
Vegetarian and vegan products, special
diet needs, own label ranges, wholefoods.

COMBE FARM FRUITS LTD
COOMBE FARM, CREWKERNE TA18 8RR
Tel:01460 72304 Fax: 01460 77349
Contact: Richard Crean
Organic fruit and confectionery
preparations for the dairy industry. Organic
frozen fruit. Soil Association members.

COUNTRY HARVEST
8 ST JAMES COURTYARD,
TAUNTON TA1 1JR
Tel: 01823 252843
Contact: H. or A. Masterton-Smith
Wholefoods, organic and gluten-free
foods, supplements, herbal and
homeopathic remedies. Pick-up point for
box schemes. Qualified staff. Deliveries to
TA1, TA2, TA3, TA4, TA6.

COURT FARM
14 CHAPEL LANE, WINFORD,
BRISTOL BS40 8EU
Tel: 01275 472335 Contact: J.R. Twine
Bio-dynamic farm for 30 years—products
from our own milk production. Natural
and fruit yoghurt, unpasteurised milk,
double cream, free range pork and beef.

CRABTREE & EVELYN
COMMERCE WAY, WALROW INDUSTRIAL
ESTATE, HIGHBRIDGE TA9 4AG
Tel: 01278 780913 Fax 01278 792815
Contact: Andrew Bowen
Manufacturer of high quality organic
preserves, marmalades and sauces. Soil
Association reg. no. P4419.

CRACKNELL'S FARM
AYLESBURY RISE, UNION DRIVE,
PICTS HILL, LANGPORT TA10 9EY
Tel: 01458 252659
Contact: Jeff Cracknell (Owner)
We produce free range additive-free
chicken, ducks and geese on our own farm.
We offer these for sale within our local area.

THE ELMS DAIRY

FRIARS OVEN FARM, WEST COMPTON,
SHEPTON MALLET BA4 4PD
Tel & Fax: 01749 890371
Contact: Gillian Stone
Goat, sheep, soya and cow dairy products
(yoghurt, milk, cream, butter), certified by
Organic Farmers & Growers. Dexter beef,
pork & lamb also certified by OF&G.

THE GREEN GROCER

THE OLD DAIRY, POOLBRIDGE ROAD,
BLACKFORD, WEDMORE BS28 4PA
Tel & Fax: 01934 713453
Contact: Quentin Isaac
Email: greengrocer@madasarfish.com
Organic fruit, vegetables and eggs. Shop is
registered with Soil Association (R4669).
Also in conversion as grower (G4668)—
fully organic from 01.01.01! Open Tues-Fri
p.m. and Sat a.m.

HAMBLEDEN HERBS

COURT FARM, MILVERTON TA4 1NF
Tel: 01823 401104 Fax: 01823 401001
Email: info@organicherbtrading.com
Website: www.hambledenherbs.co.uk
Britain's only organic dried herb specialists
supplying more than 550 different herbs
and spices in quantities from 50g upwards.
Soil Association certified.

HARVEST NATURAL FOODS

37 WALCOT STREET, BATH BA1 5BN
Tel: 01225 465519 Fax: 01225 401143
Contact: Laura Petherbridge
Email: shop@harvestfoods.fsnet
We are a GM-free store selling a wide
range of organic produce for sale: wine
and champagne, grains and mueslis, veg
(all kinds), dried fruits (all kinds), yoghurt,
milk, soya milk, tofu, tea, gluten-free,
herbs etc. We also have a delicatessen
selling fresh vegetarian and vegan
produce. See display ad.

 HIGHER RISCOMBE FARM

HIGHER RISCOMBE FARM,
EXFORD, NR. MINEHEAD TA24 7JY
Tel & Fax: 01643 831184
Contact: Rona Ayres
Email: rona@higherriscombefarm.co.uk
Website: www.higherriscombefarm.co.uk
Traditional B&B on Soil Association Hill Farm
in the heart of Exmoor National Park.
Farmers breakfast using organic ingredients.
Evening meal available. Collect the eggs,
explore the farm.

  HINTON FARMS

THE ESTATE OFFICE, HINTON HOUSE,
HINTON, CHARTERHOUSE, BATH BA3 6AZ
Tel: 01225 722946 Fax: 01225 722545
Contact: Andrew Edwards Email:
estateoffice@hintonhouse.freeserve.co.uk
Producer of organic beef and lamb.

 JENRO'S

22 WEST STREET, WIVELISCOMBE,
TAUNTON TA4 2JP
Tel: 01984 623236 Fax: 01984 629131
Contact: Richard Pakeman
We are a specialist food shop selling a
range of organic products including
vegetables, dairy products, beans, pulses,
grains, jams, marmalades, pastas,
beverages, pet food etc.

  KILMERSDON ESTATE
(LORD HYLTON)

KINGMANS FARM, FOUR WINDS,
HEMINGTON, BATH BA3 5UR
Tel: 01373 834509 Contact: D.J.C. Dukes
Growers of organic wheat, beans, oats and
barley to Soil Association symbol holder
standard. Also pedigree Ayrshire dairy herd.

LEIGH COURT FARM

ABBOTS LEIGH, BRISTOL BS8 3RA
Tel & Fax: 01275 375756
Contact: S. Miller
Email: mail@leighcourtfarm.demon.co.uk
Vegetable box scheme, Bristol Farmers'
Market (June-December), volunteers,
practical training, working with
communities, not-for-profit, promoting
local food economy. Full organic certificate
due 12/2000. Soil Association licence no.
G3034. Delivery to BS8 & BS13.

MAGDALEN FARM

MAGDALEN FARM, WINSHAM,
CHARD TA20 4PA
Tel: 01460 30277 Fax: 01460 30144
Contact: Peter Foster
Soil Association registered (no. G932)
mixed farm, beef sucklers, pigs. Field veg,
polytunnels and cereals, selling vegetables
and meat via farmers' markets, box
scheme and farm gate sales.

OSCAR MAYER LTD

FURNHAM ROAD, CHARD TA20 1AA
Tel: 01460 63781 Fax: 01460 67847
Contact: Mr B. J. Rodgers
Email: DavidJeffries@oscarmayer.co.uk
Website: www.oscarmayer.co.uk
Oscar Mayer Ltd is a major producer of
ready meals for multiple retailers &
supermarkets, currently producing five
different meals. Soil Association licensed,
we supply UK-wide.

MERRICKS ORGANIC FARM

PARK LANE, LANGPORT TA10 0NF
Tel: 01458 252901 Contact: Jane Brooke
22 acre market garden supplying farm run
box scheme with vegetables and fruit. Also
rare breed organic pork. Soil Association
reg. no. G1593.

    MILK HOUSE

THE BOROUGH, MONTACUTE TA15 6XB
Tel: 01935 823823
Contact: Elizabeth Dufton
Tiny hotel in good food guide and in
Which hotel guide. Evening meals for
residents—closed in winter.

MOLE VALLEY FARMERS LTD

HUNTWORTH MILL, MARSH LANE,
BRIDGWATER TA6 6LQ
Tel: 01278 444829 Fax: 01278 446923
Contact: Yael Rowan-Wicks
Email: mvf.feeds@farmline.com
The farmers' co-operative in the South
West, producing organic, permitted non-
organic and GM-free animal feeds for
dairy, beef, sheep, pigs and poultry.
Members of Soil Association (P2332) and
OF&G (UKP030463).

   MRS MOONS

WALTON FARM, KILMERSDON,
BATH BA3 5SX
Tel: 01761 432382 Fax: 01761 439645
Contact: Tony Davies
Email: sales@mrsmoons.com
Website: www.mrsmoons.com
Producers of the UK's first organic baking
mixes, simple and delicious to make,
available in retail or catering packs. Also
specialist organic bakers of muffins, cookies
and cakes. Soil Association registered
P3067. Deliveries nationwide.

NORWOOD FARM

BATH ROAD, NORTON ST. PHILIP BA3 6LP
Tel: 01373 834356 Fax: 01373 834884
Contact: Marcus Bradshaw (Proprietor).
Soil Association G2312. Organic butchers
selling own produce. Mixed farm open to
the public. Approved Rare Breeds Survival
Trust Centre.

OAKE ORGANICS
OAKE, TAUNTON TA4 1JA
Tel: 01823 461317 Contact: Keith Martin
Soil Association no. M49W. Box scheme
collection and deliveries of mainly own
grown organic produce in the Taunton
area and M5 corridor (Bristol, Bath, Frome,
Shepton Market, Wells, Glastonbury and
en route).

THE ORGANIC HERB TRADING CO
COURT FARM, MILVERTON TA4 1NF
Tel: 01823 401205 Fax: 01823 401001
Email: info@organicherbtrading.com
Website: www.organicherbtrading.com
Wholesalers of organic dried herbs,
supplying more than 550 different herbs,
spices and tinctures. Soil Association
certified.

 ORGANIC MILK SUPPLIERS
CO-OPERATIVE LTD
COURT FARM, LOXTON,
NR. AXBRIDGE BS26 2XG
Tel: 01934 750244 Fax: 01934 750080
Contact: Sally Bagenal (C.E.)
The largest organic milk supplier to the
dairy industry. League leader in milk price,
profit sharing schemes with buyers. All
members hold organic certificates.

ORGARDEN PRODUCE
BORDER FARM, CLOSWORTH,
YEOVIL BA22 9SZ
Tel: 01935 872483 Fax: 01935 873736
Contact: Jennifer Evans
Soil Association licence no. E07W since
1985. Have twenty 90 foot growing
houses and specialise in tomatoes,
peppers, courgettes, aubergines,
cucumbers and carrots in tunnels plus
leeks, beans, swedes outside.

PROVENDER DELICATESSEN
3 MARKET SQUARE, SOUTH PETHERTON,
SOMERSET TA13 5BT
Tel & Fax: 01460 240681
Contact: Roger Biddle
Email: sales@provender. net
Website: www.provender.net
Licensed delicatessen with large organic
selection of groceries, cheeses, dairy and
juices. Collection point for Merricks
Organic Farm Vegetables Box Scheme.
Organic frozen vegetables and ice cream.

  J.M. & M.D. PURDEY
HIGHBARN FARM, ELWORTHY,
NR. TAUNTON TA4 3PX
Tel: 01984 656104 Contact: Mark Purdey
Long established herd of Canadian Danish
Jersey cows run on all grass/clover/alfalfa
leys, producing milk for liquid, blue
cheese, clotted cream outlets (Soil
Association G0124).

RADFORD MILL FARM
TIMSBURY, BATH BA3 1QF
Tel & Fax: 01761 472549
Contact: Susan Seymour
Producers of fine organic food including
vegetables, herbs, fruit, meat and dairy
products for home delivery service in Bath
area and markets in Bath, Bristol and
Glastonbury. Soil Association no. G575.

 SEASONS WHOLEFOODS
10 GEORGE STREET, BATH BA1 2EH
Tel: 01225 469730
Contact: Peter & Anne Bassil (partners)
Take-away salads, savouries, soups etc.
Organic products available in the shop in a
designated area.

Contrary to what most economists believe, money is not neutral, i.e. different
money systems are now possible, and could make a dramatic difference in helping
us with several of our most important challenges including ecological sustainability.

Richard Douthwaite, *The Ecology of Money* (1999)

SOMERSET ORGANICS
MANOR FARM, RODNEY STOKE,
CHEDDAR BS27 3UN
Tel & Fax: 01749 870919
Contact: Richard Counsell
Email: info@somersetorganics.co.uk
Website:www.somersetorganics.co.uk
Organic meat by mail order. Online
ordering via the internet: we are the first
farmers in Europe to provide a virtual farm
tour of the farm and Somerset Levels.
Nationwide delivery. Soil Association no.
G815. See display ad.

B.H.STACEY
THE BUTCHERY, WEST STREET,
SOMERTON TA11 7PR
Tel: 01458 272285 Contact: B.H. Stacey
High class family butcher selling finest
quality locally produced beef, pork and
lamb. Soil Association registered P2751.

SUNSEED
12 SOUTH STREET, WELLINGTON TA21 8NS
Tel: 01823 662313 Fax: 01823 663202
Contact: Tony Bourne
Email: Tony@Sunseed.co.uk
Website: www.sunseed.co.uk
Most organic lines including vegetables,
yoghurts, cheese, tofu, chilled foods,
beansprouts, margarine etc. as well as
herbs, spices, books, vitamins, homeopathic
and herbal remedies plus aromatherapy oils
and natural beauty aids. Mail order
available. Therapy rooms available.

S WADDLES GREEN FARM
HARE LANE, BUCKLAND ST. MARY,
CHARD TA20 3JR
Tel: 01460 234387 Fax: 01460 234591
Contact: Charlotte Reynolds (partner)
Email: organic@swaddles.co.uk
Website: www.swaddles.co.uk
We specialise in home delivery of award
winning organic meat, pies, bacon, hams,
ready cooked meals, paté, charcuterie. Soil
Association no. P1904, Organic Farmers
and Growers nos. 12UKF070175,
11UKP010020. Winner of Soil Association
Food Awards 1994, 1995, 1996, 1997.

TOUCAN WHOLEFOODS
NO. 7 FLOYDS CORNER, THE PARADE,
MINEHEAD TA24 5UW
Tel: 01643 706101
Contact: Sally Eveleigh or Jane Hart (Partners)
A busy wholefoods shop selling a varied
selection of organic lines including
vegetables, dry goods, dairy and soya
products, and vegetarian wholefood
takeaway. We also offer nutrition and
dietary supplementary advice and
homeopathic remedies. All you'd expect
from a good wholefoods shop.

WESTAR ORGANIC VEGETABLES
MANOR FARM, HEWIS,
NR. CREWKERNE TA18 8QT
Tel: 01460 73456/07977 206530
Fax: 01460 78674
Contact: George van den Berg
Email: Georginizmir@yahoo.com
Producer organic vegetables, organic dairy.
Soil Association registration no. G2415.

THE WHOLEFOOD STORE
29 HIGH ST., GLASTONBURY BA6 9SX
Tel: 01458 831004
A large wholefood store retailing organic
dried, pre-packed foods as well as fresh
fruit and veg, dairy products and drinks.
Our aim is to provide the organic food
shopper with everything needed for a
weekly shop.

WYKE FARMS LTD
WHITE HOUSE FARM, BRUTON BA10 0PU
Tel: 01749 812424 Fax: 01749 813 614
Contact: Richard Clothier
Email: sales@wykefarms.com
Website: www.wykefarms.com
Soil Association Member. Dairy farmers
producing 10,000 tonnes cheese per
annum, 350 tonnes organic cheddar. All
sold nationally and internationally.

STAFFORDSHIRE

 BELLA HERBS
BROCTON LEYS, BROCTON,
STAFFORD ST17 0TX
Tel: 01785 663868
Contact: Beverley Squire (Owner)
Growing herbs and vegetables for
restaurant, herbalists and farmer's markets
locally. Soil Association reg. no. G778.

BESTFOODS UK LTD—FOOD INGREDIENTS
WELLINGTON ROAD,
BURTON-ON-TRENT DE14 2AB
Tel: 01283 511111 Fax: 01283 509796
Contact: Jean Cattanach
Bestfoods Ingredients specialise in the
production of stocks and bouillons for
manufacturers of prepared savoury foods.
Licensed products include organic
vegetable bouillon and organic light
bouillon. Soil Assn reg. no. P4115.

BOOTS HERBAL STORE
39/41 MERRIAL ST, NEWCASTLE ST5 2AE
Tel & Fax: 01782 617463
Contact: Keith Woolley
Email: keith.woolley@btinternet.com
Supplier of a vast range of organic foods,
essential oil, vitamins and mineral
supplements and organic herbals.

HOLGRAN
GRANARY HOUSE, WETMORE ROAD,
BURTON ON TRENT DE14 1TE
Tel: 01283 511255 Fax: 01283 511220
Contact: Alan Marson
Email: bits4bread@holgran.co.uk
Website: www.holgran.co.uk
Industrial bakery ingredients: malt, cereal,
seed ingredients and mixes for the bakery
industry. Soil Association membership.
Delivery to UK, Europe and North America.

  NATURES STORE LTD
UNIT 2, JAMAGE INDUSTRIAL ESTATE,
TALKE, STOKE-ON-TRENT ST7 1XN
Tel: 01782 794300 Fax: 01782 774698
Contact: Paul Tweedie
Email: health@naturesstore.co.uk
Website: www.naturesstore.co.uk
Natures Store, the leading wholesaler to
the independent healthfood trade, carry an
extensive range of organic products within
their 7500 line portfolio.

  THE REAL FOOD COMPANY
50 SANDBACH ROAD SOUTH, ALSAGER,
STOKE ON TRENT ST7 2LP
Tel: 01270 873322 Contact: Carol Dines
Over 300 organic grocery lines, plus box
scheme, bread, dairy, meat and fish.
Quality supplements. Organic herbal
remedies. Free local delivery on orders over
£30.00.

REGENCY MOWBRAY COMPANY LTD
HIXON INDUSTRIAL ESTATE,
HIXON ST18 0PY
Tel: 01889 270554 Fax: 01889 270927
Contact: Mrs Malbon
Email: sales@regencymowbray.co.uk
Website:
www.regencymowbray.demon.co.uk
Manufacturers of flavourings, colours, fruit
preparations, chocolate products and
emulsifiers/stablishers. Some organic
varieties of above products. Registered
with the Soil Association. Worldwide
coverage.

  S TAFFORDSHIRE ORGANIC CHEESE
NEW HOUSE FARM, ACTON,
NEWCASTLE-UNDER-LYME ST5 4EE
Tel & Fax: 01782 680366
Contact: David Deaville
Manufacture of specialist organic cheeses
from cow/ewe milk. Soil Association reg.
no. P1871.

SUFFOLK

  ASPALL
THE CYDER HOUSE, ASPALL HALL,
STOWMARKET IP14 6PD
Tel: 01728 860510 Fax: 01728 861031
Contact: Barry Chevallier Guild
Email: info@aspall.co.uk
Website: www.aspall.co.uk
Founder members of the Soil Association,
Aspall produce organic apple juice,
vinegars and cyder. All our products are
made with only the juice of whole fruits:
we do not use concentrates. Our products
are available through supermarkets and
health food retailers.

BOX FRESH ORGANICS
WOODBINE COTTAGE, UGGESHALL,
BECCLES NR34 8BH
Tel & Fax: 01502 578649
Contact: Mr J. Segrave-Daly
Organic fruit and vegetable box scheme
also supplying meat, poultry and eggs.
Part of a Soil Association small producers
group based in Suffolk. Limited range of
wholefoods. Soil Association no. P2249.

CAPEL ORGANIC MUSHROOMS
CAPEL ST. MARY, IPSWICH IP9 2LA
Tel: 01473 311245 Fax: 01473 310380
Contact: Mrs N. Redmon
Registered with UKROFS (no. 01071002)
and Soil Association. Range of brown or
white cup, open, flat or processing
mushrooms and organic compost
available.

D.J. PRODUCE
UNIT 1, GRIFFITHS YARD, GAZELEY ROAD,
MOULTON, NEWMARKET CB8 8SR
Tel & Fax: 01638 552709
Contact: D. J. Mason
OF&G cert no. 11UKP110089. Box scheme
of organic fruit and vegetables from home
and abroad, plus eggs, cheeses, flour and
general groceries. Deliver to Cambridge
and surrounding area.

 FOCUS ORGANIC FOODS
28 MARKET PLACE, HALESWORTH IP19 8AY
Tel: 01986 872899
Contact: Juan Suarez (Partner)
Our wholefood shop sells as much organic
produce as possible, including cereals,
nuts, fruits, flour, seeds, jams, sauces,
spreads, juices, pasta and vegetables.

HILLSIDE NURSERIES
HINTLESHAM, IPSWICH, IP8 3NJ
Tel: 01473 652682 Fax: 01473 652624
Contact: Alan Simpson (Proprietor)
Box scheme and vegetable growers, Soil
Association reg. no. G594. Delivery areas:
Ipswich, Felixstowe, Woodbridge,
Suffolk/N.E. Essex border.

HUNGATE HEALTH STORE
4 HUNGATE, BECCLES NR34 9TL
Tel: 01502 715009 Contact: Theresa Hale
Large range of organics stocked, including
milk, cheeses, yoghurts, bread, dried fruits,
nuts, pulses, teas, cereals, biscuits and
cakes, juices, crisps, pasta, eggs, honeys,
and jams. Range is expanding rapidly.

 MICHAEL KNIGHTS
DAGANYA FARM, NUTTERY VALE,
HOXNE, EYE IP21 5BB
Tel: 01379 668060 Contact: Michael Knights
Email: daganya@yahoo.co.uk
Vegetables in season, farm gate sales. Soil
Association reg. no. G2108.

KOPPERT UK LTD
HOMEFIELD BUSINESS PARK,
HOMEFIELD ROAD, HAVERHILL CB9 8QP
Tel: 01440 704488 Fax: 01440 704487
Contact: Julian Ives
Email: info@koppert.co.uk
Website: www.koppert.nl
Europe's largest producer of natural enemies.
Range of organic pesticides such as Bactura
W.P. for caterpillars and savona, a wide
spectrum organic pesticide. Also large range of
pest monitoring traps. Deliver to UK & Ireland.

LOAVES AND FISHES

52 THOROUGHFARE, WOODBRIDGE IP12 1AL
Tel: 01394 385650
Contact: C.M. Musson (Proprietor)
We are a natural food store specialising in organic wines, beers, vegetables, cereals, fresh fish and macrobiotic products.

LONGWOOD FARM

TUDDENHAM ST. MARY,
BURY ST. EDMUNDS IP28 6TB
Tel & Fax: 01638 717120
Contact: Matthew Unwin
Soil Association no. G669. Specialist organic meat producers, retailers of fine organic foods—meat, dairy, cheese and provisions. Huge range of over 2000 items. Nationwide plus local deliveries to postcode areas IP, NR, CB.

NATURAL FOOD STORE

NORFOLK HOUSE COURTYARD,
ST NICHOLAS STREET, DISS IP22 4LB
Contact: M. Meiracker (Partner)
We stock 'traditional' wholefoods and a big range of organic bread, cakes, fruit, vegetables and dairy goods. Our cool counter stocks our own made patés and salads, plus deli goods. We are vegetarian, catering for specialist diets. Soil Association registered.

NORTON ORGANIC GRAIN LTD

CASTLINGS HEATH COTTAGE,
GROTON, SUDBURY CO10 5ES
Tel: 01787 210899 Fax: 01787 211737
Contact: John Norton
Organic grain & pulse supplier, sourced from farms in UK, mainland Europe and elsewhere (outside EC—soya, oilseeds, grains etc.). Licensed with Soil Association (no. P2131) and OFF (SAL/97). See display ad.

OREGANO

169/171 LONDON ROAD NORTH,
LOWESTOFT NR32 1HG
Tel: 01502 582907 Fax: 01502 516675
Contact: Dawn Fellows
Health foods, vitamins, supplements and organic foods are featured in a large section in the store.

PURE ORGANIC FOOD LTD

UNIT 5C, EAST LANDS INDUSTRIAL
ESTATE, LEISTON IP16 4LL
Tel: 01728 830575 Fax: 01728 833660
Contact: John Streeter
Email: enquiries@pureorganicfoods.co.uk
Website: www.pureorganicfoods.co.uk
Quality packers of certified organic meat and poultry in domestic portions for retail trade. Organically dedicated processing plant. OF&G registered (no. UKP020415). Beef, pork, lamb, chicken, bacon, gluten-free sausages. We wholesale all over Southern England, our box scheme is nationwide.

SWALLOW ORGANICS

HIGH MARCH, DARSHAM,
SAXMUNDHAM IP17 3RN
Tel: 01728 668201
Contact: Malcolm Pinder (Proprietor)
We sell a selection of fruit and vegetables, naturally grown, from our own market garden. Also pot herbs, wild flowers (grown from seed), fuchsias, pelargoniums, etc., organic fertiliser and compost.

J.L. & C.THOROUGHGOOD

BUSHY LEY COTTAGE, ELMSETT,
IPSWICH IP7 6PQ
Tel: 01473 658671
Small farm shop selling over 20 different own produced fruit and vegetables, open mid June to November, 8 a.m.- 8 p.m., 7days a week. Please phone for large orders. Soil Association symbol no. T12E.

JAMES WHITE

WHITES FRUIT FARM
ASHBOCKING, IPSWICH IP6 9JS
Tel: 01473 890 111 Fax: 01473 890 001
Contact: Lawrence Mallinson
Email: info@jameswhite.co.uk
Website: www.jameswhite.co.uk
The pressing and bottling of a range of organic apple juices including cranberry and apple, carrot and apple, pear. Soil Association Membership no. P2648.

SURREY

BARN FIELD MARKET GARDEN
FRANKSFIELD, PEASLAKE,
GUILDFORD GU5 9SR
Tel & Fax: 01306 731310
Contact: Jane Jennifer
We grow a wide range of seasonable
vegetables and fruit, which we harvest
fresh for our weekly box scheme. Boxes
(£5-£20) are ready for collection after 3
p.m. on Fridays.

BODY AND SOUL ORGANICS
1 PARADE COURT, OCKHAM ROAD
SOUTH, EAST HORSLEY KT24 6QR
Tel: 01483 282868 Fax: 01483 282060
Contact: Sarah Webber
Email: bodyandsoul@organic-gmfree.co.uk
Website: www.organic-gmfree.co.uk
Shop and delivery service with wide range of
fruit and veg, wholefoods, dairy, wines,
beers, ciders, meat, poultry, etc.. Gluten-
free, dairy-free, special diets, over 2000
organic lines including Auro paints. Home
deliveries throughout UK—phone for details.

BREWHURST HEALTH FOOD SUPPLIES LTD
ABBOT CLOSE, OYSTER LANE,
BYFLEET KT14 7JP
Tel: 01932 354211 Fax: 01932 336235
Contact: Denise Glynn
Email: marketing@brewhurst.com
Website: www.brewhurst.com
Evernat offers the largest range of organic
products in the health food trade, from
biscuits to rice, pasta to frozen food,
Evernat has something for everyone. We
deliver nationwide to health food stores.

CHASE ORGANICS / THE ORGANIC GARDENING CATALOGUE
RIVERDENE, MOLESEY RD.,
HERSHAM KT12 4RG
Tel: 01932 253666 Fax: 01932 252707
Contact: Mike Hedges (Retail Manager)
Email: chaseorg@aol.com
Website: www.organiccatalog.com
The Organic Gardening Catalogue contains
seeds, fertilisers, composts, pest controls,
sundries and books for organic gardeners.
It is the official catalogue of the HDRA.

CHEEKY RASCALS
THE BRIARS, PETWORTH ROAD,
WITLEY GU8 5QW
Tel: 01428 682488 Fax: 01428 682489
Contact: Selina Russell
Email: cheekyrascals@aol.com
Website: cheekyrascals.co.uk
Importers of baby and toddler nursery
equipment, in particular washable nappies
and kiddy and buggy boards. Member of
the Real Nappy Association.

CLEARLY NATURAL
CAMBERLEY GU15 2SN
Tel & Fax: 01276 675609
Contact: Sarah Ropella
Email: slropella@hotmail.com
Website: www.clearlynatural.co.uk
An educational webstore and mail order
company selling natural and organic
toiletries and cosmetics. Ranges cover hair
care, body and bath products, soaps and
toothpastes for all the family including
children and babies. Organic cotton
towels, face cloths, sanitary products,
bathrobes and bed linen.

Once released, the new living organisms made by genetic engineering are able to
interact with other forms of life, reproduce, transfer their characteristics and mutate
in response to environmental influences. In most cases they can never be recalled
or contained.

Luke Anderson, *Genetic Engineering, Food, and Our Environment* (1999)

119

CONFOCO (UK) LTD
DUNCAN HOUSE, HIGH ST., RIPLEY GU23 6AY
Tel: 01483 211288 Fax: 01483 211388
Contact: Mrs A. Banyard
Email: confocouk@confocouk.com
Website: www.confocouk.com
Leading supplier of processed fruit and
vegetable products for the food industry,
including organic. Soil Assn. licence no.
P2452.

 CRANLEIGH ORGANIC FARM SHOP
LOWER BARRIHURST FARM, DUNSFORD
ROAD, CRANLEIGH GU6 8LG
Tel: 01483 272896 Fax: 01483 273486
Contact: Ray Parker
Email: organi@globalnet.co.uk
Mixed farm producing vegetables, herbs,
meat and poultry. Our farm shop also sells
produce from other local organic farms.

 FOOD FOR THOUGHT
38 MARKET PLACE, KINGSTON KT1 1JR
A large range of wholefoods, organic
foods, special diet foods and food
supplements. Fresh organics vegetables
and vegetarian takeaways.

  THE HEALTH FOOD CENTRE
62 THE BROADWAY, TOLWORTH KT6 7HR
Tel: 020 8399 3932
An ever expanding range of organic
produce, from beans to yoghurts, available
to the calling customer or via mail order.
Phone for details.

 HEALTH FOODS CHEAM VILLAGE
60 THE BROADWAY, CHEAM,
SUTTON SM3 8BD
Tel: 020 8643 5132 Contact: Mr Ahmed
Stockists of organic cereals, nuts and dried
fruits, drinks, teas, chocolate, etc. No fresh
fruit or vegetables.

 OCTAVIA'S ORGANICS
7 PRICES LANE, WOODHATCH,
REIGATE RH2 8BB
Tel: 01737 244155 Fax: 01737 244742
Contact: John Shaw
Retail shop supplying a very wide range
including fruit, vegetables, meat, dairy,
bread, cakes, wholefoods, remedies and
wines. Open 6 days a week; delivery service.

OLIVERS WHOLEFOOD STORE
5 STATION APPROACH, KEW GARDENS,
RICHMOND TW9 3QB
Tel: 020 8948 3990 Fax: 020 8948 3991
Contact: Sara Novakovic
Email: sara@oliverswholefoods.co.uk
Winner of 'Organic Community Shop of
the Year 99' and 'Health Food Store of the
Year 99'. Full organic grocer with off
licence, specialising in excellent quality
organic food—vegetables, fish, meat etc.
Also full range of natural remedies.
Nationwide mail order service for remedies.

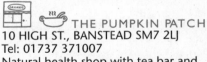 THE PUMPKIN PATCH
10 HIGH ST., BANSTEAD SM7 2LJ
Tel: 01737 371007
Natural health shop with tea bar and
vegetarian deli. Therapy centre. Organic
foods.

A farmer from Saskatchewan in Canada is being sued for growing seed without a
licence, after samples were taken from around his fields. Percy Schmeiser says that
he has been growing oilseed rape for years and freely admits to saving his seed, but
denies that it belongs to Monsanto. The problem, according to Mr. Schmeiser, is
that there are a lot of genetically engineered crops being grown in the neighbouring
area and pollen from them is blowing everywhere.

Luke Anderson, *Genetic Engineering, Food, and Our Environment* (1999)

SINGLE MARKETING LTD
HIPLEY HOUSE, HIPLEY ST.,
WOKING GU22 9LQ
Tel: 01483 771152 Fax: 01483 766808
Contact: Jeff Bayley
Email: singlemktg@aol.com
Direct sales to major national retail and
wholesale outlets/companies, with
growing organic portfolio. Soil Association
no. P2540.

SUNSHINE ORGANICS
2 KNOWLE COTTAGES, KNOWLE LANE,
CRANLEIGH GU6 8JL
Tel: 01483 268014
Contact: Amanda Porter Email:
Amanda@sunshineorganics.demon.co.uk
Website: susnshine organics.demon.co.uk
Fresh fruit and vegetables, home shopping
service supporting local Soil Association
growers. Orders taken Mon-Wed for
delivery on the following Thursday.
Delivery to GU & RH postcodes.

TAKE IT FROM HERE
UNIT 04, BETA WAY, THORPE INDUSTRIAL
PARK, EGHAM TW2 8RZ
Tel: 0800 137064 Fax: 01784 477814
Contact: Martin
Email: martin@danmarinternational.co.uk
Website: www.danmarinternational.co.uk
We are a mail-order company specialising
in exclusive Italian foods, with a range of
healthy and organic products including
organic olive oils, organic pastas, and 24
month old crack-cut parmesan.

THE WHOLEFOOD SHOP
96 HIGH ST., CROYDON CR0 1ND
Tel: 020 8686 6167 Fax: 020 8649 9375
Contact: Jen Brown
Established over 20 years ago, we sell a
great range of vegetarian, ethical and
special diet foods—much of it organic. We
also sell high quality herbal remedies and
supplements.

Because of the type of money we use at present, the prices set by the market at any given moment have nothing to do with long-term values. They are therefore entirely inadequate for determining the development path that we should select. The problem arises because the market is a human construct that works according to rules people have devised for it. Currently, those rules prevent millions of people without money from affecting the price levels in the market. Consequently, the prices that emerge from the market merely reflect the immediate wants of that fraction of the world's present population fortunate enough to have the money to be able to express them.

Richard Douthwaite, *The Ecology of Money* (1999)

Key

 Producers

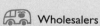 Wholesalers

 Import/Export

 Retailers

 Mail Order

 Restaurants

 Day Visits/B&B

 Farm Gate Sales

 Box Schemes/ Delivery Service

 Garden/Farm Sundries

 Manufacturers & Processors

EAST SUSSEX

 ASHURST ORGANICS

THE ORCHARD, ASHURST FARM, ASHURST
LANE, PLUMPTON, LEWES BN7 3AP
Tel: 01273 891219 Contact: Peter Haynes,
Collette Pavledis (Owners & Growers)
Organic growers operating box scheme
delivering fresh, seasonal, local produce
direct to Lewes, Brighton and surrounding
areas.

BARCOMBE NURSERIES

MILL LANE, BARCOMBE, LEWES BN8 5TH
Tel & Fax: 01273 400011
Contact: Adrian Halstead & Miles Denyer
(Growing & Box Scheme)
Large protected area for organic
vegetables, salad crops and herbs. Well
established box scheme, vegetables, fruit,
eggs, with free home delivery area
including Brighton and Hove, Haywards
Heath and Lewes.

BATTLE WHOLEFOOD

83 HIGH ST., BATTLE TN33 0AQ
Tel: 01424 772435 Email:
nick@battle-wholefood.freeserve.co.uk
Contact: N. Crawshaw
We stock a large variety of organic items
and can get more to order.'

BEANS AND THINGS

HARVEST HOME, CHUCK HATCH,
HARTFIELD TN7 4EN
Tel: 01273 477774
Contact: Dave Flintan (Manager)
Door to door deliveries of organic fruit,
veg, dairy and wholefoods to Brighton,
Newhaven, Seaford, Hove etc.

BEAUMONTS

THE RIVERSIDE CENTRE, LEWES
Tel & Fax: 01825 840089
Contact: Pam Beaumont (Owner)
Email: organic@pavilion.co.uk
Retailer of only organic foods since 1981,
the oldest in the UK.

BOATHOUSE ORGANIC FARM SHOP

Shop address: THE ORCHARD,
UCKFIELD RD., RINGMER, LEWES BN8 5RX
Tel: 01273 814188
Farm address: BOATHOUSE ORGANIC
FARM, ISFIELD, UCKFIELD TN22 5TY
Tel: 01825 750302
Contact: Martin Tebbutt Email:
shop@boathouseorganic.fsbusiness.co.uk
Website:
www.boathouseorganics.fsbusiness.co.uk
Farm shop. Home produced beef, mutton,
lamb, vegetables, flour and full range of
groceries. Quality beef available wholesale
and retail.

CORNERWEIGHS

ELM LODGE, CAUDLE STREET,
HENFIELD BN5 9DQ
Tel: 01273 492794 Contact: Susie
Email: cornerweighs@netscapeonline.co.uk
An Aladdin's cave for whole and organic
foods. Specialising in dried goods and
dietry requirements. We also stock Solgar
and Bioforce.

FINBARR'S WHOLEFOODS

57 GEORGE ST., HASTINGS TN34 3EE
Tel: 01424 443025 Contact: Carol Ridge
Wholefood shop selling a wide range of
fresh organic fruit, vegetables, wines, beers,
cider, bread, eggs and environmentally
friendly products. Delivery service.

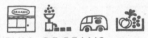

FULL OF BEANS

96 HIGH STREET, LEWES BN7 1XH
Tel: 01273 472627 Contact: Sara Gosling
We manufacture from organically
produced soya beans, tofu, tempeh and
miso, which we wholesale and retail. Also
box scheme.

GLYNDE KITCHEN GARDENS
THE STREET, GLYNDE, NR. LEWES BN8 6SX
Tel & Fax: 01273 858148
Contact: Martin Ball
An 18th-century walled kitchen garden under restoration! Producing gourmet salads, herbs, vegetable plants, handmade pickles & preserves. Gardens open weekends Easter-October, seasonal events, open days throughout the year—phone for details. Mail order anywhere. OF&G registered. Open throughout the year: Easter to end October. Phone for details.

THE GRANVILLE HOTEL
124 KINGS ROAD, BRIGHTON BN1 2FA
Tel: 01273 326 302 Fax: 01273 728 294
Contact: Mr M. Paskins
Email: granville@brighton.co.uk
Website: www.granvillehotel.co.uk
Town centre sea front hotel. Four posters, jacuzzi, water bed, organic produce (whenever possible), environmentally friendly, your rubbish recycled. Pets and their well-behaved owners welcome.

GRAPEVINE ORGANICS LTD
UNIT 5, MARINE TRADE CENTRE, BRIGHTON MARINA BN2 5UG
Tel: 01273 819055 Fax: 01273 819066
Contact: Kevan Trott
Email: sales@grapevine-organics.co.uk
Website: www.grapevine-organics.co.uk
Organic wine, beer, lager, spirits, juices and cordials delivered to your door. Available in small quantities, see our brochure for details of our large range of over 90 organic drinks. Nationwide delivery (free to BN1 and BN2).

HARVEST FORESTRY
1 NEW ENGLAND STREET, BRIGHTON BN1 4GT
Tel: 01273 689725 Fax: 01273 622727
Contact: Jenny
Email: harvestforestry@fastnet.co.uk
Website: www.harvestforestry.co.uk
Unrivalled selection of fruit, veg, dairy and other foods. Six deliveries p.w., fresh bread daily. Committed to buying locally, and now growing our own. Also organic compost, seeds, pots and more !

HARVEST SUPPLIES
HARVEST HOME, CHUCK HATCH, HARTFIELD TN7 4EN
Tel: 01342 823392
Contact: Dave Flintan (Manager)
Distribute for local growers. Retail business at home, door to door deliveries, wholesale deliveries to shops, restaurants etc. Full selection of veg, fruit, herbs and wholefoods in Sussex and Kent.

HEALTHWISE
44B COODEN SEA RD., LITTLE COMMON, BEXHILL-ON-SEA TN39 4SL
Tel: 01424 844075 Contact: Eileen Vaines
Healthfood shop stocking a range of organic goods along with the organic box scheme.

HENLEY BRIDGE INGREDIENTS LTD
BRAYS HILL, ASHBURNHAM, NR. BATTLE TN33 9NZ
Tel: 01424 892024 Fax: 01424 892015
Contact: Tony Mycock
Email: tony.mycock@lineone.net
Soil Association P4239. Suppliers of organic ingredients to food processors—sugar, chocolate, cereal, syrups, dextrose, starch, milk powders—will source anything on request.

Approximately one million small coffee farmers in Mexico have adopted fully organic production methods, increasing production by half.

Luke Anderson, *Genetic Engineering, Food, and Our Environment* (1999)

HIDDEN SPRING VINEYARD AND ORGANIC ORCHARD

VINES CROSS ROAD, HORAM TN21 OHF
Tel & Fax: 01435 812 640
Contact: Sue Mosey
Email: hidden-spring@eastbourne.org
Products of top quality organic apples and pears grown in nine acres of orchard alongside six acres of gently sloping vineyard. Members of the Soil Association, no. G1459.

HOLLY PARK ORGANICS

HOLLYPARK NORTH LANE,
GUESTLING TN35 4LX
Tel: 01424 812229 Fax: 01424 812025
Contact: Linda Beaney
Email: hollypark@supanet.com
Certified Bio-dynamic farm (BDA 303). Home produced goat's milk, cheeses, yoghurts a speciality. Vegetables and salads all year through. Culinary/medicinal herbs. Welsh lamb and Xmas turkeys.

HONEYBROOK ORGANIC PRODUCE

FRANCHISE MANOR FARM,
BURWASH TN19 7HY
Tel: 01435 883151 Fax: 01435 883964
Contact: Mrs Judy Harris
Farm shop and milk/produce deliveries providing home grown organic produce. 1998 and 1999 Organic Foods Awards winner. Soil Association member G1836.

INFINITY FOODS

FRANKLIN RD., PORTSLADE,
BRIGHTON BN41 1AF
Tel: 01273 424060 Fax: 01273 417739
Contact: Mr R. Fitzgibbon
Website: www.infinityfoods.co.uk
Leading UK wholesaler of organic foods. Soil Association no. P1465. Over 3500 organic lines in stock offering the most comprehensive range of organic products available anywhere. Delivery to the trade throughout the UK. See display ad.

INFINITY FOODS

25 NORTH RD., BRIGHTON BN1 2AA
Tel: 01273 603563 Fax: 01273 675384
Organic bread (baked on the premises), vegetables, fruit, dried fruit, nuts, pulses, grains, cruelty-free cosmetics.

LANSDOWN HEALTH FOODS

44 CLIFFE HIGH ST., LEWES BN7 2AN
Tel: 01273 474681 Contact: Cindy Holmes
Wholefoods and healthfoods shop. Organic vegetables in season, herbal and homeopathic remedies. Wide variety of organic products. Many tasty take-away snacks.

MAGPIE HOME DELIVERY

UNIT 4, LEVEL 3, NEW ENGLAND HOUSE,
NEW ENGLAND STREET,
BRIGHTON BN1 4GH
Tel: 01273 621222 Fax: 01273 626226
Contact: Daniel
Email: magpiehomedelivery@fastnet.co.uk
Website: www.magpiehomedelivery.co.uk
Home delivery of organic, quality produce for Brighton and Hove. Soil Association registered.

NEAL'S YARD REMEDIES

2A KENSINGTON GARDENS,
BRIGHTON BN1 4AL
Tel: 01273 601464
Neal's Yard Remedies manufactures and retails natural cosmetics in addition to stocking an extensive range of herbs, essential oils, homeopathic remedies and reference material.

E.M. & R.J.H. OLIVER

BLACKLANDS, CROWHURST,
BATTLE TN33 9AB
Tel & Fax: 01424 830360 Fax: 01424 830360 Contact: Marianne Oliver
An organic smallholding producing vegetables and goat's milk for family; any surplus for sale to B&B, campers and holiday guests. Architects (RIBA) for environment-conscious designs.

THE ORGANIC BABY CO

UNITS 39-40, THE ENTERPRISE CENTRE,
STATION PARADE, EASTBOURNE BN21 1BD
Tel: 01323 411515 Fax: 01323 442398
Contact: Noreen Roache
Email: sales@theorganicbabyco.com
Website: www.theorganicbabyco.com
Organic retail outlet (not just for babies
anymore). Full Baby Organix range, box
scheme distributor, bread, fresh, chilled
and frozen foods.

ORGANIC BOTANICS

PO BOX 2140, HOVE BN3 5BX
Tel & Fax: 01273 773182
Contact: Celsi Richfield
Website: www.organicbotanics.com
Superb natural skincare made with
certified organic unrefined, cool-pressed
plant oils; certified organic herbal extracts,
floral waters, aloe vera and essential oils;
natural vitamins, natural UV filter. Available
in over 250 organic and wholefood shops
nationwide. Free sample to every enquirer.

PASKINS HOTEL

18/19 CHARLOTTE ST., BRIGHTON BN2 1AG
Tel: 01273 6024 76 Fax: 01273 621973
Contact: R. Marlowe (Director)
Email: welcome@paskins.co.uk
Website: www.paskins.co.uk
Most of our food is organic and we are
justly proud of our varied vegetarian
breakfasts. Our tastefully designed rooms
are individually designed and we have a
welcoming bar.

POSTLETHWAITE'S HERBAL PRODUCTS

POSTLETHWAITE HOUSE, UNIT 2,
RUTHERFORD BUSINESS PARK,
MARLEY LANE, BATTLE TN33 0TY
Tel & Fax: 01424 774498
Contact: James Postlethwaite
Email: postleherbprod@xstream.co.uk
Soil Association licence holder P4328. We
produce a range of high concentration
herbal tinctures.

RETREAT HOUSE

ST MARY'S, CHURCH STREET,
HARTFIELD TN7 4AG
Tel: 01892 770 305 Contact: Rose Moore
Opportunity for rest, retreat and spiritual
renewal in lovely old house and garden.
Home cooking, mainly organic ingredients.
Individuals and small groups welcome (no
children). Minimum stay 2 nights.

RYE WHOLEFOODS

90 HIGH ST, RYE TN31 7JN
Tel: 01797 223495
Contact: N. C. Crawshaw Email:
Nick@battle-wholefood.freeserve.co.uk
We stock a range of organic products from
established manufacturers and will always
do our best to fulfil special orders. We also
stock organic frozen vegetables and chips.

SCHMIDT NATURAL CLOTHING

21 POST HORN CLOSE,
FOREST ROW RH18 5DE
Tel & Fax: 01342 822169
Contact: Glenn Metzner
Email: glen@natural.swinternet.co.uk
Comfortable clothing and bedding for
babies, children and adults in organic and
chemical-free cotton, wool and silk.
Organic nappies. SKAL, InNaTex, IFOAM,
Oeko-Tex and Demeter certified, Fair Trade
guidelines. Free catalogue, advice line.
Delivery to all UK and international.

SCRAGOAK FARM

BRIGHTLING RD.,
ROBERTSBRIDGE TN32 5EY
Tel & Fax: 01424 838454
Contact: David Wenman
Soil Association symbol holders no. W30S.
Organic for over 20 years. Box scheme
throughout the South-East. Farm shop
open Weds, Thurs, Fri, Sat. Box scheme of
the year 1999. Organic Farm Shop of the
year 1999. See display ad.

SEASONS FOREST ROW LTD

10-11 HARTFIELD ROAD,
FOREST ROW RH18 5DN
Also at LOWER ROAD,
FOREST ROW RH18 5DN
Tel: 01342 824673 Fax: 01342 826119
Contact: Frances Ludman (Director)
Wholesale and retail organic and Bio-dynamic meat, groceries, dairy produce, baby food, fruit and vegetables. Wooden toys, books, natural cosmetics and crafts. Fruit and veg, toys and cosmetics at Lower Road. Wholesale deliveries in Sussex only.

SEASONS OF LEWES

199 HIGH STREET, LEWES BN7 2NS
Tel: 01273 473968 Contact: Carol Mercer
Vegetarian/vegan restaurant, with 75% of ingredients organic. GM-free. Outside catering available. Weddings, buffets etc. Food from the freezer (vegetarian meals, soups, pies). Family business. Open Tues-Sat 10-5 p.m.

SEDLESCOMBE VINEYARD

CRIPP'S CORNER, SEDLESCOMBE,
NR. ROBERTSBRIDGE TN32 5SA
Tel: 01580 830715 Fax: 01580 830122
Contact: Roy Cook (M.D.)
Email: rcook91137@aol.com
Website: www.tor.co.uk/sedlescombe
England's premier organic vineyard producing English wines, fruit juices and ciders to EU organic standards. Also market organic pilsner from Bavaria and claret from France's oldest organic vineyard.

SUSSEX HIGH WEALD DAIRY PRODUCTS

PUTLANDS FARM, DUDDLESWELL,
UCKFIELD TN22 3BJ
Tel: 01825 712647 Fax: 01825 712474
Contact: Mark Hardy
Email: mhardy@agnet.co.uk
Website: www.speciality-foods.com
Producers of speciality dairy products made from organic sheep's milk and organic cow's milk. Soil Association reg. no. P1772.

TABLEHURST FARM

FOREST ROW RH18 5DP
Tel: 01342 823173
Contact: Bernie Jamieson
Bio-dynamic farm producing top quality beef, lamb, pork, poultry, eggs, leeks, potatoes, onions, garlic and flour, all available from farm shop or wholesale. Shop open Thurs - Sat, 9 to 5. Own butcher on farm.

TRINITY WHOLEFOODS

3 TRINITY ST., HASTINGS TN34 1HG
Tel: 01424 430473
Organic dried fruit, nuts, dairy products, fresh fruit and vegetables, cereals, muesli, oats, bread, pastas, biscuits and cakes, beers and wines, complementary medicines available. Soil Association no. R1595.

TROGS RESTAURANT & CAFÉ BAR

124 KINGS ROAD, BRIGHTON BN1 2FA
Tel: 01273 204655 Fax: 01273 728294
Contact: Alison Lynch
Email: granville@brighton.co.uk
Website: granvillehotel.co.uk
Gourmet organic vegetarian restaurant and café bar. Organic wine and Belgian beers. Cater for weddings and other functions.

A major US study released in 1998, thought to mirror the situation in the UK, found that every day, nine out of ten American children aged betwen six months and five years are exposed to combinations of thirteen different neurotoxic organophosphate pesticides in the food they eat, one million of them consuming unsafe levels of organophosphates, which have been shown to cause long-term damage to the developing brain and nervous system.

Tanyia Maxted-Frost,
The Organic Baby Book (1999)

WEALDEN WHOLEFOODS

PILGRIMS, HIGH ST., WADHURST TN5 6AA
Tel: 01892 783065 Fax: 01892 783351
Contact: Mrs Barbara Godsalve
(Co-ordinator)
Organic wholefood retailer with a small café.

WOODEN WONDERS

FARLEY FARM HOUSE,
CHIDDINGLEY BN8 6HW
Tel: 01825 872691 Fax: 01825 872733
Contact: Noel Hardy
(Manager, Special Projects)
Email: info@woodenwonders.co.uk
Website: www.woodenwonders.co.uk
Our in-house laser engravers can customise
finely finished practical, ornamental and
corporate gifts made from Forestry
Stewardship Council wood. Wooden
Wonders is the only wooden craft gift
manufacturer with Forestry Stewardship
Council accreditation and the Soil
Association Woodmark.

WEST SUSSEX

THE ACORN CENTRE

TODHURST SITE, BRINSBURY COLLEGE,
NORTH HEATH, PULBOROUGH RH20 1DL
Tel & Fax: 01798 873533
Contact: Mrs Rachel Tuppen
Email: Linfield@compuserve.com
Training centre for adults with learning
disabilities; we grow our own organic
vegetables which are sold through our farm
shop. Other organic produce also available.
Coffee shop. Soil Association G2586/P5118.

THE AVINS BRIDGE RESTAURANT & ROOMS

COLLEGE ROAD, ARDINGLY, HAYWARDS
HEATH RH17 6SH
Tel: 01444 892393 Contact: Becky
Email: enquiries@theavinsbridge.co.uk
Website: www.theavinsbridge.co.uk
A quiet English 'AA' rosette-winning
restaurant on the edge of Haywards Heath,
specialising in organic food and wine. Also
having beautiful five diamond rated B & B
accommodation.

BIOWISE

MOYLE DEPOT, GRAFFHAM,
PETWORTH GU28 0LR
Tel & Fax: 01798 867574
Contact: Sue Cooper
Email: woodbugs@newscientist.net
Member of International Biocontrol
Manufacturer's Association. Biological
controls for professional and amateur
growers and gardeners.

COTTON BOTTOMS

UNIT12, BROOMERS HILL PARK, BROOMERS
HILL LANE, PULBOROUGH RH20 2RY
Tel: 01798 875300 Fax: 01798 875006
Contact: Joanne Freer
Email: sales@cottonbottoms.co.uk
Website: www.cottonbottoms.co.uk
Home delivery service: modern cotton
nappies delivered, collected and laundered
for you. Pinless velcro-closing pure cotton
nappy system—kind to baby and the
environment. We deliver to NHS hospitals,
Day Nurseries and parents at home.
Postcode areas covered: TN, BN, GU, PO,
SP, SO1-51, TQ12,13,14, BH1-31, EX1-20
& 24. See display ad.

DOWN TO EARTH

12 THE MINT MARKET, GRANGE RD.,
MIDHURST GU29 9LT
Tel: 01730 815133
Totally organic retail shop selling fresh
organic fruit and veg, pulses, nuts, dry
fruits, yoghurts, cheese, butter, margarine
and Ecover products.

    FARGRO LTD

TODDINGTON LANE,
LITTLEHAMPTON BN17 7PP
Tel: 01903 721591 Fax: 01903 730737
Contact: J. McAlpine
(Director of Marketing)
Email: promos-fargro@btinternet.com
Website: www.fargro.co.uk
Horticultural wholesaler providing organic
fertiliser and a full range of biological and
organic pest control products.

   FLINT ACRES FARM

BIGNOR PARK RD., BURY GATE,
PULBOROUGH RH20 1EZ
Tel: 01798 831036
Small scale organic fruit and vegetable
producer. We also sell free range eggs and
free range pork and lamb. Thurs, Fri, Sat
10 - 5.

G&G FOOD SUPPLIES LTD
VITALITY HOUSE, 2/3 IMBERHORNE WAY,
EAST GRINSTEAD RH19 1RL
Tel: 01342 312811 Fax: 01342 315938
Contact: Jeremy Stephens
(Managing Director)
Soil Association approved contract
encapsulator of herbal and vitamin capsules.
Own label product ranges created.

GOODWOOD FARMS
HOME FARM, GOODWOOD,
CHICHESTER PO18 0QF
Tel: 01243 771615 Fax: 01243 536699
Contact: M. Mills
Production of organic beef and lamb;
registered with Soil Association.

LAINES ORGANIC FARM
47 NEWBURY LANE, CUCKFIELD RH17 5AA
Tel & Fax: 01444 452480
Contact: Toos Jeuken (Sole Proprietor)
Soil Association member. 7 1/2 acres
organic outdoor vegetables (seasonal).
Self-service farm shop.

 NATURAL WAY

33A CARFAX, HORSHAM RH12 1EE
Tel & Fax: 01403 262228 Contact: Jean Earl
Offer wide range of pre-packed wholefoods
and produce sold by well known names in
the wholefood industry. Not fresh vegetables.

   OCEANS OF
GOODNESS / SEAGREENS

1 THE WARREN, HANDCROSS RH17 6DX
Tel: 01444 400403 Fax: 01444 400493
Email: oceans@probono.org.uk
seagreens@probono.org.uk
Website: www.seagreens.com
Oceans of Goodness markets Seagreens
food products, which are harvested from
pure wild seaweeds and turned into
unique food products. Consumer and
catering packs. Soil Association no. P2446.

OLD PLAW HATCH FARM LTD
SHARPTHORNE,
EAST GRINSTEAD RH19 4UL
Tel: 01342 810652/810201
Fax: 01342 811478
Contact: Michael Duveen
Email: oldplawhatch@yahoo.co.uk
161 acre Bio-dynamic farm producing
upasteurised milk, cream and cheese
(winner in the 1999 Soil Association's Fine
Food Awards), Quark, eggs, beef, pork
sausages and smoked bacon, soft fruit,
vegetables and salads. All available
through its own farm shop which opens
seven days a week.

ROOKERY FARM EGGS
ROOKERY FARM, FLANSHAM, BOGNOR REGIS PO22 8NN
Tel: 01243 583583
Contact: Rupert Langmead
We produce organic free range eggs. OF&G members (reg. no. 11UKF02075). We grade and pack the eggs ready for sale. Deliver within about 40 mile radius. Farmers' markets.

ST. MARTIN'S TEA ROOMS
ST. MARTIN'S ST., CHICHESTER PO19 1NP
Tel & Fax: 01243 786 715
Contact: Keith Nelson
Tea rooms serving teas, scones, cakes and light meals all day using mostly organic ingredients. We also sell fresh fruit and vegetables, home made cakes, breads, scones etc., all vegetarian (plus a little smoked salmon).

SURREY ORGANICS
9 THE MALTINGS, HIGH STREET, BILLINGSHURST RH14 9JL
Tel: 01483 278380 Fax: 01483 278380
Home delivery of organically grown fruit and veg. Soil Association reg. no. P2601.

TOO GOOD ORGANICS LTD
WALNUT TREE FARM, VINNETROW ROAD, RUNCTON, CHICHESTER P20 6QB
Contact: M.C. Fleming
Email: sales@too-go.co.uk
Website: www.too-go.co.uk
Organic salad products (Iceberg, Little Gem, Romaine, tomatoes, cucumbers, peppers, celery).

WAYSIDE ORGANICS
WAYSIDE, OVING, CHICHESTER PO20 6BT
Tel & Fax: 01243 779716
Contact: Mr B. Ives
Local deliveries, farm gate sales, stall at old Spitalfields market. Salads, vegetables, fruit and herbs to Soil Association Standards (nos. G1510 & P5555). Deliveries to PO19 & PO20.

WILLOW NURSERY
44 HILL LANE, BARNHAM PO22 0BL
Tel & Fax: 01243 552852
Contact: David & Michelle Wheeler
Grow a wide range of vegetable and salad crops, sold through a year-round box scheme. Also supply fruit boxes. Deliveries within West Sussex & Hampshire. Soil Association licensed (nos. W31S & P5838).

Asteya (non-stealing) is more than illegal theft: when family farms are destroyed by agribusiness, it is theft of the countryside; when crafts are destroyed by industry, that is theft of skills; when big trawlers overfish the oceans and thus destroy small fishing villages, that is theft of livelihood. Legal or illegal, these are all ways of stealing. To follow the way of *Asteya* is to use and consume only what nature can replenish. It is a way to consume only to meet our vital needs, knowing that other peoples and creatures also need to meet their vital needs, and therefore I take only my share of things. *Asteya* is a way of living simply so that others may simply live. *Asteya* is a way of generosity. *Asteya* tells me that meanness, hoarding, accumulation, and overconsumption are thefts of nature and stealing from God.

Satish Kumar, *No Destination: An Autobiography* (revised edition 2000)

BLENDEX FOOD INGREDIENTS LTD
HETTON LYONS INDUSTRIAL ESTATE,
HETTON LE HOLE DH5 0RG
Tel: 0191 517 0944 Fax: 0191 526 9546
Contact: N.J. Robinson
Email: info@blendex.co.uk
Website: www.blendex.co.uk
Blenders of organic herbs and spices for the food industry, specifically meat, poultry and bakery. Soil Association certified no. P1654.

MANDALA WHOLEFOODS
43 MANOR HOUSE RD., JESMOND,
NEWCASTLE UPON TYNE NE2 2LY
Tel: 0191 281 0045
Contact: Gordon Bell (Partner)
Wide range of organic vegetables, fruit, grains, beans, dried fruit, juices, milk, yoghurt, tofu, breakfast cereals, also books and music.

NEAL'S YARD REMEDIES
19 CENTRAL ARCADE, NEWCASTLE UPON TYNE NE1 5BQ Tel: 0191 232 2525
Neal's Yard Remedies manufactures and retails natural cosmetics in addition to stocking an extensive range of herbs, essential oils, homeopathic remedies and reference material.

OUT OF THIS WORLD
106 HIGH ST., GOSFORTH , NEWCASTLE UPON TYNE NE3 1HB
Tel: 0191 213 5377 Fax: 0191 213 5378
Contact: Brian Hutchins/Jon Walker
Email: info@ootw.co.uk Website: ootw.co.uk
Head office of small chain of ethical and organic supermarkets in Newcastle upon Tyne, Nottingham and Cheltenham (also organic café). Selling over 4000 products, most food products certified organic plus fairly traded crafts, recycled paper and bodycare products etc. Consumer co-op with over 17,500 members.
Shop at GOSFORTH SHOPPING CENTRE, HIGH ST., GOSFORTH, NEWCASTLE UPON TYNE NE3 1JZ
Tel: 0191 213 0421
Contact: Mike Chamberlain

RISING SUN FARM
KINGS RD. NORTH, WALLSEND,
TYNE & WEAR NE28 9SL
Tel: 0191 234 0539 Fax: 0191 234 0114
Contact: D. Shanks
Email: douglashanks@risingsunfarm.co.uk
Soil Association producer no. 1490. Cereals, horticultural, pigs and cattle. Urban fringe farm providing education, day service for special needs. Open farm for the community, riding for all: lessons and hacks for the socially excluded and disadvantaged.

SCOTSWOOD NATURAL COMMUNITY GARDEN
JOHN MARLEY CENTRE, off WHICKAM VIEW, NEWCASTLE-UPON-TYNE NE15 6TT
Tel: 0191 200 4706 Fax: 0191 200 4729
Contact: Ken Bradshaw
We are a 2 acre community garden growing fruit, vegetables, wheat, herbs and wild flowers using organic Bio-dynamic methods. We also have 4 ponds and a recyclable stream. We run a volunteer programme and training courses.

TRAIDCRAFT PLC
KINGSWAY, GATESHEAD NE11 0NE
Tel: 0191 491 0591 Fax: 0191 482 2690
Contact: Joe Osman
Email: traidcraft@globalnet.co.uk
Website: www.globalnet.co.uk/~traidcraft
Importer and distributor of organic honey, tea, chocolate. Soil Association no. P2321.

> Using compost as a soil enricher ensures a healthy soil. As the organic pioneers have shown us, those communities and races with healthy soils produce the healthiest people.
>
> John Roulac, *Backyard Composting*
> (1999)

WARWICKSHIRE

  G.N.& G.A.BROWNING

FELDON FOREST FARM, FRANKTON, RUGBY CV23 9PD
Tel: 01926 632246
Contact: George Browning
Soil Assn. licence no. G2209. Producing organic cereals, fruit, vegetables, plus meat from rare breeds (Shetland cattle, Castlemilk Moorit sheep, Tamworth pigs), with free range organic eggs, table poultry and geese.

  CHARLECOTE MILL

HAMPTON LUCY, WARWICK CV35 8BB
Website: www.charlecotemill.vt9.co.uk
Contact: John Bedlington
Grinding wholemeal flour using millstones driven by water power. Registered with Soil Association for organic flour.

 CITADEL PRODUCTS

32 ST. ANDREWS CRESCENT, STRATFORD-UPON-AVON, CV37 9QL
Tel & Fax: 01789 297456
Contact: K. Heming
Manufacturers of polytunnel greenhouses for commercial and domestic use. Also suitable for animal housing, storage, etc.

DOUTHWAITE & SONS
TOWNSEND FARM, RADWAY, WARWICK CV35 0UN.
Tel: 01295 670572
Contact: Philip Douthwaite
Organic beef, organic lamb, organic potatoes, organic oats and organic wheat. Soil Association symbol no. D29M.

ELMHURST ORGANIC FARM
BOW LANE, WITHYBROOK, COVENTRY CV7 9LQ
Tel: 01788 832233 Fax: 01788 832690
Contact: Ann Pattison
Farm produced organic meat, Soil Association no. G761. Shop open 5 days a week closed Thursday, Sunday and bank holidays. Beef, pork, lamb, poultry realistic prices. Farm trail. Soil Ass. Network Farm.

HENRY DOUBLEDAY RESEARCH ASSOCIATION (HDRA)
RYTON ORGANIC GARDENS, RYTON ON DUNSMORE, COVENTRY CV8 3LG
Tel: 02476 303517 Fax: 02476 639229
Contact: Jackie Gear (Executive Director)
Email: rog@hdra.org.uk
Website: www.hdra.org.uk
The HDRA is Europe's largest organic membership organisation, researching, advising on and providing information about organic gardening, growing and food. Runs courses on a wide range of organic and related subjects at its Ryton headquarters. HDRA Consultants offer consultancy in organic waste management, organic garden design, organic scientific research (which does not involve animal experimentation), and catering and retailing. HDRA runs three demonstration gardens: at Ryton in the Midlands, Yalding in Kent (see entry under Kent) and Audley End nr. Saffron Walden in Essex. All are open to the public, with shops offering gifts and organic gardening sundries. At Ryton, the restaurant has been listed in many national guides to good food and the shop there offers in addition an extensive range of food and wine. There is also a successful vegetable box scheme operated from Ryton Organic Gardens shop and from Audley End. HDRA's advice on organic growing extends overseas to developing countries and it gives practical agricultural advice to subsistence farmers. The Heritage Seed Library preserves old vegetable varieties that would otherwise be casualties of EC legislation. HDRA spreads the organic message far and wide through TV, radio and national newspaper and magazine articles and publishes many books and leaflets. *The Organic Gardening Catalogue* produced by HDRA and Chase Organics (see under Surrey) provides a mail order service for organic gardening products, seeds, books and foods.

ROOSTERS ORGANICS
GLEBE FARM, LOZLEY,
WARWICK CV35 9SW
Tel: 01789 842501 Fax: 01789 841194
Contact: Mark Payns
Email: scorpiolimited@nsm.com
Organic producers of lamb, pork and beef
from 'rare breed' stock. Also run box
scheme for organic fruit and veg—
deliveries locally. Soil Association no.
G2541. Delivery area covered: CV3.
Farmers' markets at Stratford, Warwick,
Leamington and Kenilworth.

WARWICK HEALTH FOODS
40A BROOK ST., WARWICK CV34 4BL
Tel: 01926 494311
Contact: Mr P.R. Gooding (Partner)
Family-run business, 20 years, stockists of
all kinds of organic foods, fresh fruit and
vegetables always in stock, yeast-free bread
and other speciality organic breads
available.

WELLESBOURNE WATERMILL
KINETON RD., WELLESBOURNE CV35 9HG
Tel: 01789 470237
Traditional water powered mill that
produces organic and non-organic
wholemeal stoneground flour and organic
and non-organic plain white flour,
semolina and bran.

 ## THE WHOLEFOOD SHOP
c/o ST. ANDREWS CHURCH HOUSE,
CHURCH STREET, RUGBY CV21 3PT
Tel: 01788 567757
Contact: Dave Kerruish (Owner)
Open Thursdays and Fridays 9 a.m. -5 p.m.
Organic vegetables, fruit and wholefoods.
Recycled paper and loo rolls, essential oils,
box scheme, free deliveries, herbs and
spices.

World peace is a building block to making peace with nature. When nations fight, when bombs are dropped, it is not only human beings who are killed; natural habitats are also destroyed. But no one counts the cost of nature's demise. Making peace with nature is important even if there is no war, because war with nature leads to war between nations. Most wars are fought over resources and to protect markets. Wars are less and less political and more and more economic. All wars are wars against nature since they involve a tremendous amount of air pollution, sea pollution, and land pollution; land mines are a case in point. So the nations of the world have to agree unanimously that, whatever their dispute, diplomatic and non-violent methods will be the only course they will follow; under no circumstances will violence be used.

Of course, this will not happen overnight, but if this could be a new millennium resolution and if, step by step, the world could work toward this goal, then one day we might establish a non-violent social order. In the wake of nuclear, biological, and chemical warfare, and in the wake of global warming, ozone depletion, and world hunger, the stark choice is between non-violence and non-existence.

Satish Kumar, *No Destination: An Autobiography* (revised edition 2000)

WEST MIDLANDS

 DROP IN THE OCEAN
17 CITY ARCADE, COVENTRY CV1 3HX
Tel & Fax: 024 76 225273
Contact: R. Morris
Email: dropin@compuserve.com
Website: www.dropintheocean.com
Wholefood store with extensive organic
range including fresh fruit and vegetables.

 RYAN EVANS ORGANICS
WOLVERHAMPTON WV3 8BG
Tel: 01902 762785 Contact: Susan Evans
Can supply organic meat, fish.

 M. FINN BUTCHERS
19 STANTON RD., GREAT BARR,
BIRMINGHAM B43 5QT
Tel: 0121 357 5780
Contact: Vaughan Meers (Manager)
Chemical- and hormone-free meat and
poultry specialists. Maynards dry cure
bacon and ham. Mail order available:
phone for price list.

 RUSSELL GORMAN LTD
46 THREE SHIRES OAK RD., BEARWOOD,
WARLEY B67 5BS
Tel: 0121 429 1100
Contact: Russell Gorman
Health foods, supplements (specifically
cater for weight trainers and athletes)
specialist chiropodists including orthotics.

HARVESTIME
38 RALEIGH ST., WALSALL WS2 8RB
Tel: 01922 444546 Fax: 01922 424690
Contact: Ian Toal
Harvestime is the largest organic baker in
the UK producing sliced breads, instore
bakery breads and morning goods for
retailers across the UK.

THE HEALTH FOOD CENTRE
146-148 HIGH ST., SOLIHULL B91 3SX
Tel & Fax: 0121 705 0134
Contact: Mrs Hards
Fruit, veg, pulses, dairy, soya products,
nuts, seeds, dried fruit, jams, marmalades,
wines, soft drinks, honey, flours, rice,
breakfast mixes, muesli etc.

LIFESTYLE HEALTH FOODS
139 DAVENTRY RD., CHEYLESMORE,
COVENTRY CV3 5HD
Tel: 024 76 502147 Contact: R. Tunnicliffe
Healthfood shop.

ONE EARTH SHOP
54 ALLISON STREET, DIGBETH,
BIRMINGHAM B5 5TH
Tel: 0121 632 6909
Email: rickards@lineone.net
Contact: Tina Rickards/John Beddowes
Vegan shop—large selection of organic
food, suppliers of organic vegetable boxes.
Delviery areas covered: B13 and B14.

ORGANIC ROOTS
CRABTREE FARM, DARK LANE, KINGS
NORTON, BIRMINGHAM B38 0BS
Tel: 01564 822294 Fax: 01564 829212
Contact: Bill Dinenage
Email: info@organicroots.co.uk
Website: www.organicroots.co.uk
Organic Roots is the only farm shop in the
West Midlands wholly dedicated to the
supply of organic produce. Products
include meat, veg, poultry, bread, dairy
wholefoods, wine, herbs etc. Soil
Association no. G1880, Farm Retail
Associates.

A.R.PARKIN LIMITED

UNIT 8, CLETON STREET BUSINESS PARK,
CLETON STREET, TIPTON DY4 7TR
Tel: 0121 557 1150 Contact: Tony Hilditch
Email: enquiries@arparkin.co.uk
Website: www.arparkin.co.uk
Manufacturer and supplier of organic
spice, seasonings and ingredients.
Dedicated blending plant. Soil Association
licensed.

 ROSEMARY'S HEALTH FOODS

2/3 MANDER SQUARE, MANDER CENTRE,
WOLVERHAMPTON WV1 3NN
Tel: 01902 427520 Fax: 01902 426247
Contact: D. Gillan
Email: dunroseg@aol.com
Health foods and wholefoods retail.
Also at 3 LOWER HALL LANE,
WALSALL WS1 1RH
Tel: 01922 636640
Contact: Andrew Barker.

  S.& A.ROSSITER
TRADITIONAL FAMILY BUTCHERS

247 MARYVALE ROAD, BOURNVILLE,
BIRMINGHAM B30 1PN
Tel & Fax: 0121 458 1598
Contact: Stephen Rossiter
Traditional butchers—Birmingham's first
registered organic butcher (Soil Association
no. R2037). Fresh beef, pork, lamb and
poultry; now adding fish, bread and
cooked meat.

  SAGE WHOLEFOODS

148 ALCESTER RD., MOSELEY,
BIRMINGHAM B13 8HS
Tel & Fax: 0121 449 6909
Contact: Ken Dyke (Director)
Retailer of organic fruit and vegetables,
wide range of organic wholefoods, organic
dairy products, organic teas and coffees,
fair trade products, vegetarian and vegan
foods, vitamins and herbs.

  THE SMALL GREEN COMPANY

STOURTON FARM, STOURTON,
NR. KINVER, WEST MIDLANDS
Tel: 01803 865565 Fax: 01803 868233
Contact: Michael Hallam
Email: mhallam406@aol.com
Weekly delivery of fresh organic fruit and
vegetables, eggs, bread and groceries;
milk, meat and dairy to follow by Summer
2000; local grower links. Soil Association
reg. no. R1730. Deliveries to DY8, DY9 &
DY10.

While ancient patriarchy used the symbol of the active seed and the passive earth, capitalist patriarchy, through the new biotechnologies, reconstitutes the seed as passive, and locates activity and creativity in the engineering mind. Five hundred years ago, when land began to be colonized, the reconstitution of the earth from a living system into mere matter went hand in hand with the devaluation of the contributions of non-European cultures and nature. Now, the reconstitution of the seed from a regenerative source of life into valueless raw material goes hand in hand with the devaluation of those who regenerate life through the seed—that is, the farmers and peasants of the Third World.

Vandana Shiva, *Biopiracy* (1998)

WILTSHIRE

  AGRALAN LTD
THE OLD BRICKYARD, ASHTON KEYNES,
SWINDON SN6 6QR
Tel: 01285 860015 Fax: 01285 860056
Contact: Alan Frost (Managing Director)
Email: agralan@cybermail.co.uk
Insect monitoring systems—pheromone
and sticky traps for insect monitoring.
Enviromesh—protection of vegetable crops
against pests. Also special nets for insect
screening. Permealay—weed control
fabric. Citrox—safe horticultural
disinfectant. Revive—alternative to soil
fungicides. See display ad.

   CAUSEWAY
HEALTHFOODS AND HOMEBREW
4 CAUSEWAY, CHIPPENHAM SN15 3BT
Tel: 01249 659431
Contact: Joe & Diane Hobson
Family business established 14 years. Vast
range of products, foods and vitamins.
Emphasis on dietary needs and non-dairy.
Large homebrew section.

COLESHILL ORGANICS
59 COLESHILL, SWINDON SN6 7PT
Tel & Fax: 01793 861070
Contact: Pete Richardson
Soil Association no. G2012—16 acres of
field vegetables and protected cropping—
packing around 200 boxes weekly from
the walled garden Coleshill. Seasonal veg
delivered throughout the Vale of the White
Horse.

> Because most genes being introduced
> into GE plants come from sources
> which have never been part of the
> human diet, there is no way of
> knowing whether or not the products
> of these genes will cause allergic
> reactions.
>
> Luke Anderson, *Genetic Engineering,*
> *Food, and Our Environment* (1999)

DEVERILL TROUT FARM & PURELY
ORGANIC FARM SHOP
LONGBRIDGE DEVERILL, WARMINSTER
Tel: 01985 841093 Fax: 01985 841268
Email: purely@organic96.freeserve.co.uk
Website: www.purelyorganic.co.uk
Organic trout reared in sparkling spring
water flowing from organic watercress
beds. Trade enquiries welcome. Open to
the public 7 days a week on A350
Warminster to Blandford. Farm shop selling
fresh fruit and vegetables, fresh and
smoked trout, fresh watercress, dairy
products, dry goods and groceries, £5 &
£10 veg/fruit boxes with free delivery. Soil
Assn. no. G3015. See display ad.

EASTBROOK FARM ORGANIC MEATS
EASTBROOK FARM, BISHOPSTONE,
NR. SWINDON SN6 8PW
Tel: 01793 790460 Fax: 01793 791239
Contact: Jane Faulkes
Email: info@helenbrowningorganics.co.uk
Website:
www.helenbrowningorganics.co.uk
Eastbrook Farm Organic Meats supplies a
full range of fresh organic meat, bacon,
cured ham and sausages nationwide to
retailers, the catering trade and direct to
consumers through our home delivery
service. We guarantee the highest levels of
animal welfare, with all our livestock being
reared on chemical-free pastures. Soil
Association symbol no. P535.

   FURZE COTTAGE
FURZE COTTAGE, TEFFONT MAGNA,
NR. SALISBURY SP3 5QU
Tel: 01722 716285. Contact: Carol Jacobs
Farm gate fruit and vegetables, herbs and
eggs. Soil Association symbol numbers
J125 and RJ125. Please ring for details and
to place orders.

M. & A. HARVEY
GOULTERS MILL, NETTLETON,
W. CHIPPENHAM SM14 7LL
Tel & Fax: 01249 782555
Contact: A. Harvey
We produce lamb and beef, turkey for the
Christmas market and have sheep and
Highland cattle for sale for breeding
purposes. We also have paying guests to
stay. Soil Association no. G2641. Deliveries
made all over UK.

 KIT FARM
SOUTHVIEW, LITTLE CHEVERELL,
DEVIZES SN10 4JL
Tel: 01380 818591 Fax: 01380 816487
Contact: Lynn Rooke & Peter Edwards
Email: kit.farm@rooke.cix.co.uk
We produce top quality beef animals. They
are sired by Sussex bulls, single suckled and
finished on grass. They yield tender,
succulent, marbled meat. Soil Association
symbol no. G1941.

 LAKESIDE EGGS
LAKESIDE STABLES, STEEPLE LANGFORD,
SALISBURY SP3 4NH
Tel: 01722 790786 Contact: Jill Delaney
Poultry—free range eggs from organic
hens living in small colonies. Soil
Association licensed (no. G2215).

MALMESBURY WHOLEFOODS
29 ABBEY ROW, MALMESBURY SN16 0AG
Tel: 01666 823030
Contact: Steve Cox (Owner)
Fruit and vegetables, milk, cheese, juices,
cordial, flour and meat delivered within 15
miles radius of Malmesbury.

MANOR FARM PARTNERSHIP
MANOR FARM, GRAFTON,
MARLBOROUGH SN8 3DB
Tel: 01672 810735 Fax: 01672 810735
Contact: Pip Browning
Organic farm, cattle, cereals, potatoes. Soil
Association registered.

PERTWOOD ORGANIC CEREAL CO
LOWER PERTWOOD FARM, NR. HINDON,
SALISBURY SP3 6TA
Tel: 01747 820720 Fax: 01747 820499
Contact: Mark Houghton Brown
Range of organic breakfast cereals
processed from own produce: oat based,
wheat-free, GMO-free muesli with
delicious fruits, porridge oats, crunchy with
raisins and almonds, crunchy with mixed
nuts. UK coverage. Large quantities
available.

 PERTWOOD
ORGANICS CO-OPERATIVE LTD
THE OLD BARN AT LORDS HILL,
LOWER PERTWOOD FARM, LONGBRIDGE
DEVERILL, WARMINSTER BA12 7DY
Tel: 01985 840646 Fax: 01985 840649
Contact: Miranda Tunnicliffe
Email: mail@pertwood-organics.co.uk
Website: www.pertwood-organics.co.uk
Soil Association certified farm-based box
scheme, wholesale, market stalls in Bradford-
on-Avon, Wells, Frome and Salisbury. Over
80 different kinds of fruit and vegetables.

 E. & J. PHILLIPS LTD
3 HIGH ST., MALMESBURY SN16 9AA
Tel: 01666 822355 Contact: Teresa Francis
Bakers and confectioners who also produce
organic bread. Established 1870. Soil
Association reg. no. P1721.

 PURELY ORGANIC
BATH RD., DEVIZES SN10 1QE
Tel: 01380 730011 Fax: 01985 841268
Email: purely@organic96.freeserve.co.uk
Website: purelyorganic.co.uk
Selling a complete range of organic food
products including vegetables, fruit, meat,
trout, watercress, groceries, dairy products
etc. Free home delivery within 25 miles,
also veg/fruit boxes. See display ad.

PURE ORGANICS LTD
STOCKPORT FARM, STOCKPORT RD.,
AMESBURY SP4 7LN
Tel: 01980 626263 Fax: 01980 626264
Contact: Pauline Stiles
Email: mail@pureorganics.co.uk
Website: www.pureorganics.co.uk
Soil Association no. P2269. Award winning
manufacturer of frozen, organic,
convenience foods. 'For Georgia's Sake'
from Pure Organics—range includes kids'
organic range, burgers, pizzas, sausages,
ready meals etc. EC licence, Higher Level
approved EFSIS site.

RUSHALL FARM SHOP
DEVIZES RD., RUSHALL, PEWSEY SN9 6ET
Tel: 01980 630335 Fax: 01980 630095
Contact: Lesley Walford
Email: info@rushallorganics.co.uk
Website: www.rushallorganics.co.uk
Organic farm shop open Tuesday to
Saturday. Bread baked and cakes baked
daily with Rushall organic wholemeal flour.
Rushall organic beef, pork and lamb, dairy
products, fruit and vegetables etc. Soil
Association reg. no. W09S.

S. & J. ORGANIC GROWERS
THE WALLED GARDEN, SCHOOL LANE,
CASTLE COMBE, CHIPPENHAM SN14 7HH
Tel: 01249 783294 Fax: 01249 783427
Contact: Juliet Fay/Steve Merritt
Email: sjorganics@btinternet.com
Soil Association reg. nos. G2343, P2343.
Producers of vegetables, eggs and pigs.
Home delivery of all certified organic
produce: vegetables, fruit, eggs, bread,
preserves, chicken, pork, beef, lamb, bacon,
hams, gammons and sausages. Delivery
area covers Bath, Bradford-on-Avon,
Trowbridge, Westbury, Chippenham and
surrounding areas.

STONES IN MARLBOROUGH
HUGHENDEN YARD,
MARLBOROUGH SN8 1LT
Tel: 01672 515200
Restaurant (Avebury) and café
(Marlborough) selling entirely our own
food and baking with extensive use of
fresh and organic ingredients from our
own gardens and local growers.

STONES RESTAURANT
AVEBURY SN8 1RF
Tel: 01672 539514
Email: mike@avebury.net
See entry above.

SWINDON PULSE
WHOLEFOOD CO-OP
27 CURTIS ST., SWINDON SN1 5JU
Tel: 01793 692016 Contact: Julie Smith
We are an old-style shop committed to
providing a wide range of vegetarian
organic products including fruit and veg,
cereals, pulses, sauces, pastas, spreads,
beverages, cosmetics and wines.

TRACKLEMENTS
THE DAIRY FARM, PINKNEY PARK,
SHERSTON, MALMESBURY SN16 0NX
Tel: 01666 840851 Fax: 01666 840022
Contact: Guy Tullberg
Email: sales@tracklements.co.uk
Website: www.tracklements.co.uk
Chutneys, sauces, jellies, mustards and
dressings (accompaniments to meat, fish
and cheese). Members of Soil Association.

TRAFALGAR FISHERIES
BARFORD FISH FARM,
DOWNTON SP5 3QF
Tel: 01725 5106148 Fax: 01725 511165
Contact: John Williams
Email: info@trafish.com
Website: www.trafish.com
Trout farm. Soil Association P5061. Supply
catering trade and major multiples.

WESTWOOD FARM
RODE HILL, COLERNE,
NR. CHIPPENHAM SN14 8AR
Tel: 01225 742854 Contact: Mrs J. Trotman
Registered with Soil Association (licence
no. G2362). Seasonally grown organic
vegetables, herbs and soft fruits. Delicious
farmhouse organic preserves. Local
deliveries only. Produce available at local
WI market.

WISE SAGE WHOLEFOOD
8 HIGH ST., CALNE SN11 0BS
Tel: 01249 812675
Contact: Terry Page (Proprietor)
Wholefood shop selling organic fresh
produce, dried products and a wide range
of natural products.

From Simikot it was seven days of walking to cross the Himalayas. Five sherpas accompanied our party of nine. The tents, food, kerosene, sleeping bags, and the rest of the gear were carried on yaks, mules, and horses driven by a group of herdsmen. We started climbing on a steep path immediately out of town. It was up and up and up, a good taste of the climbs to come. We followed the Humla Karnali River, which was flowing fast. At night we found either terraces or tiny meadows by the river to camp. This part of Nepal is one of the most remote and requires a special trekking permit. People live here in small settlements. The houses were beautifully built with earth and wood. Terraced villages clung to the mountain slopes. Hardworking mountain men, women, and children were bringing down brushwood and grass for the winter. Wild herbs, apricots, walnuts, and gooseberries lined the slopes in between the maize and millet, marijuana and hemp.

People wore beautifully knitted and woven clothes and heavy necklaces of silver with huge turquoise and coral beads. Their faces were weathered by sun, wind, and hard work, yet they radiated laughter in abundance.

We followed the traditional trade route, along which sheep and goats carry loads of ten kilograms each in handmade wool and leather pannier bags. They also carry grains to Tibet and bring back much desired and precious Tibetan salt. This was the middle of September, nearly the end of the trading season. The shepherds and goatherds were returning from Tibet with salt.

The paths were so steep that even the goats were panting and flopping down to rest. So you can imagine us, the unaccustomed travellers. The steepest of them all was Nara Lagna Pass, a continuous ascent reaching a huge rock cairn festooned with prayer flags at an altitude of 15,000 feet. Even though we had been walking for days and were somewhat acclimatized, every few minutes we had to stop to catch our breath. The pace of walking had to be extremely slow, but then neither speed nor time was any object.

Satish Kumar, *No Destination: An Autobiography* (revised edition 2000)

WORCESTERSHIRE

P.J. BALL
MIDDLE WOODSTON, LINDRIDGE,
TENBURY WELLS WR15 8JG
Tel: 01584 881244 Contact: Mrs P.J. Ball
Top fruit—apples, plums, damsons.

BEEWELL
4 ROYAL ARCADE, PERSHORE WR10 1AG
Tel: 01386 556577 Contact: Jen Cleese
We stock a good range of organic fresh
and dried produce; weekly supply of fresh
veg and fruit. Organic meats and poultry.
Café uses organic produce when possible.

THE COTTAGE HERBERY
MILL HOUSE, BORASTON,
NR. TENBURY WELLS WR15 8LZ
Tel: 01584 781575 Fax: 01584 781483
Contact: Kim Hurst
Open Sundays only, 10-6, May to July.
Producing organic peat-free herbs,
aromatics, medicinal plants, scented
foliage plants and herbaceous plants.

CRIDLAN & WALKER
23 ABBEY ROAD, MALVERN WR14 3ES
Contact: Christoph
Organic meat, vegetables, butter, milk,
apple juice, pear juices etc.

THE DOMESTIC FOWL TRUST
HONEYBOURNE PASTURES,
HONEYBOURNE, EVESHAM WR11 5QG
Tel: 01386 833083 Fax: 01386 833364
Contact: Mrs Landshoff
Email: dft@honeybourne.demon.co.uk
Website: mywebpage.net/domestic-fowl-trust
Suppliers of high quality poultry housing
and equipment. Traditional and hybrid
poultry, ducks and geese. Mail order
service. Full countrywide delivery. Open to
the public.

ELYSIA NATURAL SKIN CARE
19/20 STOCKWOOD BUSINESS PARK,
STOCKWOOD, NR. REDDITCH B96 6SX
Tel: 01386 792622 Fax: 01386 792623
Contact: Yvonne Rowse
Email: enquiries@drhauschka.co.uk
Website: www.drhauschka.co.uk
Elysia distributes the Dr Hauschka skin care
range, holistic products using organically
grown herbs and plants from certified Bio-
dynamic farms. The products and
ingredients are not tested on animals.

FERTILE FIBRE
KNIGHTON-ON-TEME,
TENBURY WELLS, WR15 8LT
Tel: 01584 781575 Fax: 01584 781483
Contact: Rob Hurst
Seed and multipurpose composts, coir
blocks, fertilizers and cocoashells. Mail
order throughout most of mainland UK.
Soil Association symbol holder. Write for
free sample and information pack.

GREENLINK ORGANIC FOODS
9-11 GRAHAM RD.,
GREAT MALVERN WR14 2HR
Tel: 01684 576266 Contact: Mike Gattiss
Soil Association reg. no. R1656. One-stop
organic shop and café with delivery
service.

KITE'S NEST FARM
BROADWAY WR12 7JT
Tel: 01386 853320 Fax: 01386 853621
Contact: Rosamund Young
We sell totally organic beef. Cattle live in
family groups in natural free-ranging herd.
No bought-in food ever used during last
25 years. Ring first.

OAKFIELD FARM
PRODUCTS LIMITED
MAIN STREET, WILLERSEY,
BROADWAY WR12 7PJ
Tel: 01386 858580 Fax: 01386 852585
Contact: Hugh Owens
Soil Association reg. nos. P2526, P2110,
P2253. Mushroom grower—all organic
grades of chestnut mushrooms and various
exotic varieties of mushrooms, also
organic. Delivery nationwide.

   ORGANIC PLANET
BRANSFORD SERVICE STATION & STORES,
HEREFORD ROAD, BRANSFORD,
WORCESTER WR6 5JB
Tel: 01905 333348 (a.m.)
01886 833474 (p.m.) Fax: 01905 333348
Contact: Mrs C. Powell
Email: organicplanet@fsmail.net
Soil Association Member. We provide a
wide choice of organic foods: groceries,
fresh bread, and dairy products, milk, fruit
and vegetables, wine and meats. We
provide a box scheme and a delivery
service. We deliver within Worcester and
Malvern areas.

   OXTON ORGANICS
BROADWAY LANE, FLADBURY,
PERSHORE WR10 2QF
Tel & Fax: 01386 860477
Contact: J. Eldridge
Email: oxtons@hotmail.com
We grow organic vegetables (members of
the Soil Association) and sell our
vegetables and fruit direct to the public via
our box scheme.

PERSHORE COLLEGE
AVONBANK, PERSHORE WR10 3JP
Tel: 01386 552443 Fax: 01386 556528
Contact: John Edgeley
Email: postmaster@pershore.ac.uk
Website: www.pershore.ac.uk
5 hectare organic fruit and vegetable
production unit. Training courses and
consultancy, apple juicing. Greengrowers
Organic Product Ltd. Soil Association reg.
nos. G532, P2016. Farmers' markets.

RED DEER HERBS LTD
EARL'S CROOME, WORCESTER WR8 9DF
Tel: 01386 750734 Contact: Alan Mole
Email: enquiries@reddeerherbs.co.uk
Website: www.reddeerherbs.co.uk
RDH import and grow herbs for the food
manufacturing industry. We will supply from
1kg to 1tonne. M&S, Sainsbury, Waitrose,
Asda and Tesco sell products with our herbs.
Deliveries nationally and to Europe.

 ROSEMARYS HEALTH FOODS
10 THE SHAMBLES, WORCESTER WR1 2RF
Tel: 01905 612190
Contact: Dea Childe (Manager)
Health foods and wholefoods retail.

  SONG OF THE EARTH
73 ALBERT RD., MALVERN WR14 1RR
Tel & Fax: 01684 892533
Contact: Fiona Hopes
Email: hopes.family@cwcom.net
Individual and special gardens created by a
qualified and experienced designer,
working with the subtle energies of the
land to create sustainable landscapes that
are ecologically sound, practical,
productive and beautiful.

 W.O. STEELE & SONS
CHAPEL FARM, NETHERTON,
NR. PERSHORE WR10 3JG
Tel & Fax: 01386 710379
Contact: Adrian Steele
850 acre mixed organic farm selling
milling wheat and oats, beef, lamb, wool,
potatoes, breeding sheep. Soil Association
(S37M) and Graig Farm membership.

 SUNSHINE HEALTH
SHOP & ORGANIC BAKERY
3 VINE STREET, EVESHAM WR11 4RE
Tel: 01386 443 757
Contact: Fran Cameron (Manager)
Soil Association members, retail fresh
organic fruit and vegetables weekly, many
other organic health foods and
supplements.

EAST YORKSHIRE

 ANGLIA OILS LTD
KING GEORGE V DOCK, HULL HU9 5PX
Tel: 01482 701271 Fax: 01482 709447
Contact: Steve Tate
Email: state@angliaoils.co.uk
Importing, processing and packaging,
organic extra virgin olive, safflower, sesame
and sunflower oils, palm oil (and fractions).
Certified by the Soil Association (reg. no.
P966.

CRANSWICK COUNTRY FOODS
INGLEMIRE LANE, COTTINGHAM,
HULL HU16 4PJ
Tel: 01482 848180 Fax: 01482 876146
Contact: J. Brisby
Email: jim.brisby@cranswick.co.uk
Producers of fresh pork, sausage, cooked
meats.

  FOSTON GROWERS
FOSTON ON THE WOLDS,
DRIFFIELD YO25 8BJ
Tel: 01262 488382 Contact: Jenny Webb
Glasshouse crops—helda beans, tomatoes,
courgettes, peppers and mixed salad
leaves.

GREEN GROWERS
1 STATION COTTAGES, WANSFORD RD.,
NAFFERTON, DRIFFIELD YO25 8NJ
Tel: 01377 255362
Contact: Dr G.M. Egginton (Owner)
A smallholding producing a wide range of
vegetables, fruit, herbs plants, comfrey
liquid, for local sale. Teach organic
gardening through talks and visits. Host
member of WWOOF. Soil Association
symbol no. G2175.

 HIDER FOOD IMPORTS
WILTSHIRE ROAD, HULL HU4 6PA
Tel: 01452 561137 Fax: 01452 565668
Contact: Deirdre Mills
Email: mail@hiderfoods.co.uk
Registered with the Soil Association (no.
P4325). Categories: nuts, dried fruits,
savoury mixes, muesli. Deliver countrywide.

SLATER ORGANICS
16 CROSS ST., ALDBROUGH,
HULL HU11 4RW
Tel: 01964 527519 Contact: Bob Slater
Soil Association reg. no. G1917. Grow field
vegetables and run box scheme.

WHEELBARROW FOODS
3 THORNGARTH LANE,
BARROW ON HUMBER DN19 7AW
Tel: 01469 530721
Wheelbarrow foods produces vegetables,
fruit and herbs to Soil Association standard.
Farm gate sales. Local delivery to shops.
Vegetable box scheme. Small shop.
Distribution point.

Government test results published in
September 1999 in the Working Party
on Pesticide Residues (WPPR) Annual
Report confirm concerns over pesticide
in our food. All supermarket and shop-
bought non-organic oranges, and most
pears, lettuces, yams, and chocolate
were found to contain residues,
including some from chemicals whose
use is prohibited in the UK.

Tanyia Maxted-Frost,
The Organic Baby Book (1999)

NORTH YORKSHIRE

  ALLIGATOR

104 FISHERGATE, YORK YO10 4BB
Tel: 01904 654525
Contact: Arfer, Steve or Peter
Wholefoods, fruit and vegetables, organic
wherever possible at sensible prices. Orders
made up for collection or delivery.

BRUNSWICK ORGANIC NURSERY

APPLETON RD., BISHOPTHORPE,
YORK YO23 2RF
Tel & Fax: 01904 701869
Contact: Adam Myers
Charity working with adults who have
learning difficulties, producing vegetables
and fruit to Soil Association standards, (no.
G1903). Perennials, herbs, vegetables and
plants in pots. Also run a craft workshop.

CAMPHILL VILLAGE TRUST—
BOTTON VILLAGE

BOTTON VILLAGE, DANBY,
WHITBY YO21 2NJ
Tel: 01287 660871 Fax: 01287 660888
Contact: E. Wennekes (Grower)
Email: botton@camphill.org.uk
Website: www.camphill.org.uk
Botton Village is a Camphill Village Trust
community for adults with special needs
based on 5 mixed farms which are run on
Bio-dynamic principles.

CAMPHILL VILLAGE TRUST—
LARCHFIELD COMMUNITY

STOKESLEY RD., HEMLINGTON,
MIDDLESBROUGH TS8 9DY
Tel: 01642 593688 Fax: 01642 595778
Contact: Atkinson, Pink, Smith (Co-workers)
Producers of real organic meat, vegetables,
seasonal fruit, bread etc. Also hand crafts—
weaving and wooden toys.

COUNTRY PRODUCTS

11A CENTRE PARK, MARSTON BUSINESS
PARK, TOCKWITH, YORK YO26 7QF
Tel & Fax: 01423 358858
Contact: Mark Leather
Email: countryproducts@fsbdial.co.uk
Website: www.countryproducts.co.uk
Wholesale and retail supplier of quality
dried fruits, nuts, spices and other fine
foods. Own mixes of muesli, fruits and
nuts. Contract packer, Soil Association no.
P1987.

DEMETER SEEDS STORMY HALL

STORMY HALL FARM, BOTTON VILLAGE,
DANBY, WHITBY YO21 2NJ
Tel: 01287 661369 Fax: 01287 661369
Email: stormy.hall.botton@camphill.org.uk
Producer, processor, and retailer of Bio-
dynamic seed (organic certification UK 6),
specialising in vegetable, herb and flower
seeds.

  EL PIANO

15-17 GRAPE LANE, YORK YO1 7HU
Tel: 01904 610676
Contact: Maggi or Astrid
Email: el.piano@collage.co.uk
Open 10 a.m. - 12.30 a.m. (i.e. after
midnight), closed Sundays. Non-licensed,
hispanic, informal, vegetarian. Function
rooms, event-catering inside or out.
Children welcome all hours. Retail: organic
meat, spanish foods, ceramic and rugs.
Publishers of York's *Little Issue*.

  FIRST SEASON

1 ST. ANN'S LANE, WHITBY YO21 3PF
Tel: 01947 601608
Contact: Keith Mollison (Partner)
Wide range of organic food including
bread, margarine, butter, cheese, dairy,
dried fruits. Distributor of organic fruit and
vegetable boxes.

FOUNTAINS DAIRY PRODUCTS LTD
KIRKBY MALZEARD HG4 3QD
Tel: 01765 658212 Fax: 01765 658732
Contact: Gail Hill
Email: reaks@zoo.co.uk
Registered with the Soil Association. Manufacturer of organic cheese including Cheddar, Red Leicester, Cheshire, Wensleydale and Double Gloucester. See display ad.

GOOSEMOOR ORGANICS
WARFIELD LANE, COWTHORPE, NR. WETHERBY LS22 5EU
Tel & Fax: 01423 358887
Email: vegebox@goosemoor.org.uk
Website: www.goosemoor.org.uk
Wholesaler, grower, importer and pre-packer registered with the Soil Association. The company is fully committed to social, environmental and ethical practices, which are in place in its day to day running. BBC Good Food Awards finalist.

  THE GREEN HOUSE
5 STATION PARADE, HARROGATE HG1 1UF
Tel: 01423 502580 Contact: Bob Fisher
Shop selling probably the widest organic food and drink selection in Yorkshire. Totally GMO-free. Also sells vegetarian and special diet foods. Delivery within approx 5 miles of shop.

HUNTERS OF HELMSLEY
13 MARKET PLACE, HELMSLEY Y062 5BL
Tel: 01439 771307 Fax: 01439 771307
Contact: Jennie
Specialist retail food outlet—high class delicatessen and luxury foods, keeping foods that are not available in supermarkets. Bakery, dairy produce, meats, cooked, raw, game—condiments, preserves, dry goods.

  G.A. KIRK & SON
THE ABATTOIR, NUNNINGTON, YORK YO6 4DE
Tel: 01439 748242 Fax: 01439 788546
Contact: Richard Kirk (Director)
Soil Association no. P2160. We are a small country abattoir able to slaughter any animals, and will deliver (if a volume) by arrangement.

 THE LITTLE DELICATESSEN
3 HIGH STREET, TADCASTER LS24 9AP
Tel: 01937 833244
Contact: Wendy Preston
High class delicatessen with a wide range of wholefoods: organic beer and organic lager.

NATURE'S WORLD
LADGATE LANE, ACKLAM, MIDDLESBROUGH TS5 7YN
Tel: 01642 594895 Fax: 01642 591224
Unique environmental centre with organic demonstration gardens, forest garden and working River Tees model.

  C.F. & E.T. PADMORE
BANK HOUSE FARM, GLAISDALE, WHITBY YO21 2QA
Tel & Fax: 01947 897297
Contact: Chris or Emma Padmore
Frozen organic lamb and beef. Telephone before to check availability. Soil Assn no. G1135.

M. & P. SELLERS
(THE ORGANIC FARMSHOP)
THE ORGANIC FARM SHOP, STANDFIELD HALL, WESTGATE CARR RD., PICKERING YO18 8LX
Tel & Fax: 01751 472249 Contact: Mike
One of the biggest selections of organic produce in Yorkshire. Home grown beef. Home made burgers and sausages (pork) and vegetarian frozen meals; box scheme in Ryedale; wholesale throughout Yorkshire.

SMITHY FARM SHOP
BALDERSBY, THIRSK YO7 4PN
Tel: 01765 640676 Contact: Susan Brown
Retail Graig Farm beef, pork, lamb
vegetables, dairy produce.

R.TURK
BRAY'S FARM HOUSE, WEST END,
SUMMERBRIDGE, HARROGATE HG3 4AE
Tel: 01943 880404 Contact: R. Turk
Organically produced meat (turkeys,
ducks, bantams, lamb, pork), eggs, fruit.
Live chicks and young poultry. Christmas
turkeys and ducks need to be ordered by
August 30th.

VILLAGE CRAFT FLOURS
THORPE MILL, GREWELTHORPE,
NR. RIPON HG4 3BS
Tel & Fax: 01765 658534
Contact: G.T. & J. Roberts (Directors)
We are millers and wholesalers of organic
wholewheat and Wood's range of quality
flours, retailing in N. Yorks area and coast
to coast.

WILD GINGER VEGETARIAN BISTRO
behind THE GREEN HOUSE, 5 STATION
PARADE, HARROGATE HG1 1UF
Tel: 01423 566122 Fax: 01423 520056
Contact: Rachel Melton
Email: wildginger@veganvillage.co.uk
Website: www.veganvillage.co.uk/wildginger
100% vegetarian foods, freshly prepared
and home made. Large choice for vegans,
also gluten/dairy/wheat/sugar-free and
other exclusion diets catered for. Licensed,
selling organic wines and beer. Regular
gourmet evenings and special events.

YORK BEER SHOP
28 SANDRINGHAM ST., FISHERGATE,
YORK YO1 4BA
Tel & Fax: 01904 647136
Contact: Eric Boyd (Partner)
Specialist retailer of beers, wines, ciders
and cheeses. Organic products available in
all these categories.

YORKSHIRE GARDEN WORLD
MAIN RD., WEST HADDLESEY,
NR. SELBY YO8 8QA
Tel & Fax: 01757 228279
Contact: Carole Atkinson Email:
carole@yorkshiregardenworld.freeserve.co.uk
Website:
www.yorkshiregardenworld.freeserve.co.uk
Member of the Yorkshire Tourist Board and
Herb Society at Banbury. We specialise in
designing and planning herb gardens,
specialist growers of organic herbs,
heathers and conifers. Display gardens.
Mail order catalogue available.

> By denying the creativity of nature
> and other cultures, even when that
> creativity is exploited for commercial
> gain, 'intellectual property rights'
> becomes another name for intellectual
> theft and biopiracy. Simultaneously,
> people's assertion of their customary,
> collective rights to knowledge and
> resources is turned into 'piracy' and
> 'theft'.
>
> Vandana Shiva, *Biopiracy* (1998)

Key

 Producers
 Wholesalers
 Import/Export
 Retailers
 Mail Order
 Restaurants
 Day Visits/B&B
 Farm Gate Sales
 Box Schemes/ Delivery Service
 Garden/Farm Sundries
 Manufacturers & Processors

SOUTH YORKSHIRE

BEANIES WHOLEFOODS
205-207 CROOKES VALLEY ROAD,
SHEFFIELD S10 1BA
Tel & Fax: 0114 268 1662
Contact: Y. Williams
Soil Association no. R1731. Shop, and
delivery service within Sheffield. Organic
fruit and veg, box scheme, bread,
wholefoods, vegetarian and vegan, wine,
dairy etc. Workers co-operative.

THE DRAM SHOP
21 COMMONSIDE, SHEFFIELD S10 1GA
Tel: 0114 268 3117 Contact: Linda Taylor
Specialist off licence wines, beers, ciders
and spirits.

HEELEY CITY FARM
RICHARDS RD., SHEFFIELD S2 3DT
Tel: 0114 258 0482 Contact: Kevin Quinn
(Horticultural Manager)
We sell organic vegetables and other
products in season. We provide training
courses in organic horticulture and
agriculture.

MEADOWLANDS
THE PEAK PARK VISITOR CENTRE,
LANGSETT BARN, LANGSETT, BARNSLEY
Tel: 0114 283 0322 Fax: 0114 288 7941
Contact: Robert Hanna
Email: meadowlands@dial.pipex.com
Website: www.meadowlands.org.uk
Wildflower meadow and grass seed of UK
provenance. Herbal extracts from wild
flora.

POTTS BAKERS (EST 1891)
STANLEY ROAD, STAIRFOOT,
BARNSLEY S70 3PG
Tel: 01226 249175 Fax: 01226 249175
Contact: Andrew Potts
Specialist bakers of organic bread, cakes,
morning goods and Christmas baking,
available in our shops and at farmers'
markets in Yorkshire. Wholesale suppliers
to shops, restaurants, supermarkets. Soil
Association reg. no. P4477.

THE REAL BREAD BAKEHOUSE LIMITED
56 MARSH HOUSE ROAD,
SHEFFIELD S11 9SP
Tel: 0114 262 1212 Fax: 0114 236 2722
Contact: John Coatman
Email: john@realbread.freeserve.co.uk
Wholesale bakery—bread and wholesale
confectionery. Deliveries to shops and co-
ops etc. Deliveries to the following
postcode areas: S, DE, NG and LS. Soil
Association registered (no. P4265).

YORKSHIRE ORGANIC EARTH
33 DEVONSHIRE DRIVE, HALLBALK,
BARNSLEY S75 1EE
Tel: 0385 901215 Email:
stuartallen@yorkshireorganicearth.fsnet.co.uk
Highly commended 1998 (vegetables),
Highly commended 1999 (eggs). Summer
seasonal vegetables. Some farm gate sales.

Cities need to endeavour to become centres of civilisation, not of mobilisation. We need to implement the vision of cities as places of creativity, of conviviality and above all else of settled living. Cities can be places of beauty, with great public spaces and buildings, as well as places for intimate community living.

Herbert Girardet, *Creating Sustainable Cities* (1999)

WEST YORKSHIRE

BEANO WHOLEFOODS

36 NEW BRIGGATE, LEEDS LS1 6NU
Tel & Fax: 0113 243 5737 (24 hours)
Contact: Carol, Mary, James
Email: info@beanowholefoods.co.uk
Website: www.beanowholefoods.co.uk
Fresh organic fruit and vegetables
delivered to us on Wednesdays. Organic
bread and organic vegan/vegetarian take-
outs, and sandwiches daily. Vast range of
organic foods stocked. Delivery service
within Leeds area. Soil Association reg. no.
R2282.

BEANSTALK

FELL EDGE BUNGALOW, MOORSIDE LANE,
ADDINGHAM LS29 9JY
Tel: 01943 831103 Fax: 01943 839199
Contact: Alan Stevens
Email: h@beanstalkorganix.demon.co.uk
Soil Association licence P4995. Free home
delivery of organic vegetables, fruit, milk,
cheese, eggs, meat, fish, bread, beer, wine
and 2000 other lines. Packed to customers
requirements. Delivery areas covered: West
Yorks, North Yorks, East Lancs.

BRADFORD WHOLEFOODS LTD

AT THE CELLAR DOOR PROJECT,
THE OLD SCHOOL, FAIRFIELD RD., SHIPLEY
Tel: 01422 202648
Contact: Jack First (Owner)
Specialist organic retailer including direct
supplies of organic produce and over 100
other organic foods. Only open on
Thursdays.

BRICKYARD ORGANIC FARM

BADSWORTH, NR. PONTEFRACT WF9 1AX
Tel & Fax: 01977 617327
Contact: John Brock (Grower)
Brassicas, salad (polytunnels), and wide
range of vegetables on 35 acres. Soil
Association licensed.

 DE RIT (UK) LTD

TENTERFIELDS BUSINESS PARK,
LUDDENDENFOOT, HALIFAX HX2 6EJ
Tel: 01422 885523 Fax: 01422 884629
Contact: George Carroll
Our range covers organic cakes, biscuits,
rice cakes, crispbreads, conserves,
vegetable preserves, herbs and spices,
tomato products, mayonnaise, pasta,
sweets and snacks. We also supply organic
commodities, some of which are especially
suitable for manufacturers.

FOOD THERAPY

11 NORTHGATE, HALIFAX HX1 1UR
Tel: 01422 350 826 Fax: 01422 362 106
Contact: K. Benson (Owner)
Voted best health food store in UK 1995.
Wide range of organic fruit and veg, plus
ever-expanding quality organic product
range. Ordering service for non-stock
items: if it's available, we can obtain it.

HALF MOON WHOLEFOODS

6 HALF MOON ST.,
HUDDERSFIELD HD1 2JJ
Tel: 01484 456392 Fax: 01484 310161
Contact: Judith Beresford
Email: sales@halfmoon-healthfoods.co.uk
Website: www.halfmoon-healthfoods.co.uk
We are a wholefood store specialising in
organic lines, vegetables, breads, dairy
products, eggs, beers and wines. Our
organic box scheme has been established
12 years. Soil Association membership
applied for.

  NATURAL CHOICE

72 WESTBOURNE RD., MARSH,
HUDDERSFIELD HD1 4LE
Tel: 01484 513162
Contact: Graham Rusworth (Owner)
15 years experience selling wholefoods and
organics. New larger range now available,
also our own organic bread and rye bread.
Box scheme and delivery service.

ORGANIC ALTERNATIVES

KERSHAW'S GARDEN SHOPPING CENTRE,
HALIFAX ROAD, BRIGHOUSE HD6 2QD
Tel: 01484 713435/719288
Fax: 01484 400563 Contact: Mark Yates
Email: mwjyates@hotmail.com
Organic Alternatives offers a range of fine
organic foods including meats, beer and
wine, ice cream, per food, organic
fertilizers and composts. We also offer a
box scheme and free delivery service. Free
tasting every weekend. Ordering service
for non stock items.

P.A. & S.J. SNOWDEN

HAWTHORNE HOUSE FARM,
DUNKESWICK, HAREWOOD,
LEEDS LS17 9LP
Tel: 0113 288 6254 Fax: 0113 288 6754
Contact: P.A. Snowden
Family farm with increasing organic
acreage producing potatoes, cereals and
fat lambs. Member of Soil Association (reg.
no. G1630) and BOF.

SUMA WHOLEFOODS

DEAN CLOUGH, HALIFAX HX3 5AN
Tel: 01422 345513 Fax: 01422 349429
Contact: Ric Lihou
Email: info@suma.co.uk
Website: www.suma.co.uk
Vegetarian workers co-operative with over
2000 organic lines. Wholesale, export,
brand name. One of the longest
established in the country.

VINCEREMOS WINES AND SPIRITS LTD

19 NEW ST., LEEDS LS18 4BH
Tel: 0113 205 4545 Fax: 0113 205 4546
Contact: Harriet Walsh
Email: info@vinceremos.co.uk
Website: www.vinceremos.co.uk
The UK's longest established organic wine
specialists. We also supply organic beers,
ciders, juices and spirits. Free catalogue,
friendly service and nationwide delivery.
Run HDRA Organic Wine Club. See
display ad.

WEST RIDING ORGANICS

147 BRIGHTS BUILDINGS, NEW MILL RD.,
HONLEY, HUDDERSFIELD HD7 2QE
Tel: 01484 609171 Fax: 01484 661956
Contact: Julian Chambers (Proprietor)
Email: westridingorganics@btinternet.co.uk
Website: www.organicsuk.com
Manufacturers of Nature's Own and Bio-
Pak organic composts (Soil Association
registered). Module, blocking, potting and
grow bags all supplied. Trade enquiries
welcome.

The challenge of biodiversity conservation is to enlarge the scope of economies based on diversity and decentralization, and shrink the scope of economies based on monocultures, monopolies, and non-sustainability. While both kinds of economies use biodiversity as an input, only economies based on diversity produce diversity. Monoculture economies produce monocultures.

Vandana Shiva, *Biopiracy* (1998)

Northern Ireland

ARKHILL FARM SHOP
25 DRUMCROONE ROAD,
GARVACH, L'DERRY BT51 4EB
Tel: 02829 557920 Contact: Paul Craig
Member of IOFGA (licence no. 1003).
Organic egg producer, goat's milk, organic
pork and lamb, fruit and vegetables. We
have an open farm with education centre
and B&B for people wishing to stay or
work on the farm.

**CAMPHILL
COMMUNITY—CLANAGOBAN**
CLANAGOBAN, DRUDGETON ROAD,
OMAGH, CO. TYRONE BT78 1TJ
Tel: 02882 256111 Fax 02882 256114
Contact: Martin
Email: martinsturn@x-stream.co.uk
Mixed Demeter veg farm. Sale of home
produced salami and some veg.

**CAMPHILL
COMMUNITY—HOLYWOOD**
8 SHORE ROAD, HOLYWOOD,
CO. DOWN BT1 89HX
Tel: 02890 423203 Fax: 02890 397818
Contact: Miriam Muller
Vegetarian meals in café, eco-filtered
water, everything organic. We also train
and employ people with special needs and
cover all organic foods in the shop, except
meat. We provide a home bakery, café and
shop selling organic foods.

  TOM GILBERT
12 BALLYLAGAN ROAD, STRAID,
BALLYCLARE, ANTRIM BT39 9NF
Tel: 028 9332 2867 Fax: 02893 322129
Contact: Tom Gilbert
Email: Ballylagan@aol.com
Producer of organic beef, lamb, poultry
and vegetables. Soil Association reg. no.
G1513. Farm shop with comprehensive
range of groceries open Friday afternoons
and all day Saturday.

  LIFETREE
37 SPENCER ROAD, DERRY BT47 6AA
Tel: 02871 342865 Fax: 02871 347880
Contact: Mrs A. Munro
Email: ckm@iol.ie
Health food shop run by qualified therapist
with medical background, specialising in
foods for special diets. Box scheme weekly
with selection of seasonal fruits and
vegetables.

> For many millions of people the late
> 20th-century world economic system
> is violent and destructive, unfree and
> disorderly. We must transform it into a
> 21st-century system designed and able
> to meet the needs of people and the
> Earth, including their needs for
> freedom and peace and order.
>
> James Robertson, *Transforming
> Economic Life* (1998)

Key

 Producers

 Mail Order

 Wholesalers

 Import/Export

 Retailers

 Box Schemes/
Delivery Service

 Restaurants

 Day Visits/B&B

 Farm
Gate Sales

 Box Schemes/
Delivery Service

 Garden/Farm
Sundries

 Manufacturers
& Processors

Scotland

ARGYLL & BUTE

 ARGYLL HOTEL
ISLE OF IONA PA76 6SJ
Tel: 01681 700 334 Fax: 01681 700 510
Contact: Claire Bachellerie
Email: reservations@argyllhoteliona.co.uk
Website: www.argyllhoteliona.co.uk
Small friendly hotel on the beautiful island of
Iona. We grow our own organic vegetables
and serve local organic meat, as well as
regular meals and vegetarian options.
Excellent wines.

 MILLSTONE WHOLEFOODS
15 HIGH STREET, OBAN PA34 4BG
Tel & Fax: 01631 562704
Contact: Ray Grant
Wholefood shop with wide range of
organic produce.

 R. & H. VERNON
RASHFIELD FARM, BY KILMUN PA23 8QT
Tel: 01369 840237 Fax: 01369 840237
Contact: Henrietta Vernon
Email: ailldeachd@rashfield
Pedigree highland cattle, specialising in the
famous original 'Buara Dubh' black cattle
of the Western Isles.

BORDERS

  BEAN MACHINE
GREATRIDGEHALL, KELSO TD5 7PD
Tel & Fax: 01573 460346
Contact: George McDonald (Partner)
Home delivery of organic fruit, vegetables
and wholefoods to Edinburgh, Lothian and
the Borders and Berwick on Tweed on a
weekly basis.

GARVALD HOME FARM LTD
DOLPHINTON, WEST LINTON EH46 7HJ
Tel: 01968 682238 Contact: John &
Shelagh Brett (Joint Managers)
Demeter no. 237. Small community farm
with people with special needs producing
beef, lamb, table poultry, cereals, mixed
vegetables etc. Meat sold through local
butcher in Biggar, S. Lanarkshire.

CENTRAL

ORGANIC FARMERS SCOTLAND
BLOCK 2, UNIT 4, BANDEATH INDUSTRIAL
ESTATE, THROSK, STIRLING FK7 7XY
Tel: 01786 817581 Fax: 01786 816100
Contact: Murray Cameron Email:
enquiries@organicfrmssco.demon.co.uk
Website: Soon!
Scottish producer marketing co-operative
organic beef, lamb, cereals, animal
feedstuffs, etc. Delivery to all of UK.

DUMFRIES AND GALLOWAY

 CAMPHILL
VILLAGE TRUST—LOCH ARTHUR
LOCH ARTHUR COMMUNITY FARM AND
CREAMERY, BEESWING DG2 8JQ
Tel: 01387 760296 Contact: Barry Graham
Bio-dynamic Demeter standard beef, lamb,
dairy produce—Farmhouse cheese, soft
cheese, yoghurt and cream cheese. Trade
enquiries welcome and we run a mail order
service for our Cheddar cheese. Small
bakery producing a range of organic
breads. Farm shop Mon - Fri.

CREAM O'GALLOWAY DAIRY CO LTD
RAINTON, GATEHOUSE OF FLEET,
CASTLE DOUGLAS DG7 2DR
Tel: 01557 814040 Fax: 01557 814040
Contact: Wilma Dunbar (Director)
Email: info@creamogalloway.co.uk
Website: www.creamogalloway.co.uk
Farm made luxury organic dairy ice cream
and frozen yoghurt in innovative flavours.
Farm, nature trails and ice cream parlour
open to the public April to October. Soil
Association membership P2928. The farm
is also a Soil Association member (G2554).

LOW CRAIGLEMINE FARM HOLIDAYS
LOW CRAIGLEMINE, WHITHORN,
NEWTON STEWART,
WIGTOWNSHIRE DG8 8NE
Tel & Fax: 01988 500730
Contact: Kirsty Hurst
Email: craiglemine@freeuk.com
130 acre livestock farm—sheep, beef,
smallholding animals near coast. Members
of SOPA and Soil Association.

NETHERFIELD FARM
NETHERFIELD FARM, BEESWING,
DUMFRIES DG2 8JE
Tel & Fax: 01387 730217
Contact: J.M. Anderson
Offering rest, care, rejuvenation, in
Galloway hills. Home cooking/baking using
organic/Bio-dynamic produce. Own fruit
and veg. Warm welcoming atmosphere,
beautiful garden. Hauschka massage and
facial treatments also available.

THE ROSSAN
AUCHENCAIRN,
CASTLE DOUGLAS DG7 1QR.
Tel: 01556 640269 Fax: 01556 640278
Contact: Mrs Bardsley
Long established guesthouse in large
organic garden. Specialising in vegetarian,
vegan and medical diets, plus local meat if
required. Edge of village, near the sea, well
behaved dogs welcome.

SUNRISE WHOLEFOODS
49 KING ST., CASTLE DOUGLAS DG7 1AE
Tel: 01556 504455
Contact: Pauline Tilbury (Owner)
Email: pstilb@sunrise-whofo.demon.co.uk
Wholefood shop, specialising in organic dried
and fresh foods; fruit and veg, cheese, wine,
bread, books. SOPA symbol holder. Fresh veg
daily from smallholding in summer.

FIFE

BELLFIELD ORGANIC NURSERY
STRALHMIGO, CUPAR KY14 7RH
Tel & Fax: 01337 860764
Contact: Irene Alexander
Grower of organic vegetables. Home
delivery service.

CRAIGENCALT FARM ECOLOGY CENTRE
CRAIGENCALT FARM,
KINGHORN KY3 9YG
Tel & Fax: 01592 891567
Contact: Ronnie Mackie
Email: ricard_neil@compuserve.com
The Craigencalt Farm Ecology Centre is
used by schools and adult groups for
ecological studies, weekend study groups
and various craft/arts persons. Visitors are
welcome to take part, walk, bird watch,
chat to members, even pitch in with the
various projects underway.

ORGANIC MEAT & PRODUCTS SCOTLAND LTD
JAMESFIELD FARM,
ABERNETHY KY14 6EW
Tel: 01738 850498 Fax: 01738 850 741
Email: alan.dickenson@ukonline.co.uk
Website: www.jamesfieldfarm.co.uk
Next day home delivery organic and free
range meats, beef, lamb, pork, poultry and
game. Farm shop. SOPA member no.
421/98/1421.

PILLARS OF HERCULES FARM SHOP
PILLARS OF HERCULES,
FALKLAND KY15 7AD
Tel: 01337 857749 Contact: Bruce Bennett
Email: mail@pillars.co.uk
Website: www.pillars.co.uk
Organic smallholding producing wide
range of vegetables and fruit. Also eggs,
poultry, and lamb. Farm shop also stocks
wholefoods, meat and dairy products. Soil
Association no. B26C. Delivery areas—Fife
and Edinburgh. See display ad.

SCOTMED HERBS
GARDEN BY THE LOCH
CRAIGENCALT FARM, KINGHORN KY3 3YG
Tel: 01592 874027
Contact: Alan Steedman Email:
asteedman@scotmedherbs.freeserve.co.uk
Soil Association registered producer and
retailer of culinary and medicinal herb pot
plants and fresh cut herbs. At the farm shop,
an extensive range of herb plants and cut
herbs is also available, as well as herbal
products and gifts. Shop open 1st April - 30th
October: Wed to Fri 1-6 p.m., Sat & Sun 11
a.m. to 5 p.m. Also open on public holidays.

SPECIALIST POTATOES LTD
GRANARY BUSINESS CENTRE,
COAL ROAD, CUPAR KY15 5YQ
Tel & Fax: 01334 656360
Contact: Alan Romans
Soil Association registered processor
specialising in joint operations with either
Soil Association or Scottish Organic
Producers Association. Growers and
merchants of organic seed potatoes. We
supply mainly to the UK and Europe.

GRAMPIAN

BIODYNAMIC SUPPLIES
LORIENEEN, BRIDGE OF MUCHALLS,
STONEHAVEN, ABERDEEN AB39 3RU
Tel & Fax: 01569 731756
Contact: Paul Van Midden
Specialist supplies to Bio-dynamic
gardeners, farmers and Demeter symbol
holders.

CROFT ORGANICS
SKELLARTS CROFT, DAVIOT,
INVERURIE AB51 0JL
Tel: 01467 681717 Fax: 01467 681718
Contact: Vic Hunter
SOPA certified box system. Veg grown on
SOPA registered land. Assorted veg and
fruit sales, organic wines also. Organic
herd of blonde d'Aquitaine cattle.

J. W. FRASER
BURNORRACHIE, BRIDGE OF MUCHALLS,
STONEHAVEN AB39 3RU
Tel: 01569 730195
Contact: John & Maggie (Owners)
Organic veg and pork to Demeter
standards. High quality veg sold locally
and wholesale all over Scotland. Supply
other box schemes.

HOUSE OF EDEN SCOTLAND
EDEN PLACE, DENHEAD, KINGSWELLS,
ABERDEEN AB15 8PT
Tel & Fax: 01224 749288
Contact: Michelle Herd
Email: michelle@edenplace.fsnet.co.uk
Website: www.house-of-eden.co.uk
A friendly, convenient and efficient
business supplying a comprehensive range
of non-perishable organic food by mail
order. A member of the Soil Association.

HOWEGARDEN UK LTD
AUCHTURLESS, TURRIFF,
ABERDEEN AB53 9EN
Tel: 01888 511808 Fax: 01888 511565
Contact: Tom Rossiter Email:
tom.rossiter@howegarden.sprint.com
Website: www.howegarden.co.uk
Soil Association member, packing organic
produce for major supermarket chains.
Specialise in locally grown produce.

LEMBAS
LORIENEEN, BRIDGE OT MUCHALLS,
STONEHAVEN, ABERDEEN AB39 3RU
Tel & Fax: 01569 731746
Contact: Paul Van Midden
Growers and distributors of Demeter and
organically grown vegetables and fruit.
Delivery area covered: Aberdeenshire.

MACRAE HOLDINGS
GHILLIE AND GLEN, BURGHMUIR PLACE,
INVERURIE AB51 4FS
Tel: 01467 625700 Fax: 01467 624209
Contact: Roy Cunningham
Email: roy@macrae.co.uk
A processor of ready-to-eat seafood
products, including organic smoked Scottish
salmon, organic salmon paté, organic trout
paté, organic smoked trout fillets and
organic Scottish salmon gravadlax. Licence
B2493. Deliveries to UK and EEC.

SCOTTISH AGRICULTURAL COLLEGE
CRAIBSTONE ESTATE, BUCKSBURN,
ABERDEEN AB21 9YA
Tel: 01224 711072 Fax: 01224 711293
Contact: David Younie
Email: d.younie@ab.sac.ac.uk
Website: www.sac.ac.uk/organic-farming
Two organic mixed farms (research and
demonstration), provision of advice as part
of Scottish Executive Organic Aid Scheme,
organic telephone helpline (01224
711072). Diploma, masters and distance
learning courses in organic farming.

104 HOLBURN ST., ABERDEEN AB10 6BY
Tel: 01224 593959 Fax: 01224 458958
Contact: Michael Noble
Email: info@totalorganics.com
Website: www.totalorganics.com
We supply only certified organic foods (over
1600 lines): fresh fruit and veg, chilled
foods, fresh meat and poultry, groceries,
beers and wines, natural remedies and
bodycare products. We are certified with
the Soil Association. We cater for many
people on special diets.

COLIN J.WARD
BRIDGEFOOT, NEWMACHER AB21 7PE
Tel: 01651 862041 Contact: Colin Ward
Soil Association no. G1071. A small mixed
farm delivering vegetables, fruit and eggs
in the Aberdeen area through its prize
winning box scheme.

HIGHLAND

MARJ DONALDSON
13 NEWTON KINKELL,
MUIR OF ORD IV6 7RB
Tel: 01349 861791
Contact: Marj Donaldson
Soil Association symbol holder, providing
fresh and frozen lamb in autumn and
winter.

THE HEALTH SHOP
20 BARON TAYLOR'S STREET,
INVERNESS IV1 1QG
Tel: 01463 233 104 Fax: 01463 718 144
Contact: Martin Sellar
Email: healthshopinvern@aol.com
We are delighted to offer you a large range
of organic products: just get in contact
and we'll do the rest! Look forward to
hearing from you.

HIGHLAND WHOLEFOODS
UNIT 6, 13 HARBOUR RD.,
INVERNESS IV1 1SY
Tel: 01463 712393
Email: hihoco@enterprise.net
Free delivery service throughout Northern
Scotland. Cash and carry warehouse in
Inverness. Over 800 organic lines stocked,
including chilled and frozen. Soil
Association reg. no. P2113.

PETER & THERESE MUSKUS
LAIKENBUIE, NAIRN IV12 5QN
Tel: 01667 454630
Email: muskus@bigfoot.com
Website: www.bigfoot.com/muskus
Soil Association reg. no. G2210. Watch roe
deer and osprey on tranquil croft with
beautiful outlook over trout loch amid
birch woods. Near Inverness and Moray
Firth. Top quality chalet, caravan and tipi,
safe for children.

OLD PINES RESTAURANT WITH ROOMS
SPEAN BRIDGE,
BY FORT WILLIAM PH34 4EG
Tel: 01397 712324 Contact: Suline
Email: goodfood@oldpines.co.uk
Website: www.oldpines.co.uk
A rare combination of relaxed informality
and unusually good food where only your
enjoyment and the food are taken seriously.
Restaurant of the Year 2000 in the *Good
Food Guide.*

PHOENIX COMMUNITY STORES LTD
THE PARK, FINDHORN BAY,
MORAY IV36 3TZ
Tel: 01309 690110 Fax: 01309 690933
Contact: David Hoyle
Email: phoenix@findhorn.org
Website: www.phoenixshop.com
A full service community store featuring an
extensive range of organic/fine foods with
associated wholesale bakery and organic
farm projects.

POYNTZFIELD HERB NURSERY
BLACK ISLE, BY DINGWALL IV7 8LX
Tel & Fax: 01381 610352
Contact: Duncan Ross
Specialists in organic/Bio-dynamic culinary,
aromatic and medicinal herb plants and
seeds; 450 varieties of rare, unusual and
popular plants. Demeter standards. Please
send 4 x 1st class stamps for informative
mail order catalogue.

RHANICH FARM
RHANICH RD., EDDERTON, TAIN IV19 1LG
Tel: 01862 821265
Contact: Pam Shaw (Partner)
High welfare farm, can arrange visits.
Producers of organic vegetables, goat's
milk, cheese, eggs, yoghurt, sheepskins,
fleeces, wool. Camping on hill farm,
member of WWOOF and Compassion in
World Farming.

ANTHONY WALKER
EASTER ACHNACLOICH, ARDROSS,
ALNESS IV17 0XP
Tel: 01349 882226 Contact: A. Walker
Upland farm, mainly sheep.

LOTHIAN

 THE CALEDONIAN
BREWING CO LTD
42 SLATEFORD ROAD,
EDINBURGH EH11 1PH
Tel: 0131 337 1286 Fax: 0131 313 2370
Contact: Stephen Crawley
Email: info@caledonian-brewery.co.uk
Website: www.caledonian-brewery.co.uk
Producer of the award winning organic beer,
Golden Promise. Member of the Soil
Association.

 ALLAN CAMPBELL
63 INVERLEITH ROW,
EDINBURGH EH3 5PX
Tel & Fax: 0131 552 3486
This is a High Street shop selling organic
meat and poultry, eggs and cheeses.

DAMHEAD ORGANICALLY GROWN
FOODS
32A DAMHEAD, OLD PENTLAND RD.,
LOTHIANBURN, EDINBURGH EH10 7EA
Tel: 0131 445 1490 Fax: 0131 445 5848
Contact: Susan Gerard
Email: sgerard@compuserve.com
Wholesalers & growers. Importers of fruit
and vegetables and wholefoods retailers
via farm shop, home delivery and mail
order of all organic foods (including meat,
dairy produce, poultry, fish etc).

EAST COAST ORGANIC BOXES
24 BOGGS HOLDINGS,
PENCAITLAND EH34 5BD
Tel & Fax: 01875 340227
Contact: Mike Callender
Email:
ECOBOX@eastcoastorganics.freeserve.co.uk
Farm Box Scheme offering fresh produce
and a wide range of organic supplies. Home
delivery or collection points throughout
Edinburgh and Lothians. Bio-dynamic
registered no. 295.

 THE ENGINE SHED
GARVALD COMMUNITY ENTERPRISES LTD.,
19 ST. LEONARD'S LANE,
EDINBURGH EH8 9SD
Tel: 0131 662 0040 Fax: 0131 667 5319
Contact: M. MacDonald
Email: engineshed@aol.com
Community workshops producing tofu
products, bread and snacks. We also have
a health food shop and café open 7 days a
week.

 GO ORGANIC LTD
24 BOSWALL RD., EDINBURGH EH5 3RN
Tel & Fax: 0131 552 2706
Contact: Sheila Ross
Email: email@goorganic.co.uk
Website: www.goorganic.co.uk
Organic soups, sauces, curries. No GMOs,
no artificial thickeners or flavours, no
colours, no hype—no compromise—just
the best pure organic ingredients. Soil
Association registered.

 HELIOS FOUNTAIN
7 GRASSMARKET, EDINBURGH EH1 2HY
Tel: 0131 229 7884 Fax: 0131 622 7173
Contact: Jos Bastiaensen (Director)
Friendly wholefood vegetarian coffee house
using some organic produce to make food
ranging from the wholesome to the
positively wicked. Also a rather unusual shop.

NATURE'S GATE
83 CLERK STREET, EDINBURGH EH8 9JG
Tel & Fax: 0131 668 2067
Contact: Gill Bainbridge
Wholefood shop with a full range of
organic, vegetarian, vegan and macrobiotic
products, including fruit and veg, chilled
foods and wines. Soil Association symbol
no. R1827. Open Mon, Wed, Thurs & Fri
10-7, Tues & Sat 10-6, Sun 12-4.

NEAL'S YARD REMEDIES

46A GEORGE ST., EDINBURGH EH2 2LE
Tel: 0131 226 3223
Neal's Yard Remedies manufactures and retails natural cosmetics in addition to stocking an extensive range of herbs, essential oils, homeopathic remedies and reference material.

THE NEW LEAF

20 ARGYLE PLACE, MARCHMONT, EDINBURGH EH9 1JJ
Tel: 0131 228 8840
Contact: Linda Goodman
Small, friendly shop specialising in natural and organic foods. Fresh organic milk, dairy produce, bread, fruit and vegetables. Soil Association member.

ISLE OF MULL

FINDHORN FOUNDATION

ISLE OF ERRAID, FIONPHORT, ISLE OF MULL PA66 6BN
Tel: 01681 700384 Contact: Paul Johnson
Organic vegetable and fruit garden, small dairy herd on tidal islet off Mull; intentional ecological community open for paying guests mid-August to mid-July.

ORKNEY ISLANDS

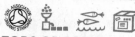

THE ORKNEY SALMON COMPANY LTD

CROWNESS POINT, HATSTON, KIRKWALL, ORKNEY KW15 1RG
Tel: 01856 876101 Fax: 01856 873846
Contact: Kirsty McCallum
Email: kamccallum@aol.com
Growers, packers and processors of organic farmed salmon. UK-wide distribution. Member of Soil Association (no. P2924).

TODS OF ORKNEY

THE GRANARY, NORTH END RD., STROMNESS KW16 3AG
Tel: 01856 850873 Fax: 01856 850213
Contact: James Stockan (Director)
Website: www.stockan-and-gardens.co.uk
Soil Association reg. no. P1905. Established over 200 years, we produce oatcakes, shortbread and other biscuits to the highest standard. The range includes sugar-free, wholemeal and organic oatcakes and petticoat tails.

ISLE OF SKYE

GLENDALE SALADS

KORNELIUS & BRIDGET HAGMANN 19 UPPER FASACH, GLENDALE, ISLE OF SKYE IV55 8WP
Tel & Fax: 01470 511349
Contact: K. Hagmann
Salads, herbs, veg and soft fruit for hotels and restaurants, and to the public through a box scheme. Varieties selected for flavour and attractiveness. Delivered chilled on regular runs several times a week. SA certificate G2263. Deliveries to IV55, IV51 & IV49.

SKYE AND LOCHALSH PERMACULTURE RUBHA PHOIL FOREST GARDEN

PIER RD., ARMADALE, ISLE OF SKYE IV45 8RS
Tel: 01471 844420 Contact: A.M. Masson
Email: skye.mail@virgin.net
Members of HDRA, Soil Association and Permaculture Association, and Centre for Alternative Technology Ecosite. Herbs, vegetables, displays and demonstration of alternative systems, (bothy) accommodation, woodland walk, otter/seal bird hide, solitude in wilderness. Organic grower. Soil Assn. licence no. GC5025/G4609.

STRATHCLYDE

BARWINNOCK HERBS

BARRHILL KA26 0RB
Tel: 01465 821338 Contact: Dave Holton
Email: herbs@barwinnock.com
Website: www.barwinnock.com
Garden and nursery with hardy plants from
a cool climate, propagated and grown
without any chemical fertilisers or
pesticides. Culinary and medicinal herbs
available by mail order.

BUTTERWORTHS ORGANIC NURSERY

GARDEN COTTAGE, AUCHINLECK ESTATE,
CUMNOCK KA18 2LR
Tel: 01290 551088
Contact: John Butterworth (Proprietor)
Soil Association reg. no. G1075. Fruit tree
nursery growing to official organic
standards since 1991. Specialists in
varieties, and advice for difficult sites. Mail
order service, visitors by arrangements
Catalogue at www.webage.co.uk/apples or
send 2 x 1st class stamps.

EPO GROWERS

KENNELS COTTAGE, HARDGATE,
DUMBARTON G81 5QR
Tel: 01389 875337
Contact: Echo Mackenzie
We grow and sell organic vegetables, herbs
and soft fruit under a Community Supported
Agriculture subscription system. Deliveries to
households in Glasgow and NW area; use
compost, manure and rock dust for fertility.

EVERGREEN WHOLEFOODS

18 NITHSDALE RD., POLLOCKSHIELDS,
GLASGOW G41 2AN
Tel: 0141 422 1303
Contact: Deborah Donohoe
Vegetarian wholefood shop with a large
selection of organic fresh fruit and veg,
grains, flour, yoghurts, spreads, nuts and
dried fruits, bread, beverages, eggs,
snacks, ice cream, ready meals.

CAROL FREIREICH

1 BURNSIDE COTTAGES,
SUNDRUM, BY AYR KA6 5JX
Tel: 01292 570617
Organic blackcurrants, redcurrants, and top
fruit in season (July-October). Collection
only.

GLENDRISSAIG GUEST HOUSE

GLENDRISSAIG, NEWTON STEWART RD.,
GIRVAN KA26 0HJ
Tel & Fax: 01465 714631
Contact: Findlay & Kate McIntosh
Modern detached country house with
welcoming atmosphere and wonderful
views. Spacious rooms with en suite
facilities. Traditional home cooking
including vegetarian meals with our own
organic produce and spring water.

GREENCITY WHOLEFOODS

23 FLEMING ST., GLASGOW G31 1PQ
Tel: 0141 554 7633 Fax: 0141 556 5589
Contact: Alan Macbeth
Email: greencity@net.ntl.com
Website: www.websites.ntl.com/~greencity
Wholesaler of natural and organic and
vegetarian wholefoods throughout
Scotland. Certified organic by the Soil
Association (licence no. P2370).

NATURALLY

8 FINLARIG STREET, SOUTH ROGERFIELD,
GLASGOW G34 0AD
Tel & Fax: 0141 773 3241
Contact: Diana Schad
Member of Real Nappy Association.
Fabulous choice of natural baby goods and
children's clothes, natural toiletries, soft
and wooden toys, books on natural
parenting and cartoon-free children's
books.

SCOTTISH HERBAL SUPPLIES
108 KINNELL AVENUE,
GLASGOW G52 3RZ
Tel & Fax: 0141 882 7001
Contact: M. Robertson
Email: sshm@herbalmedicine.org.uk
Website: www.herbalmedicine.org.uk
Medical herbalists with established mail
order supply of organic herbs and essential
oils. Soil Association no. P2020.

     S.O.S.

SCULLIONS ORGANIC SUPPLIES
143 STAMPERLAND GARDENS,
CLARKSTON, GLASGOW G76 3LJ
Tel: 0141 638 6200: Fax: 0141 881 1373
Contact: Joyce Scullion Email:
orders@scullionsorganicsupplies.co.uk
Website: www.scullionsorganicsupplies.co.uk
Glasgow's first all organic retailer
established December 98. SOPA certified
products on offer: dairy, fruit and veg,
bakery, meats, poultry, fish, general
groceries, toiletries and skincare.

   S TAIR ORGANICS

S TAIR ORGANICS
11 THE YETTS, TARBOLTON KA5 5NT
Tel: 01292 541369 Fax: 0870 1215831
Contact: Steve Hilbourne
Email: steve@cairngorms.com
We are a small market garden supplying to
a box scheme, but also high quality
saladings to local hotels. Soil Association
symbol no. G2036. Deliveries within the
KA5 area.

SUNDRUM ORGANICS
UNIT 5, HIGH HOUSE INDUSTRIAL ESTATE,
AUCHINLECK KA18 2AL
Tel & Fax: 01290 426770
Contact: Steve Wall
Email: sales@sundrum.force9.co.uk
Website: www.sundrum.co.uk
SA Symbol R1574. Vegetarian and vegan
only. Deliver to postcodes G, KA, ML, PA,
DG.

   TOTAL ORGANICS

168 KILMARNOCK RD., SHAWLANDS,
GLASGOW G41 3PG
Tel: 0141 401 8050 Fax: 0141 401 8051
Contact: Martin Fraser
Email: glasgow@totalorganics.com
Website: www.totalorganics.com
We supply only certified organic foods (over
1600 lines): fresh fruit and veg, chilled
foods, fresh meat and poultry, groceries,
beers and wines, natural remedies and
bodycare products. We are certified with
the Soil Association. We cater for many
people on special diets.

TAYSIDE

HIGHLAND HEALTH STORE
7 & 16 ST. JOHN ST., PERTH PH1 5SP
Tel: 01738 628102 Fax: 01738 447541
Contact: John Ritchie
Organic wholefoods—cereals, nuts, dried
fruit, herbal teas, coffees, condiments,
chocolate, biscuits, chilled produce, bread,
gluten-free products, soya milks, juices.

LURGAN FARM SHOP
DRUMDEWAN, BY ABERFELDY PH15 2JQ
Tel: 01887 829303 Fax: 01887 829303
Contact: Sally Murray
Members of SOPA (no. 200), we specialise
in home-produced blackface lamb and
Highland beef. Organic vegetables and
fruit, large range of organic groceries,
hand-made preserves and ready meals
prepared in shop kitchen. Mail order, veg
boxes and delivery service to PH
postcodes.

Wales

CARMARTHEN-SHIRE

BLACK MOUNTAIN FOODS
CWMCOCHIED, CWMDU,
LLANDEILO SA19 7EE
Tel & Fax: 01558 685018
Contact: Peter Mitchell
Soil Association certified (G1802)
wholesaler of meat and poultry. Weekly
deliveries to London, Midlands and the M4
corridor. Specialist suppliers to retail
butchers.

FRONUN FARM ORGANIC VEGETABLES
FRONUN, ABERGWILI,
CAMARTHEN SA32 7EP
Tel & Fax: 01267 223 979
Contact: Greg Nutgens
Email: fronun@merlinshill.freeserve.co.uk
We are a small organic market garden
growing a wide range of salads and
vegetables including unusual products such
as florence fennel, ruby chard, sugar snap
peas, horseradish and oyster mushrooms.

E.L.HARRIS
TYCOCH FARM, TALIARIS,
LLANDEILO SA19 7UU
Tel: 01558 685388 Contact: E. L. Harris
Organic grass grazing for livestock, cattle
and sheep. Soil Association licensed
organic farm.

HERBS AT MYDDFAI
BEILIGLAS, MYDDFAI,
NR. LLANDOVERY SA20 0QB
Tel: 01550 720494 Contact: Gill Swan
Email: beiliglas@aol.com
Small nursery specialising in aromatic and
medicinal plants, display garden in
peaceful surroundings. Friendly B&B or
self-catering cottage with a wide range of
vegetables available in season.

IECHYD DA
11 BROAD ST., LLANDOVERY SA20 0AR
Tel: 01550 720703
Contact: Mr J. Nisbett (Proprietor)
General health foods etc., organic fresh
veg, dried fruit, yoghurts, coffee, cider
vinegar, tofu, bread, tea, soya milk, rice,
pasta, flour, oats and bran.

JAC BY THE STOWL—HUMUNGUS FUNGUS
PEHRHIW HOUSE, LLANDDEUSANT,
LLANGADOG SA19 9YW
Tel & Fax: 01550 740306
Email: mushrooms.jac@virgin.net
Website: www.jac-by-the-stowl.co.uk
Soil Association licenced (nos.
GC5020/P4068 & R5236). Growers of
organic shiitake mushrooms and producers
of organic mushroom spawn.

ORIEL JONES AND SON LTD
TEIFI PARK, LLANBYDDER SA40 9QE
Tel: 01570 480284 Fax: 01570 480260
Contact: Meinir Thomas
Lamb, beef meet processing and packing
plant. Abattoir.

MAESTROYDDYN ORGANICS

MAESTROYDDYN FACH, HARFORD,
LLANWRDA SA19 8DU
Tel: 01558 650774 Contact: S. J. Wallis
Producers of organic beef from traditional
Hereford cattle and lamb from Portland
Llanwendg, Dorset Horn and Rough Fell
sheep. Soil Association reg. no. G4251.

ORGANICS TO GO

WERNDOLAU FARM, GOLDEN GROVE,
CARMARTHEN SA32 8NE
Tel: 0800 458 2524 (Freephone)
Fax: 01558 668088 Contact: Roger Hallam
Email: mail@organics2go.co.uk
Website: www.organics2go.co.uk
Soil Association registered delivery service
of vegetables & fruit—order from 40+
varieties each week or various size boxes.
Delivery in London, Bristol, Cardiff,
Carmarthenshire. See display ad.

CEREDIGION

GARTHENOR

GARTHENOR, LLANIO ROAD,
NR. TREGARON SY25 6UR
Tel & Fax: 01570 493347
Contact: Chris and Sally King
Garthenor is a small farm specialising in
minority breeds of sheep for traditional
meat, fine fleeces and knitting yarn. Also
free range eggs, vegetables in season and
self-catering holiday annexe. Soil
Association licence no. G4388.

GO MANGO WHOLEFOODS

4+5 BLACK LION MEWS, HIGH ST.,
CARDIGAN SA43 1HJ
Tel: 01239 614727 Fax: 01239 613653
Contact: Chris and Jane Abri
Wholefood shop with organic aims. Large
range and friendly staff.

THE HIVE ON THE QUAY

CADWGAN PLACE,
ABERAERON SA46 0BU
Tel: 01545 570445 Contact: Sarah Holgate
Housed in a converted coal wharf
overlooking Aberaeron Harbour, our café-
restaurant specialises in local seafood,
salads and European cooking—the honey
ice cream is a must. All seasonal—please
phone.

LLUEST GROWERS

LLUEST Y CONSCIENCE, TREFENTER,
ABERYSTWYTH SY23 4HE
Tel: 01974 272218 Contact: John Crocker
Small family business growing a wide
range of in season vegetables and salads to
Soil Association standards. Licence no.
G2225.

MAETHY MEYSYDD

16 CHALYBEAT ST., ABERYSTWYTH SY23
Tel: 01970 612946
Contact: D.M. Parkin (Proprietor)
Home made bread, organic flours, grains,
cereals, fruit, nuts, pulses, chocolate,
yoghurts, seeds, wine, beer, tea, herbs.
Delivery service.

MULBERRY BUSH

2 BRIDGE STREET, LAMPETER SA48 7HG
Tel: 01570 423317 Fax: 01570 423317
Contact: Stella Smith
Friendly shop selling organic food, wines,
herbal and dietary supplements, vegetarian
food and pet food.

ORGANIC FARM FOODS

LLAMBED ENTERPRISE PARK,
TREGARON RD., LAMPETER SA48 8LT
Tel: 01570 423099 Fax: 01570 423280
Widest range of fresh fruit and vegetables
available for supermarkets, wholesalers,
retailers and processors.

PENBRYN ORGANIC CHEESE
TY-HEN, SARNAU, LLANDYSUL SA44 6RD
Tel & Fax: 01239 810347
Contact: Mrs A. Degen
Email: penbryn.cheese@talk21.com
Members of Soil Association (no. G528)
and Specialist Cheesemakers Association.
Family business producing organic cheese
since 1989 using a unpasteurised milk
from our own Friesian/MRI herd.

RACHEL'S ORGANIC DAIRY
UNIT 63, GLANYRAFON INDUSTRIAL
ESTATE, ABERYSTWYTH SY23 2AE
Tel: 01970 625805 Fax: 01970 626591
Contact: Lindsay Collin and Margaret Oakley
Email: enqs@rachelsdairy.co.uk
Website: www.rachelsdairy.co.uk
Rachel's Dairy Organic dairy products,
made solely from fresh liquid milk, organic
fruit, organic sugar and live cultures. No
flavours, colours, preservatives or stabilisers
used. Soil Association member. Nationwide
coverage.

REBBECK & HOLDEN
BWLCHWERNEN FAWR, LLANGYBI,
LAMPETER SA48 8PS
Tel: 01570 493244 Contact: Nick Rebbeck
Email: nick.rebbeck@virgin.net
Soil Association Symbol no. H09WW.
Established 1973. Ayrshire dairy herd of
60, 6 x beef cross Welsh Black 12 acres of
oats, 12 acres of carrots. Farmed at 750
feet.

RIVERSIDE HEALTH
ADPAR, NEWCASTLE EMLYN SA38 9EE
Tel: 01239 710965
Contact: Simon (Owner)
Small friendly wholefood shop with a fair
selection of organic foods including an
organic fruit and veg section.

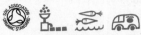

THE TREEHOUSE
14 BAKER ST., ABERYSTWYTH SY23 2BJ
Tel: 01970 615791
Contact: Jane Burnham (Owner)
We have a ten acre market garden growing
vegetables and fruit which are retailed in
our organic food shop and made into
delicious meals in our restaurant.

TROPICAL FOREST PRODUCTS
PO BOX 92, ABERYSTWYTH SY23 1AA
Tel & Fax: 01970 832511
Contact: David Wainwright (M.D.)
Email: tfp@netmatters.co.uk
Soil Association no. P923. Importers,
packers and sellers of exotic honey. We
have a particular interest in promoting the
produce of traditional regional artisans.
Our Zambian and Tanzanian honey and
wax carry Soil Association approval.

WELSH INSTITUTE
OF RURAL STUDIES
UNIVERSITY OF WALES,
ABERYSTWYTH SY23 3AL
Tel: 01970 622248 Fax: 01970 622238
Contact: Dr N.H. Lampkin (Co-ordinator)
Email: nhl@aber.ac.uk Website:
www.wirs.aber.ac.uk/research/organic
Research and development of organic
farming systems (techniques, economics,
policy); BSc degree in agriculture with
organic agriculture; training courses for
producers; Welsh organic demonstration
farm network; 40 hectare organic beef and
sheep unit.

WINDSOR HEALTH CENTRE
42 TERRACE RD., ABERYSTWYTH SY23 2AE
Tel: 01970 612915 Fax: 01970 627055
Contact: M.T. Lawrence
Email: win01@btinternet.co.uk
Comprehensive range of high quality hypo
allergenic and good selection of organic
non fresh foods and comestibles.

CLWYD

   BRYN COCYN

ORGANIC BEEF & LAMB
BRYN COCYN, LLANNEFYDD,
DENBIGH LL16 5DH
Tel: 01745 540207 Contact: Patrick Noble
Farm shop selling home produced beef
and lamb from our long-established
organic upland farm. Soil Association
license no. G727.

 COUNTRY KITCHEN
10 SEAVIEW ROAD,
COLWYN BAY LL29 8DG
Tel: 01492 533329
Contact: David or Sally Frith
General independent natural food store in
business for 15 years: vitamin
supplements, organic products, pre-
ordered organic fruit and vegetables
available from shop from 11 a.m. weekly
on Fridays. Willing to order individual
requirements. Free delivery possibly within
five mile radius of shop on orders of £25
minimum.

GLAMORGAN

 BEANFREAKS LTD
3 ST. MARY ST., CARDIFF CF1 2AT
Tel & Fax: 02920 251671
Contact: Kevin Bowles (M.D.)
Supply of organic and wholefoods,
aromatherapy, allergy and cholesterol
testing service.
Also at 7 CARADOC RD., CWMBRAN
Tel: 01633 482507
And at 5 CHARTIST TOWERS,
UPPER DOCK ST., NEWPORT
Tel: 01633 666150
And at SWISS HERBAL REMEDY STORE,
18 NOLTON ST., BRIDGEND
Tel: 01656 661441

  GREEN CUISINE
87 WESTVILLE ROAD, PENYLAN,
CARDIFF CF23 5DF
Tel & Fax: 029 20498721
Contact: A. & M. Robinson
Email: greencuisine@talk21.com.
A customer choice home delivery service
from twelve page price list (meat, poultry,
eggs, dairy, groceries, fruit, veg, baked
goods, cleaning products)—not a box
scheme! OF&G no. 11UKOP00116.

 NEAL'S YARD REMEDIES
23-25 MORGAN ARCADE, CARDIFF CF1 2AF
Tel: 02920 235721
Neal's Yard Remedies manufactures and
retails natural cosmetics in addition to
stocking an extensive range of herbs,
essential oils, homeopathic remedies and
reference material.

   PENCOED ORGANIC GROWERS
FELINDRE NURSERIES, FELINDRE,
PENCOED CF35 5HU
Tel: 01656 861956 Contact: Yvonne Leslie
Produce seasonal vegetables and sell these
mainly from the farm gate over 10 months
of the year. Members of BOF, Soil
Association and HDRA.

 PULSE WHOLEFOODS
171 KINGS ROAD, CANTON,
CARDIFF CF1 9DE
Tel: 02920 225873 Contact: Ronnie Kaye
An independent wholefood shop selling
organic fruit and vegetables, wine and
wholefoods offering a friendly and helpful
service.

  SPICE OF LIFE
1 INVERNESS PLACE, ROATH,
CARDIFF CF2 4RU
Tel: 02920 487146
Wholefood shop running box scheme.

SUNSCOOP PRODUCTS LTD

UNITS K1/K2 COEDCAE LANE,
INDUSTRIAL ESTATE, LLANTRISANT,
PONTYCLUN CF72 9HG
Tel: 01443 229229 Fax: 01443 228883
Contact: John Llewellyn
Manufacturers of organic and non-organic
savoury nut products for the independent
wholesale and multiples trades. Soil
Association membership no. P2570.

URBAN ORGANICS

32 SPLOTT RD., SPLOTT, CARDIFF CF24 2DA
Tel: 029 2040 3399
Email: sales@urbanorganics.co.uk
Website: www.urbanorganics.co.uk
The only licensed organic shop in Cardiff.
Licensed with the Soil Association (P4406)
selling whole range of food from shop with
a doorstep delivery scheme in and around
Cardiff. No meat.

GWENT

ABERGAVENNY FINE FOODS

CASTLE MEADOWS PARK,
ABERGAVENNY NP7 7RZ
Tel: 01873 850001 Fax: 01873 850002
Contact: B.J. Craske
Email: sales@abergavenny.uk.com
Producers and importers of a wide range of
organic dairy products. Soil Association
approved manufacturers, processors and
packers.

IRMA FINGAL-ROCK

64 MONNOW ST., MONMOUTH NP5 3EN
Tel: 01600 712372
Contact: Tom Innes (Partner)
Email: irmafingalrock@msn.com
Website: www.rockwines.co.uk
Cheese, wine, ciders and perry, eggs,
bread, butter, olive oil, etc. Also fruit and
vegetables to order.

KEDDIE SAUCEMASTERS LTD

PRINCE OF WALES INDUSTRIAL ESTATE,
ABERCARN NP1 5AR
Tel: 01495 244721/246855 Fax: 01495
244626 Contact: Lisa Holman
Email: lholman@costa.co.uk
Manufacturer of an extensive range of
quality sauces for the retail, industrial and
catering sector. We can offer an array of
pack formats from sachets, bottles, jars,
catering to bulk formats. We are Soil
Association approved.

LITTLE MILL FARM

LLANFAENOR, NEWCASTLE,
MONMOUTH, NP25 5NF
Tel: 01600 780449
Contact: M. & A. Eggleton (Partners)
Soil Association no. G661. Small organic
farm, wildlife award winner, glorious
countryside, offering B&B by day or by
week and half board at weekends, using
our own organic meat, eggs, vegetables
and fruit.

MEDHOPE ORGANIC GROWERS

TINTERN, CHEPSTOW NP6 7NX
Tel: 01291 689797 Contact: Sally Field
Soil Association no. F02WW. Expanding
organic market garden with retail shop
open daily. Plants and refreshments also
available. Delivery service to Chepstow and
surrounding area NP6.

WHITEBROOK ORGANIC GROWERS

FLAT 2, THE RECTORY, LLANVACHES,
CALDICOT NP26 3AY
Tel: 01633 400406 Contact: Mr P. Cooper
We are organic growers producing a wide
range of vegetables, salads and a wide
range of pulses, dried fruit juices etc.
Deliver to CF5, CF4, CF3, CF2, CF1, NP4,
NP44, NP6 & NP9. Soil Association reg.
no. G59W.

WYE VALLEY PLANTS
THE NURTONS, TINTERN NP16 7NX
Tel & Fax: 01291 689253
Contact: A. Wood
Growing/selling 1000+ types of herbacious perennials including very comprehensive range of herbs. 2 acre plantsman's garden open daily except Tuesday, notable for collections of hostas, salvias and grasses.

WYEDEAN WHOLEFOODS
113 MONNOW STREET,
MONMOUTH NP25 3EG
Tel & Fax: 01600 715429
One-stop organic shopping with over 700 organic lines. Dairy and eggs, meat and poultry, bread, fruit, vegetables and commodity lines.

GWYNEDD

ANGLESEY SEA SALT CO
BRYNSIGNCYN, ANGLESEY LL61 6TQ
Tel: 01248 430871 Fax: 01248 430213
Contact: Kelly Lovitt
Email: enq@seasalt.co.uk
Website: www.seasalt.co.uk
Pure, white, organically certified (by Soil Association) sea salt, produced from the fresh waters around Anglesey. Also sea salt with organic spices. Range of eclectic salt bowls. Carriage at cost for small orders, UK wide. Free delivery for larger orders.

DIMENSIONS
15 HOLYHEAD RD., BANGOR LL57 2EG
Tel & Fax: 01248 351562
Contact: Miss Noorjahan Begum
Soil Association no. 1857. Natural food store with a huge range of organic wholefoods, fruit and veg. We have weekly deliveries within Bangor and Menai Bridge.

PENTRE BACH HOLIDAY COTTAGES
PENTRE BACH, LLWYNGWRIL,
NR. DOLGELLAU LL37 2JU
Tel: 01341 250294 Fax: 01341 250885
Contact: Margaret Smyth
emai: orgd@pentrebach.com
Website: www.pentrebach.com
Dinner, bed & breakfast, holiday cottages, free range (GMO-free) eggs, organic fruit and veg in small quantities. Offer Land Rover tours into hills to visit standing stones and find energy lines. Permaculture enthusiasts.

RHOSFAWR NURSERIES
RHOSFAWR, PWLLHELI LL53 6YA
Tel: 01766 810545
Contact: Janet Kidd (Owner)
Soil Association member no. G08WW. Small nurseries selling garden plants, etc. and organic produce. Also touring caravan and camping park.

The European Commission . . . set up the European Federation of Biotechnology Task Group on Public Perception on Biotechnology, which is specifically designed to deal with public resistance. Millions of pounds of taxpayers' money have been allocated to projects designed to persuade people of the benefits of genetic engineering.

Luke Anderson, *Genetic Engineering, Food, and Our Environment* (1999)

PEMBROKESHIRE

D. W. & C. M. EVANS
CAERFAI FARM, ST. DAVIDS,
HAVERFORDWEST SA62 6QT
Tel & Fax: 01437 720548
Contact: Wyn Evans
Email: wyn.evans@farming.co.uk
Website: www.caerfai.co.uk
Soil Association reg. no. G1644. In the
Pembrokeshire coast National Park, 140
acre organic dairy farm producing
unpasteurised milk and home made
cheeses, early potatoes. Sales from farm
shop and box schemes. Camping and self
catering cottages.

R. F. & C. HARRIS
PENBANC, GLANRHYD,
CARDIGAN SA43 3PG
Tel: 01239 881285
Contact: Richard or Catherine
Email: family.harris.penbanc@ukgateway.net
Soil Association reg. no. C1276. Dairy
farm, sell milk through AXIS. We also sell
calves and Sept-born Dorset lambs.
Members of WWOOF, COG.

T. R. E. & A. T. LATTER
PENRHIW, GOODWICK SA64 0HS
Tel: 01348 873315
Contact: Tom & Ann Latter
Soil Association reg. no. G1445. Mixed
organic farm, dairy, beef, cereals, potatoes.
Self-catering accommodation.

THE OLD RECTORY
CASTLEMARTIN SA71 5HW
Tel & Fax: 01646 661447 B&B
reservations: 01646 661677
Contact: Christopher & Emma
Younghusband
Bed and Breakfast—formerly ran Hill
House, Pewsey, Wiltshire.

THE ORGANIC WOOL COMPANY
PWLL-Y-BROGA, PONTFAEN,
FISHGUARD SA65 9TY
Tel: 07973 382813
Contact: Douglas Whitelaw (Sole Trader)
Email:
DouglasWhitelaw@organicwool.freeserve.co.uk
Manufacturer of wool products using the
wool from organic sheep. The sheep are
not dipped in OPs and the wool is washed
in soap, without the use of chemicals or
bleaches.

PENCRUGIAU
ORGANIC FARM SHOP
PENCRUGIAU, FELINDRE, FARCHOG
CRYMYCH SA41 3XH
Tel & Fax: 01239 881265
Contact: Mike Ray
Soil Association reg. no. R28WW. Grower
of a wide range of vegetables, salad and
herbs from our own farm shop, wholesale,
and delivery to retail outlets, restaurants
etc. Stockist of fruit.

THE PUMPKIN SHED
THE PUMPKIN SHED ORGANIC WALLED
GARDEN, LLANUNWAS, SOLVA SA62 6PJ
Tel: 01437 721949
Contact: Magda Piessens
We grow herbs and vegetables in an
organic walled garden. In the garden shop
we sell herb products and we have a small
herb nursery. Open April-November.
Closed Sundays.

> Two early founders of America, George
> Washington and Thomas Jefferson,
> were strong advocates of crop rotation,
> composting and other methods of
> ensuring continuing healthy soils.
>
> John Roulac, *Backyard Composting*
> (1999)

THE RESPONSIVE EARTH TRUST
PLASDWBL BIODYNAMIC FARM,
MYNACHLOG DDU, CLYNDERWEN,
DYFED SA66 7SE
Tel: 01994 419352 Contact: A. Kleinjans
Plasdwbl Farm is a Charitable Trust, run for
the benefit of students wishing to gain
practical experience in Bio-dynamic
farming and gardening, We have a Welsh
Black herd and two Jersey milkers, The farm
is 40 ha and on 4ha we grow vegetables
and forage. We make our own butter,
cheese and bread. Demeter cert. no. 111.

M. R. & T. SARRA— THE ORGANIC FARM SHOP
UPPER MILL MOOR FARM, PORTFIELD
GATE, HAVERFORDWEST SA62 3LT
Tel & Fax: 01437 762323
Contact: Romeo Sarra
150 acres organic producing potatoes,
cabbages, swedes, carrots, eggs, cereals
and beans for livestock feed. Retail shop,
full range of groceries, fruit and veg. Soil
Association certified (no. G621). Delivery
to box schemes. Specialise in potatoes,
delivered UK, direct by pallet.

WELSH HOOK MEAT CENTRE LTD
WOODFIELD, WITHYBUSH ROAD,
HAVERFORDWEST SA62 4BW
Tel: 01437 768876 Fax: 01437 768877
Email: ordering@welsh-organic-meat.co.uk
Website: www.welsh-organic-meat.co.uk
Wholesale catering butchers specialising in
pork, beef, lamb, veal and poulty, home
made sausages and burgers. Twice weekly
deliveries to London and M4 corridor. Soil
Association no. P1773. See display ad.

WHOLEFOODS OF NEWPORT
EAST STREET,
NEWPORT/TREFDRAETH SA42 0SY
Tel & Fax: 01239 820773
Contact: Reg Atkinson
Retailers of natural foods, specialising in
local produce. Frozen and chilled foods,
ready meals and snacks, lots of organics
including fruit and vegetables, cheeses and
wines, alternative remedies, body care.
Delivery service to SA42 postcode area.

POWYS

BACHELDRE WATERMILL
CHUCHSTOKE, MONTGOMERY SY15 6TE
Tel & Fax: 01588 620489
Contact: Tony Jay (Partner)
Email: jay@bacheldremill.freeserve.co.uk
Website: www.go2.co.uk/bacheldremill
Soil Association reg. no. P1638. Millers of
stoneground strong organic and traditional
flours, for baking and other products.
Organic flours commended in 1999
Organic Food Awards. Self catering
apartments to let adjacent to watermill.
Touring caravan site also.

BHC (HONEY SUPPLIERS) LTD
UNIT 3, FFRWDGRECH INDUSTRIAL
ESTATE, BRECON LD3 8LA
Tel: 01874 622335 Fax: 01874 623141
Email: bhchoney@aol.com
Website: bhchoneysuppliers.co.uk
Pack organic honey as certified by the Soil
Association (reg. no. P1059).

Pinkerton private detective agency, which used to supply employers with auxilaries
to break trade unions, has been hired by Monsanto to check that farmers are not
saving seeds. . . . A freephone hotline has also been set up to encourage farmers to
tell on their neighbours for seed-saving.

Luke Anderson, *Genetic Engineering, Food, and Our Environment* (1999)

BLOOMING THINGS

Y BWTHYN, CYMERAU, GLANDYFI,
MACHYNLLETH SY20 8SS
Tel: 01654 781256 Fax: 01654 781256
Contact: Dale & Wyn Garnes
Family run organic nursery, Soil Association
registered (no. G2319). Producing herb,
vegetable and wild flower plugs and pots
for growing on/planting out. Retail through
mail order. Wholesale inquiries welcome.

**CENTRE FOR ALTERNATIVE
TECHNOLOGY**

MACHYNLLETH SY20 9AZ
Tel: 01654 702400 Fax: 01654 702782
Contact: Marketing Officer
Email: help@catinfo.demon.co.uk
Website: www.cat.org.uk
Established in 1974, the Centre for
Alternative Technology is an internationally
renowned display and education centre,
promoting practical ideas and information
on technologies which sustain rather than
damage the environment. The Centre
inspires and enables people to soften their
impact on the natural world in a number
of different, but interrelated ways:
demonstrating working alternative
technologies, developing the Alternative
Technology Association, publishing a
quarterly magazine *Clean Slate*, operating a
range of exciting educational services,
running a residential courses programme,
promoting a mail order service of books
and products, offering an alternative
technology information service.

**COMPOST
TECHNOLOGY LTD**

TREWERN, WELSHPOOL SY21 8EA
Tel & Fax: 01938 570678
Contact: Edwin Kentfield
Manufacturers of Cluck!, the unique high
analysis organic fertiliser. Uses a new
patented process to obtain 5-5-5 analysis.
Deliver to UK, except N. Ireland and
offshore.

GOOD FOOD DISTRIBUTORS

35 DDOLE ROAD INDUSTRIAL ESTATE,
LLANDRINDOD WELLS LD1 6DF
Tel: 01597 824720 Freephone 0800
833068 Fax: 01597 824760
Contact: K. Powell (Owner)
Email: gfd.wholesale@btinternet.com
Website: www.goodfooddistributors.co.uk
Weekly delivery service to all parts of Wales
and West Midlands, Gloucestershire,
Lancashire, Herefordshire, Worcestershire,
Cheshire. We stock a comprehensive range of
approved and certified products associated
with the wholefood and healthfood trades,
including branded names, fruit, flour, rice,
grains, pulses, cereals, nuts, seeds, herbs.

GRAIG FARM ORGANICS

DOLAU, LLANDRINDOD WELLS LD1 5TL
Tel: 01597 851655 Fax: 01597 851991
Contact: Bob & Carolyn Kennard (Owners)
Email: sales@graigfarm.co.uk
Website: www.graigfarm.co.uk
Soil Association reg. no. P1501. Award
winning range of organic meats, including
our specialities such as Welsh Mountain
mutton, fish and pies. Mail order service
includes wide range of other organic
produce including dairy, par-baked bread
and wines. See display ad.

GWALIA FARM

GWALIA CEMMAES,
MACHYNLLETH SY20 9P2
Tel: 01650 511 377
Contact: Olivia Chandler
Peaceful smallholding with goats, hens and
sheep. Mountain views of southern
Snowdonia, excellent walking. Wholefood
vegetarian cooking using own vegetables,
fruit, eggs, milk. Machynlleth and Centre
for Alternative Technology 9 miles. Spring
water.

NETHERBOURNE FOODS LTD
UNIT 7, IRFON BUSINESS COMMUNITY, GARTH RD., BUILTH WELLS LD2 3NL
Tel: 01982 552012 Fax: 01982 552018
Contact: Geoff York
Email: netherbourne.foods@virgin.net
Soil Association accredited P1891. Teas, coffee and speciality beverages. Branded, private label and contract pack.

ORGANIGO
1 TOWER STREET, CRICKHOWELL NP8 1BL
Tel: 01873 811112 Fax: 01873 811037
Contact: James Goodsir
Email: shop@organigo.co.uk
Website: www.organigo.co.uk
New, purely organic shop specialising in vegetarian and vegan food and drink. Fresh bread, fruit and veg, dairy products and ice cream. Wines, beer, cider and spirits. Good Welsh section.

PRESTEIGNE WHOLEFOOD CO-OP
RADNOR BUILDINGS, PRESTEIGNE LD8 2AT
Tel: 01544 267392
A health food shop providing a full range of organic wholefoods, organic bread, organic fruit and vegetables, delicatessen, natural remedies and supplements.

PRIMROSE ORGANIC CENTRE
FELINDRE, BRECON LD3 0ST
Tel: 01497 847636 Contact: Paul Benham
Wide variety of vegetables, fruit and herbs grown sustainably to Soil Association symbol standard. Education courses on organic and sustainable food production. Retreat accommodation.

THE QUARRY CAFÉ
13 MAENGWYN ST.,
MACHYNLLETH SY20 8EB
Tel: 01654 702624
Contact: Michael Tomlinson
We are a wholefood café using organic flour, vegetables and other ingredients as available.

THE QUARRY SHOP
21 MAENGWYN ST.,
MACHYNLLETH SY20 8EB
Tel: 01654 702624
Contact: Michael Tomlinson
We sell organic flour, rice, oats, muesli, dried fruit, tea, coffee, marmalade, honey, pasta, yoghurts, bread, rolls, cider, vinegar, soya products, wines, beers etc.

D. RAIKES
TREBERFYDD, BWLCH, BRECON LD3 7PX
Tel: 01874 730205
Soil Association reg. no. G964. Enterprise consists of an organic Welsh Black suckler herd and beef finishing unit.

In 1996, when the UK Advisory Committee on Novel Foods and Processes approved riboflavin (vitamin B2) that had been produced with GE bacteria, they accepted as evidence of safety, data which only identified contaminants present at levels greater than 0.1%. This is clearly inadequate—in the case of L-tryptophan, the level of contamination was far less than 0.1%, and yet proved fatal.

Luke Anderson, *Genetic Engineering, Food, and Our Environment* (1999)

ASSOCIATIONS
and Organisations including Certification Bodies, Charities, Clubs, Local Groups, Education, Research and Development

ABERDEEN BIODYNAMIC LANDTRUST
BEANNACHAR, BANCHORY-DEVENICK, ABERDEEN AB12 5YL
Tel: 01224 861200 Contact: Andy Plant
Purchase of agricultural land to hold in trust for Bio-dynamic or organic food production, and support businesses renting that land.

ADAS TERRINGTON
TERRINGTON ST. CLEMENT, KINGS LYNN PE34 4PW
Tel: 01553 828621 Fax: 01553 827229
Contact: Dr Bill Cormack
(Research Team Manager)
Email: bill.cormack@adas.co.uk
Website: www.adas.co.uk
Producer of organic potatoes, vegetables, cereals and pulses to UKROFS standard. Research into stockless arable organic rotations, organic pig production, organic production of sugar beet and energy use farming systems.

AGROFORESTRY RESEARCH TRUST
46 HUNTERS MOON, DARTINGTON, TOTNES TQ9 6JT
Contact: M. Crawford
Email: mail@agroforestry.co.uk
Website: www.agroforestry.co.uk
Nursery supplying plants and seeds by mail order. Also publications on agroforestry, tree crops, fruits, nuts and forest gardening.

APPLIED RURAL ALTERNATIVES
10 HIGHFIELD CLOSE, WOKINGHAM, BERKS RG40 1DG
Tel: 0118 962 7797 Contact: D.S. Stafford
Education of the general public in organic farming and growing issues by visits, meetings and publication of papers. Send SAE for details and programmes.

BIODYNAMIC AGRICULTURAL ASSOCIATION (BDAA)
PAINSWICK INN PROJECT, GLOUCESTER STREET, STROUD, GLOUCESTER GL5 1QG
Tel & Fax: 01453 759501
Contact: Bernard Jarman
Email: bdaa@biodynamic.freeserve.co.uk
Website: www.anth.org.uk/biodynamic
Part of a worldwide movement promoting the unique Bio-dynamic approach to organic agriculture arising from Rudolf Steiner's spiritual scientific research. It operates the well respected Demeter Symbol (UK), publishes journal *Star & Furrow* and offers apprentice training in Bio-dynamic farming and gardening. A wide range of books is available.

BUTTERFLY CONSERVATION
PO BOX 222, DEDHAM, COLCHESTER CO7 6EY
Tel: 01206 322342 Fax: 01206 322739
Contact: Mrs D. Swillion
Email: butterfly@cix.compulink.co.uk
National conservation charity dedicated to saving wild butterflies, moths and their habitats.

CAMPHILL COMMUNITY— HOLYWOOD
8 SHORE ROAD, HOLYWOOD, CO. DOWN BT1 89HX
Tel: 02890 423202 Fax: 02890 397818
Contact: Miriam Muller
Vegetarian meals in café, eco-filtered water, everything organic. We also train and employ people with special needs and cover all organic foods in the shop, except meat. We provide a home bakery, café and shop selling organic foods.

CAMPHILL VILLAGE TRUST— OAKLANDS PARK
OAKLANDS PARK, NEWNHAM, GLOS GL14 1EF
Tel: 01594 516550 Fax: 01594 516821
Working community with people with special needs. Soil Association reg. no.

VOIM, Demeter 101. Involved with regional land training (Bio-dynamic), vegetables, herbs and fruit for wholesaling and box scheme. Work opportunities for many levels of ability.

CANON FROME COURT
NR LEDBURY, HEREFORDSHIRE HR8 2TD
Tel: 01531 670203 Contact: The Secretary
Email: Windflower@btinternet.com
Organic farming community comprising 18 households living in Georgian house and stable block set in 35 acres of park and farmland. WWOOFer and potential community members welcome.

CENTRE FOR ALTERNATIVE TECHNOLOGY
MACHYNLLETH, SY20 9AZ
Tel: 01654 702400 Fax: 01654 702782
Contact: Andy Rowland (Visitor Manager)
Email: help@catinfo.demon.co.uk
Website: www.cat.org.uk
Established in 1974, the Centre for Alternative Technology is an internationally renowned display and education centre, promoting practical ideas and information on technologies which sustain rather than damage the environment. The Centre inspires and enables people to soften their impact on the natural world in a number of different, but interrelated ways: demonstrating working alternative technologies, developing the Alternative Technology Association, publishing a quarterly magazine *Clean Slate*, operating a range of exciting educational services, running a residential courses programme, promoting a mail order service of books and products, offering an alternative technology information service.

COMMUNITY COMPOSTING NETWORK
67 ALEXANDRA RD., SHEFFIELD S2 3EE
Tel & Fax: 0114 258 0483
Contact: David Middlemas (Co-ordinator)
Email: ccn@gn.apc.org
Website: www.chiron-s.demon.co.uk/ccn
A national network of over 125 members promoting the environmental, social and economic benefits of community composting.

COMPASSION IN WORLD FARMING
CHARLES HOUSE, 5A CHARLES ST., PETERSFIELD, HANTS GU32 3EH
Tel: 01730 264208 Fax: 01730 260791
Email: compassion@ciwf.co.uk
Website: www.ciwf.co.uk
Pressure group lobbying and campaigning to improve conditions for livestock and poultry. See display ad.

CRAIGENCALT ECOLOGY CENTRE
CRAIGENCALT FARM, KINGHORN, FIFE KY3 9YG
Tel & Fax: 01592 891567
The Craigencalt Farm Ecology Centre is used by schools and adult groups fior ecological studies, weekend study groups and various arts/crafts persons. Visitors are welcome to come to take part, walk, birdwatch or even to pitch in with the various environmental projects.

DARTINGTON TECH—THE REGIONAL CENTRE FOR ORGANIC HORTICULTURE
WESTMINSTER HOUSE, 38/40 PALACE AVENUE, PAIGNTON, DEVON TQ3 3HB
Tel & Fax: 01803 867693
Contact: Jenny Pidgeon (Project Manager)
Email: jpidgeon@rcoh.co.uk
Website: www.rcoh.co.uk
The RCOH is an education and resource centre for the promotion of organic gardening and horticulture. We offer courses for professionals and amateurs at our Soil Association certified site (G1402).

DEMETER STANDARDS COMMITTEE OF THE BIODYNAMIC AGRICULTURAL ASSOCIATION
17 INVERLEITH PLACE, EDINBURGH EH3 5QE
Tel: 0131 624 3921 Contact: Fiona Mackie
Inspection, certification and information service for Bio-dynamic production.

EARTHWORM CO-OP LTD
WHEATSTONE, LEINTWARDINE SY7 0LH
Tel: 01547 540461 Contact: Hil Mason
Suppliers of willow for basket making, hurdles etc; venue for low cost hire for camps, courses, meetings. Demonstration wetland system and organic/veganic gardens. WWOOF host farm.

ECOTRICITY
AXIOM HOUSE, STATION ROAD,
STROUD, GLOS GL5 3AP
Tel: 01453 756111 Fax: 01453 756222
Contact: Vicki Evans/Clare Summers
Email: info@ecotricity.co.uk Website:
www.ecotricity.co.uk (under construction)
Ecotricity founded the UK's 'green'
electricity market in 1996. Ecotricity is now
the undisputed market leader in Europe.

ELM FARM RESEARCH CENTRE
HAMSTEAD MARSHALL, NEWBURY,
BERKSHIRE RG20 0HR
Tel: 01488 658298 Fax: 01488 658503
Contact: Lawrence Woodward (Director)
Email: efrc@compuserve.com
Research, advice, education on organic
farming and sustainable land use. Advisory
service provides consultancy. Research
contracts (EU, MAFF, other), educational
material. Publications, regular bulletin,
organic farm (beef and cereals).

EMERSON COLLEGE
HARTFIELD ROAD, FOREST ROW,
EAST SUSSEX RH18 5JX
Tel: 01342 822238 Fax: 01342 826055
Contact: Belinda Hammond
Email: mail@emerson.org.uk
Website: www.emerson.org.uk
Every summer we offer a one week
introductory course in Bio-dynamic
Agriculture and Gardening. From
September 2001 we will be running a 4
year full time training in Bio-dynamic
Agriculture, accredited by a Dutch college.

FARMS FOR CITY CHILDREN
NETHERCOTT HOUSE, IDDESLEIGH,
WINKLEIGH, DEVON EX19 8BG
Tel: 01837 810573 Fax: 01837 810866
Contact: Clare Morpurgo Email:
ffcc@nethercott-house.freeserve.co.uk
Website: nethercott-house.freeserve.co.uk
An educational charity, Farms for City
Children runs 3 farms, one organically,
where urban children come to stay and
help the farmers. They learn to work
together for the common good and gain a
sense of achievement.

FEDERATION OF CITY FARMS & COMMUNITY GARDENS
THE GREENHOUSE, HEREFORD ST.,
BEDMINSTER, BRISTOL BS3 4NA
Tel: 0117 923 1800 Fax: 0117 923 1900
Contact: Diane Godwin
(Information Worker)
Email: farmgarden@btinternet.com
Charity supporting community farms and
gardens. A membership lead organisation
working on behalf of community managed
farms and gardens, mainly in urban areas.
FCFCG works with the Soil Association,
NFU and others to promote healthy
organic food.

THE FOOD COMMISSION
94 WHITE LION STREET, LONDON N1 9PF
Tel: 020 7837 2250 Fax: 020 7837 1141
Contact: Ian
Email: foodcomm@compuserve.com
Website: www.foodcom.org.uk
The Food Commission campaigns for safer,
healthier food in the UK. Our magazine,
The Food Magazine, reports on genetic
engineering, additives, pesticides, food
irradiation, food labelling and animal
welfare. Sample copies available.

FRIENDS OF THE EARTH
26-28 UNDERWOOD ST., LONDON N1 7JQ
Tel: 020 7490 1555 Fax: 020 7490 0881
Contact: Info & Enquiries officer
Email: info@foe.co.uk
Website: www.foe.co.uk
Environment group with a food and Biotech
Campaign. Friends of the Earth is one of the
UK's leading pressure groups, campaigning
on a wide range of local, national and
international environmental issues. For
information on membership, publications or
your nearest local group in England, Wales
or Northern Ireland, contact the
Information and Enquiries Officer.

THE GENETICS FORUM
94 WHITE LION STREET, LONDON N1 9PF
Tel: 0171 837 9229 Fax: 0171 837 1141
Contact: Mark Raby (Co-ordinator)
Email: geneticsforum@gn.apc.org
Website: www.geneticsforum.org.uk
A charity focussing on issues concerning
genetic engineering—the UK's only public
interest group exclusively devoted to policy
development, campaigns and publications
on genetic engineering from a social,
ethical and environmental perspective.

GENEWATCH UK

THE COURTYARD, WHITECROSS ROAD,
TIDESWELL, BUXTON,
DERBYSHIRE SK17 8NG
Tel: 01298 871898 Fax: 01298 872531
Contact: Dr Sue Mayer
Email: gene.watch@dial.pipex.com
Website: www.genewatch.org
Independent policy research group which
works on the ethics and risks of genetic
engineering. Publish bi-monthly briefings,
available on subscription.

JOAN & ALAN GOULD

WOODRISING, THORN LANE,
GOXHILL, DN19 7LU
Tel: 01469 530356
Contact: Joan & Alan Gould
Email: alan@agolincs.demon.co.uk
Always willing to help with advice after a
lifetime of organic producing.

GREEN CITY CENTRAL

42-46 BETHEL ST., NORWICH NR2 1NR
Tel: 01603 631007 Contact: Tigger
The shop acts as a contact point for local
veg box scheme and is stockist of a wide
range of organic and GMO-free foods. A
resource centre offering meeting space,
offices and other facilities to local and
regional voluntary groups.

GREENPEACE UK

CANONBURY VILLAS, LONDON N1 2PN
Tel: 0171 865 8100 Fax: 0171 865 8200
Email: gp-info@uk.greenpeace.org
Website: www.greenpeace.org.uk
Environmental campaigning organisation.
Includes action against genetically modified
foods.

HENRY DOUBLEDAY RESEARCH ASSOCIATION (HDRA)

RYTON ORGANIC GARDENS,
RYTON ON DUNSMORE,
COVENTRY CV8 3LG
Tel: 024 76 303517 Fax: 024 76 639229
Contact: Jackie Gear (Exec. Director)
Email: rog@hdra.org.uk
Website: www.hdra.org.uk
The HDRA is Europe's largest organic
membership organisation, researching,
advising on and providing information
about organic gardening, growing and
food. Runs courses on a wide range of
organic and related subjects at its Ryton
headquarters. HDRA Consultants offer
consultancy in organic waste
management, organic garden design,
organic scientific research (which does not
involve animal experimentation), and
catering and retailing. HDRA runs three
demonstration gardens, at Ryton in the
Midlands, Yalding in Kent (see entry under
Kent) and Audley End nr. Saffron Walden in
Essex. All are open to the public with shops
offering gifts and organic gardening
sundries. At Ryton, the restaurant has been
listed in many national guides to good
food and the shop there offers in addition
an extensive range of food and wine.
There is also a successful vegetable box
scheme operated from Ryton Organic
Gardens shop and from Audley End.
HDRA's advice on organic growing extends
overseas to developing countries and it
gives practical agricultural advice to
subsistence farmers. The Heritage Seed
Library preserves old vegetable varieties
that would otherwise be casualties of EC
legislation. HDRA spreads the organic
message far and wide through TV, radio
and national newspaper and magazine
articles and publishes many books and
leaflets. The Organic Gardening Catalogue
produced by HDRA and Chase Organics
(see under Surrey) provides a mail order
service for organic gardening products,
seeds, books and foods.

THE HORTICULTURAL CORRESPONDENCE COLLEGE

FREEPOST, LACOCK, CHIPPENHAM,
WILTSHIRE SN15 2BR
Tel: 0800 378918 (24hrs freephone)
Contact: Mrs Janet Elms
Email: hc.college@btinternet.com
Website: www.btinternet.com/~ hc.college
Home study courses including Organic
Gardening (Soil Association symbol),
Conservation Studies, Herbs for Pleasure &
Profit, Garden Design, Leisure Gardening
plus preparation for Royal Horticultural
Society exams and Royal Forestry Society
exams. Also agriculture courses.

INTERNATIONAL FEDERATION OF ORGANIC AGRICULTURAL MOVEMENTS (IFOAM)
OEKOZENTRUM, IMSBACH, D-66636 THELEY, GERMANY
Tel: +(49) 6853-5190 Fax: +(49) 6853 30110
Contact: Bernward Geier (Exec. Director)
Email: IFOAM@t-online.de
Website: www.ifoam.org
IFOAM is the world umbrella organisation of the organic agriculture movement with 750 members. It offers publications like the directory *Organic Agriculture Worlwide* and the magazine *Ecology and Farming*, and organises international conferences and workshops.

IRISH ORGANIC FARMERS AND GROWERS ASSOCIATION (IOFGA)
ORGANIC FARM CENTRE, HARBOUR RD., KILBEGGAN, CO. WEST MEATH, IRELAND
Tel: +(353) 0506 32563 Fax: +(353) 0506 32063 Contact: Eva Draper
Email: iofga@tinet.ie
Website: www.irishorganic.ie
IOFGA is a company limited by guarantee, open to farmers, growers, consumers and others interested in the production of healthy food and the protection of the environment. IOFGA operates an inspection and certification scheme, publishes a magazine *Organic Matters* and practical information for organic farmers and growers. Producers and processors registered with IOFGA may display the IOFGA symbol on their products and produce. Details of IOFGA registered producers, processors, wholesalers and those offering box delivery, market stalls are available directly from IOFGA.

THE KINGCOMBE CENTRE
TOLLER PORCORUM, DORCHESTER DT2 0EQ
Tel: 01300 320684 Fax: 01300 321409
Email: nspring@kingcombe-centre.demon.co.uk
Website: www.kingcombe-centre.demon.co.uk
Day and residential courses on natural history, conservation and other subjects inspired by the idyllic surroundings. Large organically managed garden. Organic and locally produced food. Brochure available on request.

LACKHAM COLLEGE
LACOCK, CHIPPENHAM, WILTSHIRE SN15 2NY
Tel: 01249 443111 Fax: 0249 444474
Contact: Trevor Arnes
Email: lackham@rmplc.co.uk
A range of qualifications both part-time and full-time: City & Guilds Organic Gardening, Certificate in Organic Horticulture, National Certificate in Organic Horticulture, HND & HNC in organic crop production.

LAND HERITAGE
POUND CORNER, WHITESTONE, EXETER EX4 2HP
Tel: 01647 61099 Fax: 01647 61134
Contact: Pauline Huggins
Email: 101500.2204@compuserve.com
Website: www.hiroona.freeserve.co.uk
Registered landowning charity letting farms to tenants who farm organically. Continually seeking funds for further land purchase. Membership of Sustain (formerly SAFE Alliance). See display ad.

LITTLE ASH ECO-FARM
THROWLEIGH, OKEHAMPTON, DEVON EX20 2GQ
Tel & Fax: 01647 231394
Contact: Dr M. Kiley-Worthington & Alex Armstrong
Courses in animal welfare, animal minds, improved husbandry, self sustaining small ecological agriculture, farm walks and nature trail. Soil Association licensed beef, lamb, dairy products,cereals, vegetables, boxes, llamas, horses. Organic wool and fine fibres and garments.

MICHAEL LITTLEWOOD
TROUTWELLS, ROADWATER, NR WATCHET, SOMERSET TA23 ORN
Tel & Fax: 01984 641 330
Contact: Michael Littlewood Email: michael@ecodesigner.freeserve.co.uk
Organic landscape and garden designer. Producer of companion planting chart and designer for all types of sustainable projects anywhere, from eco villages to eco gardens.

LOWER SHAW FARM
SHAW, SWINDON, WILTSHIRE SN5 9PJ
Tel & Fax: 01793 771080
Contact: Andrea Hirsch
Email: enquiries@lsfarm.globalnet.co.uk
Website: www.swindonlink.com/lsfarm

Courses and conference centre. Programme of courses and workshops, also centre available for hire. Organic garden, chickens, sheep and ducks. SAE for details.

MOVEMENT FOR COMPASSIONATE LIVING
6 KINCROSS CRESCENT, LUTON LU3 3JS
Tel: 01582 753904 Contact: Sam Taylor
Email: Sam.Taylor1@btinternet.com
Website:
http://pages.unisonfree.net/mcl/#A
MCL publishers leaflets, booklets, and a quarterly journal *New Leaves*, it aims to inspire, inform and give practical advice on achieving a vegan lifestyle. Various booklets are produced on food, food growing, trees and the environment.

NATIONAL ASSOCIATION OF FARMERS' MARKETS
SOUTH VAULTS, GREEN PARK STATION, GREEN PARK RD., BATH BA1 1JB
Tel: 01225 787914 Fax: 01225 460840
It is generally accepted by most farmers' markets that stallholders must have grown, bred, caught, pickled, brewed or baked the goods themselves. Their main emphasis is to help local producers and processors to sell their goods direct to the public, near their source of origin, creating benefits for them and the local community.

THE NATIONAL INSTITUTE OF MEDICAL HERBALISTS
56 LONGBROOK STREET, EXETER, DEVON EX1 6AH
Tel: 01392 426022
Website: www.btinternet.com/~nimh
Professional body of practising medical herbalists. Offers details/information on all aspects of Western herbal medicine and how to source a qualified practitioner. Details on education & research available.

NORFOLK ORGANIC GARDENERS
6 OLD GROVE COURT, NORWICH NR3 3NL
Tel: 01603 403415
Contact: Janet Bearman
Email: norfolkorganic@cwcom.net
Website: www.norfolkorganic.mcmail.com
Local group of Soil Association and HDRA. We aim to promote the organic movement in Norfolk by increasing public awareness of organic methods of farming and gardening.

THE NORTH WALES ORGANIC GROWERS AND PERMACULTURE GROUP
PEN-Y-BRYN, TALWRN, LLANGEFNI, YNYS MON LL77 7SP
Tel: 01248 723639 Contact: Kath Turner
Group of 50 members who hold meetings, run courses, have talks, plant swaps, show videos, arrange trips to other organic and permaculture farms etc. Produce a newsletter. Have set up a farmers' market and forest garden project. Future projects include setting up a box scheme, community woodland, eco centre.

THE ORGANIC CONSULTANCY
101 ELSENHAM ST., LONDON SW18 5NY
Tel: 020 8870 5383 Fax: 020 8870 8140
Contact: Simon Wright
Email: simon@organic-consultancy.com
Website: www.organic-consultancy.com
I help companies develop organic processed food and drink. I am a board member of UKROFS and sit on two Soil Association processing committees.

ORGANIC FARMERS AND GROWERS LTD
THE ELIN CENTRE, LANCASTER ROAD, SHREWSBURY SY1 3LE
Tel: 01743 440512 Fax: 01743 461481
Organic Farmers and Growers is the 2nd largest sector body in the UK, licensed to certify all aspects of organic productions processing and retailing, with well over 1000 participating members.

ORGANIC FARMERS SCOTLAND
BLOCK 2, UNIT 4, BANDEATH INDUSTRIAL ESTATE, THROSK, STIRLING FK7 7XY
Tel: 01786 817581 Fax: 01786 816100
Contact: Murray Cameron Email: enquiries@organicfrmssco.demon.co.uk
Website: Soon!
Scottish producer marketing co-operative organic beef, lamb, cereals, animal feedstuffs, etc. Delivery to all of UK.

ORGANIC FOOD FEDERATION
UNIT 1, MANOR ENTERPRISE CENTRE, MOWLES MANOR, ETLING GREEN, DEREHAM NR20 3EZ
Tel: 01362 637314 Fax: 01362 637980
Contact: J. Wade (Executive Secretary)
Trade federation for the organic food industry representing manufacturers and processors of organic foods and importers

of finished product and raw materials and ingredients. Authorised by United Kingdom Register of Organic Food Standards (UKROFS) as a certifying body for above categories. Representation at governmental, EEC and non-governmental level. Lobbying, trade information, etc. Certified members can use the federation symbol on packaging.

OTLEY COLLEGE

OTLEY, IPSWICH, SUFFOLK IP6 9EY
Tel: 01473 785543 Fax: 01473 785353
Contact: R. Staines
Email: course_enquiries@otleycollege.ac.uk
Website: www.otleycollege.ac.uk
Otley provides a wide range of training in organics, conservation and sustainable systems, including Commercial Organic Production, Holistic Horticulture, Horticultural Therapy, an HNC in sustainable environments, plus conventional agricultural & horticultural courses.

PENRHOS SCHOOL OF FOOD & HEALTH

KINGTON HR5 3LH
Tel: 01544 230720 Fax: 01544 230754
Contact: Martin Griffiths
Email: daphne@penrhos.co.uk
Website: www.penrhos.co.uk
Chef/nutritionist runs courses on food and health. Soil Association no. E2051. Green Cuisine 2000, eco/organic events. See display ad.

PERMACULTURE LONDON

c/o JUDITH HANNA, 15 JANSONS ROAD, LONDON, N15 4JU
Email: jehanna@gn.apc.org
Contact: Judith Hanna
Design for Sustainability: Consultancy & Courses. 'Permaculture' is an internationally recognised approach to designing that is nature-friendly, people-friendly and based on 'fair shares'. We provide design consultancy, two-day introductory courses and 72-hour certificate courses.

PERSHORE COLLEGE

AVONBANK, PERSHORE, WORCS WR10 3JP
Tel: 01386 552443 Fax: 01386 556528
Contact: John Edgeley
Email: Postmaster@pershore.ac.uk
Website: www.pershore.ac.uk
5-hectare organic fruit and vegetable production unit. Training courses and consultancy, apple juicing. Greengrowers Organic Product Ltd. Member of Soil Association (reg. nos G532, P2016). Farmers' markets.

PLANTS FOR A FUTURE

THE FIELD, HIGHER PENPOL, ST. VEEP, LOSTWITHIEL, CORNWALL PL22 0NG
Tel: 01208 873554
Contact: Elaine Avery (Coordinator)
Day visits and tours, courses on woodland gardening, permaculture, nutrition, research, information, demonstration and supply of edible and otherwise useful plants. Plants for a Future is a registered charity researching and demonstrating ecologically sustainable vegan organic horticulture in the form of woodland gardening and other permacultural practices.

PRIMROSE ORGANIC CENTRE

FELINDRE, BRECON LD3 0ST
Tel: 01497 847 636 Contact: Paul Benham
Wide variety of vegetables, fruit and herbs grown sustainably to Soil Association symbol standard. Education courses on organic and sustainable food production. Retreat accommodation.

PROPER JOB

3 FERNLEIGH, NEW ST., CHAGFORD TQ13 8BD
Tel & Fax: 01647 432616
Contact: Jo Hodges
Email: properjob@chagfd.freeserve.co.uk
Community business. Holistic co-op. Developing from waste to resource issues. Especially composting, collecting compostables, education/consciousness raising. Organic veg production and sale in our community shop/café. Setting up training in related issues. Organic collection round.

Associations etc

RARE BREEDS SURVIVAL TRUST
NATIONAL AGRICULTURE CENTRE,
KENILWORTH CV8 2LG
Tel: 024 7669 6551 Fax: 024 7669 6706
Contact: Richard Lutwyche
Email: postmaster@rare-breeds.com
Website: www.rare-breeds.com
A national charity devoted to the
preservation and conservation of rare
breeds of farm livestock. The trust's
traditional breeds meat marketing scheme
includes some organic produce.

THE REAL NAPPY ASSOCIATION
PO BOX 3704, LONDON SE26 4RX
Tel: 020 8299 4519
Contact: Maeve Murphy & Gina Purrman
The Real Nappy Association is the central
source for information and advice on all
nappy related issues, for local authorities,
health professionals, the media and
individuals. For free parent information
pack send a large sae with two stamps.

REDFIELD COMMUNITY
BUCKINGHAM RD., WINSLOW MK18 3LZ
Tel: 01296 713661 Fax: 01296 714983
Contact: Chris Reid (Secretary)
Email: 106031.2416@compuserve.com
Intentional community in its 21st year.
Includes 17 acre organic smallholding.
Regular events on communities and co-
operative living. See display ad.

THE RESPONSIVE EARTH TRUST
PLASDWBL BIODYNAMIC FARM,
MYNACHLOG DDU, CLYNDERWEN,
DYFED SA66 7SE
Tel: 01994 419352 Contact: A. Kleinjans
Plasdwbl Farm is a Charitable Trust, run for
the benefit of students wishing to gain
practical experience in Bio-dynamic
farming and gardening, We have a Welsh
Black herd and two Jersey milkers. The farm
is 40 hectares and on 4 hectares we grow
vegetables and forage. We make our own
butter, cheese and bread. Demeter certified
(no. 111).

RUSKIN MILL
OLD BRISTOL RD., NAILSWORTH GL6 0QE
Tel: 01453 837500 Fax: 01453 837512
Contact: Julian Pyzer
Café and shop, crafts, exhibitions,
workshops, concerts, storytelling and talks.
Part of special needs further education
college with Bio-dynamic market garden
and mixed farm.

SCOTTISH AGRICULTURAL COLLEGE
CRAIBSTONE ESTATE, BUCKSBURN,
ABERDEEN AB21 9YA
Tel: 01224 711072 Fax: 01224 711293
Contact: David Younie
(Organic Farming Specialist)
Email: d.younie@ab.sac.ac.uk
Two organic mixed farms (research and
demonstration), provision of advice as part
of Scottish Executive Organic Aid Scheme,
organic telephone helpline (01224
711072). Diploma, masters and distance
learning courses in organic farming.

SCOTTISH ORGANIC PRODUCERS ASSOCIATION (SOPA)
MILTON OF CAMBUS, DOUNE,
PERTHSHIRE FK16 6HG
Tel & Fax: 01786 841657
Contact: Carolyn Beattie
Email: contact@sopa.demon.co.uk
Certifying organisation. SOPA promotes
the interests of organic producers in
Scotland under the Scottish Organic label.
It operates a verification and certification
system for organic produce approved by
UKROFS.

SEA SPRING PHOTOS
LYME VIEW, WEST BEXINGTON,
DORCHESTER, DORSET DT2 9DD
Tel: 01308 897892 Fax: 01308 897735
Email: joy.michaud:btinternet.com
Contact: Joy Michaud
A slide library specialising in organic
agriculture and horticulture. Organic
Holdings registration number is available
with each image. Vegetable photographs
normally include variety, name and
management details.

SKYE AND LOCHALSH PERMACULTURE, RUBHA PHOIL FOREST GARDEN
PIER RD., ARMADALE, ISLE OF SKYE IV45 8RS
Tel: 01471 844420
Contact: A.M. Masson (Owner-Guardian)
Memer of HDRA, Soil Association and
Permaculture Association, and Centre for
Alternative Technology Ecosite. Herbs,
vegetables, displays and demonstration of
alternative systems, holiday
accommodation, woodland walk,
otter/bird hide, solitude in wilderness.

THE SOIL ASSOCIATION
BRISTOL HOUSE, 40-56 VICTORIA STREET,
BRISTOL BS1 6BY
Tel: 0117 929 0661 Fax: 0117 925 2504
Email: info@soilassociation.org
Website: www.soilassociation.org
The Soil Association exists to research,
develop and promote sustainable
relationships between the soil, plants,
animals and people in order to produce
healthy food and other products while
protecting and enhancing the
environment. The Soil Association is a
membership charity founded in 1946 to
campaign for and assist organic food
production. We produce a quarterly
magazine for our members called *Living
Earth* and a more specialist magazine
Organic Farming for farmers and
growers. The Soil Association has been at
the forefront of the campaign against GM
foods, guaranteeing that there is no
place for GMOs in organic food or
farming.

SOIL ASSOCIATION CERTIFICATION
LTD.
BRISTOL HOUSE, 40-56 VICTORIA STREET,
BRISTOL, BS1 6BY
Tel: 0117 914 2405
Fax: 0117 925 2504
Email: cert@soilassociation.org
Soil Association Certification Limited is the
largest of the UK certification bodies and
currently inspects and certifies over 70% of
UK licensed organic producers and
processors. We certify to the Soil
Association Standards for Organic Food
and Farming which are respected
worldwide. The well known Soil
Association Organic Symbol, featured in
this book and displayed on much organic
food and packaging, is widely recognised
and trusted by consumers.

STALLCOMBE HOUSE
SANCTUARY LANE, WOODBURY
SALTERTON, DEVON EX5 1EX
Tel: 01395 232373
Contact: Ms G. Ritchie-Smith
Residential care home for people with
learning difficulties producing fresh
organic garden produce, free range eggs
and granola with maximum involvement
from residents.

SUSTAIN
94 WHITE LION ST., LONDON N1 9PF
Tel: 020 7 837 1228 Fax: 020 7 837 1141
Email: sustain@sustainweb.org
Website: www.sustainweb.org
Formerly the Sustainable Agriculture, Food
and Environment Alliance and the National
Food Alliance. Campaigns for sustainable
food and farming.

THE SUSTAINABLE LIFESTYLES
RESEARCH CO-OP LTD
POND COTTAGE EAST,
CUDDINGTON RD., DINTON,
BUCKS HP18 0AD
Tel: 01296 747737 Fax: 01296 748278
Contact: Mike George
Email: mike.george@euphony.net
70 acre permaculture farm run by a
workers co-op. Organic box scheme, free
range eggs, subscription livestock,
community orchard, public access and
involvement. Developing eco-housing,
craft workshops, education facilities,
permanent wetlands alongside river
Thame.

TURNERS' FIELD PERMACULTURE
COMPTON DUNDON, SOMERTON,
SOMERSET TA11 6PT
Tel: 01458 442192 Contact: Ann Morgan
Email: annmorgan@ukf.net
Developing $3^1/2$ acres as a residential
organic permaculture garden—learning
and teaching skills and knowledge in all
aspects of ecologically and socially
sustainable living.

UNITED KINGDOM
REGISTER OF ORGANIC FOOD
STANDARDS (UKROFS)
NOBEL HOUSE, 17 SMITH SQUARE,
LONDON SW1P 3JR
Tel: 020 7238 5915
The United Kingdom certification authority
for organically produced foods.

WELSH INSTITUTE OF RURAL
STUDIES
UNIVERSITY OF WALES, ABERYSTWYTH,
CEREDIGION SY23 3AL
Tel: 01970 622248 Fax: 01970 622238
Contact: Dr N.H. Lampkin (Co-ordinator)
Email: nhl@aber.ac.uk Website:
www.wirs.aber.ac.uk/research/organic
Research and development of organic
farming systems (techniques, economics,

policy); BSc degree in agriculture with organic agriculture; training courses for producers; Welsh organic demonstration farm network; 40-hectare organic beef and sheep unit.

WHITEHOLME FARM
WHITEHOLME, ROWELTOWN, CARLISLE, CUMBRIA CA6 6L5
Tel: 016977 48058/48331
Contact: Mike Downham
Soil Association symbol (G797A) certified organic beef, lamb and pork, sold direct from the farm to private customers locally. Also sale of organically certified breeding and store cattle. Organic resources centre (day or residential visits) opening October 2000.

WILLING WORKERS ON ORGANIC FARMS (WWOOF)
PO BOX 2675, LEWES, EAST SUSSEX BN7 1RB
Tel & Fax: 01273 476286
Contact: Fran Whittle
Email: fran@wwoof-uk.freeserve.co.uk
Website: www.phdcc.com/wwoof
A worldwide exchange network where bed and board and practical experience are given in return for work on organic farms for holiday breaks, travel or changing to a rural life.

WOMENS ENVIRONMENTAL NETWORK
87 WORSHIP ST., LONDON EC2A 2BE
Tel: 020 7481 9004 Fax: 020 7481 9144
Email: wenuk@gn.apc.org
Website: www.gn.apc.org/wen
WEN aims to educate, empower and inform on matters. Campaigns include encouraging local organic food growing projects, waste minimisation, health and the environment, sanitary protection and nappies.

WORLD ORGANIC COMMODITY EXCHANGE LTD (WOCX)
THE WHITE HOUSE, KINGS RIDE, ASCOT, BERKSHIRE SL5 7JR
Tel: Fax: Contact: Jo-Anne Johnston
Email: jo@wocx.net www.wocx.net
Website: www.wocx.net
The single global source of certified organic products. Visit our website or contact Jo-Anne Johnston for further information.

Y DRAIG GOCH
BLAENCWMBYCHAN, FELONGGWM-UCHAF, NANTGAREGM CARMARTHEN, DYFED SA32 7QA
Contact: R. Williams
Holistic centre for the preservation of the natural environment for the benefit of human beings using self-sustaining renewable energy sources for self-realisation.

Now one of the most exclusive villages in which to own a house, East Portlemouth was in the last century a somewhat run down hamlet populated by sailors, fishermen and wreckers. Owned by the absent Duke of Cleveland, his agents informed him that as the villagers would not work the land properly and only cared for the sea, it was a needless expense to keep them as tenants. In something akin to the 18th and 19th century Highland Clearances, almost half the population was evicted and their cottages demolished, then the land was made into three large farms. In 1880 Portlemouth's plight came to the attention of the national press, and as a result the Duchess of Cleveland paid for the restoration of the parish church.

Jane Fitzgerald, *Off the Map* (2000)

PUBLISHERS AND PUBLICATIONS

Many of the organisations in the previous section produce their own publications.

COUNTRY SMALLHOLDING
STATION RD., NEWPORT,
SAFFRON WALDEN, ESSEX CB11 3PL
Tel: 01799 540922 Fax: 01799 541367
Contact: Helen Sears (Editor)
Email: helen@countrysmallholding.com
Website: www.countrysmallholding.com
Published monthly, it covers organic growing, small scale poultry management and breeds, waterfowl, sheep, goats, bees, rabbits, trees, crafts, DIY, cookery, country courses and events, competitions and reader offers. Mail order book and video service—over 800 titles. Call for free sample issue.

ECO-LOGIC BOOKS
19 MAPLE GROVE, BATH BA2 3AF
Tel: 01225 484472 Fax: 0117 9420164
Contact Peter Andrews
Email: books@eco-logic.demon.co.uk
Specialise in mail order selling of books that provide practical solutions to environmental problems including permaculture, organic gardening, eco-design and energy efficiency. All

GREEN BOOKS
FOXHOLE, DARTINGTON, TOTNES,
DEVON TQ9 6EB
Tel: 01803 863260 Fax: 01803 863843
Email: sales@greenbooks.co.uk
Website: www.greenbooks.co.uk
The publishers of this book, as well as many others on organics and related subjects. They include *The Organic Baby Book, The Organic Baby & Toddler Cookbook,* and *Genetic Engineering, Food and Our Environment.* See display ad.

HEALTH FOOD BUSINESS
CLAREMONT HOUSE, 12-18 CLAREMONT
RD., WEST BYFLEET, SURREY KT14 6DY
Tel: 01932 336325 Fax: 01932 353670
Contact: Tracy McLoughlin
Email: healthfdmg@aol.com
Health Food Business trade magazine is sent free of charge to all registered named buyers of Natural organic foods, drinks, toiletries, herbals and dietary supplements. Serve UK & Eire mostly but available worldwide.

THE ORGANIC BABY BOOK & THE ORGANIC BABY & TODDLER COOK BOOK
Tel: 01803 863260 Contact: Paul Rossiter
Email: greenbooks@gn.apc.org Website: www.theorganicbabybook.co.uk
Reviews over 600 organic products for parents/baby—nappies, babyfoods, clothing, bedding, toys, toiletries, etc. Nutrition and health advice by leading experts. Cookbook has juice and seasonal meal recipes. £7.95/£6.95

ORGANIC GARDENING MAGAZINE
PO BOX 29, MINEHEAD,
SOMERSET TA24 6YY
Tel & Fax: 01984 641 212 Contact:
Geoffrey Bevan
Email: organic.gardening@virgin.net
The essential magazine for the organic gardener. 100% chemical-free. The UK's only organic monthly news-stand gardening magazine. Practical hands-on advice on every aspect of the garden—vegetables, fruit, ornamentals, ponds, wildlife. Write or phone for a free trial copy.

PERMACULTURE MAGAZINE & PERMANENT PUBLICATIONS
THE SUSTAINABILITY CENTRE,
EAST MEON, HANTS GU32 1HR
Tel: 01730 823311 Fax: 01730 823322
Contact: Maddy Harland (Editor)
Email: info@permaculture.co.uk
Website: www.permaculture.co.uk
Publishers of *Permaculture Magazine,* books and the Earth Repair catalogue. 400 books, videos and publications about all aspects of sustainable living.

POSITIVE NEWS
5 BICTON ENTERPRISE CENTRE,
CLUN, SHROPSHIRE SY7 8NT
Tel: 01588 640022 Fax: 01588 640033
Contact: Shauna Crockett-Burrows
Email: positive.news@btinternet.com
Website: www.positivenews.org.uk
Positive news is a not-for-profit company publishing a quarterly international newspaper reporting on the people, events and influences that are creating a positive future. Subscribers receive a full colour magazine, *Living Lightly,* which explores these ideas in greater depth.

RESURGENCE MAGAZINE
FORD HOUSE, HARTLAND, BIDEFORD,
DEVON EX39 6EE
Tel: 01237 441293 Fax: 01237 441203
Contact: Angie Burke
Email: ed@resurge.demon.co.uk
Website: www.resurgence.org
An international forum for ecological and
spiritual thinking, with many influential
contributors, described by *The Guardian* as
"the spiritual and artistic flagship of the
Green Movement". Sample copy available
on request.

SMALLHOLDER MAGAZINE
editorial HOOK HOUSE, WIMBLINGTON,
MARCH, CAMBS PE15 0QL
Tel: 01354 741538 Fax: 01354 741182
Email: edit@smallholder.co.uk
Contact: Liz Wright
Although not purely organic, we do cover
organics on a regular basis. We do
promote good animal welfare and
discourage intensive methods.

SOIL ASSOCIATION
Produce many publications, reports etc.
See above under Associations.

WORLDLY GOODS
10-12 PICTON ST, BRISTOL BS6 5QA
Tel: 0117 9420165 Fax: 0117 9420164
Contact: Peter Andrews
Email: wg@eco-logic.demon.co.uk
Specialise in wholesale/trade sales of books
that provide practical solution to
environmental problems, permaculture,
organic gardening etc.

ETHICAL INVESTMENT

THE ECOLOGY BUILDING SOCIETY
FREEPOST, 18 STATION RD., CROSS HILLS,
NR. KEIGHLEY, W. YORKS BD20 7EH
Tel: 0845 674 55566 (local rate) Fax:
01535 636166
Email: info@ecology.co.uk
The Ecology uses the money deposited by
savers to provide green mortgages, such as
the purchase of land and construction of
buildings, including homes, that support
organic food production. See display ad.

THE ETHICAL INVESTMENT
CO-OPERATIVE LTD
VINCENT HOUSE, 15 VICTORIA RD.,
DARLINGTON, CO. DURHAM DL1 5SF
Tel: 01325 267228 Fax: 01325 267200
Contact: Ian Harland, Andy Woodmancy
Email: greeninvest@gn.apc.org
Independent financial advisers specialising
in ethical/environmental investments and
pensions. Members of : Soil Association,
Friends of the Earth, Sustrans, Amnesty,
PETA, CPRE.

TRIODOS BANK
BRUNEL HOUSE, 11 THE PROMENADE,
CLIFTON, BRISTOL BS8 3NN
Tel: 0800 328 2181 for free information on
banking services for organisations
Tel: 0500 008720 for personal savings
details
Fax: 0117 973 9303 Email:
mail@triodos.co.uk Website:
www.triodos.co.uk
Triodos Bank's unique Organic Saver
Account offered in partnership with the
Soil Association, gives you a secure and
rewarding way to target your savings to
organic enterprises. We provide full
banking services for organic food and
farming enterprises, including current and
investment accounts, overdrafts and loan
facilities. As Europe's leading ethical bank
we have financed a wide range of organic
businesses over many years and
understand the needs and dynamics of the
sector. Contact us for more details. See
display ad.

FARMERS' MARKETS

**The information below has kindly been supplied
by the National Association of Farmers' Markets.**

Abbreviations: Borough Council BC   District Council DC   County Council CC

BEDS

LEIGHTON BUZZARD
THE HIGH ST
Tel: 01525 371920
Contact: Rachel Bond, Leighton
 & Linslade Town Council
3rd Sat monthly
 9 a.m.-3.30 p.m.

BERKS

READING
OLD CATTLE MARKET
Tel: 0118 901 5201
Contact: Mark Hillyer, Reading
 Council
May 6, 20; June 3, 17; July 1,
 15; Aug 5; Sept 2, 23; Oct 7,
 21; Nov 4, 18; Dec 2, 23,
 9 a.m. –1 p.m.

MAIDENHEAD
GROVE RD. CAR PARK
Tel: 01628 416538
Contact: Kath Pinto
2nd Sunday monthly
 10 a.m.–1 p.m.

BRISTOL

BRISTOL
CORN ST
Tel: 0117 922 4016
Contact: Steve Morris, Bristol
 City Council
Wednesday weekly,
 9.30 a.m.–3 p.m.

CAMBS

CAMBRIDGE
MARKET SQ
Tel: 01223 547524
Contact: Annette Joyce,
 Cambridge City Council
Sundays weekly, 10.30
 a.m.–4.30 p.m.

CHESHIRE

CHESTER
CHESTER MARKET, PRINCESS
 ST
Tel: 01244 402340
Contact: Julie Chew/Janet
 Fowles, Chester City Council
3rd Wednesday monthly,
 8 a.m.–4.30 p.m.

CREWE & NANTWICH
NANTWICH TOWN SQUARE
Tel: 01270 537424
Contact: Phil Riding, Crewe &
 Nantwich BC
Last Saturday monthly,
 10 a.m.–3 p.m.

KNUTSFORD
SILK MILL ST, behind
 permanent market
Tel: 07801 015258 / 01244
 603373
Contact: Gaynor Bowen-Jones,
 Cheshire CC
1st Saturday monthly,
 9 a.m.-3 p.m.

CORNWALL

LOSTWITHIEL
COMMUNITY CENTRE
Tel: 01840 250586
Contact: Joy Cheeseman
Fortnightly, 10 a.m.-2 p.m.

ST.AUSTELL
CORNERSTONE CAFÉ, BAPTIST
 CHURCH HALL, TRINITY ST
Tel: 01726 74507
Contact: Barbara Giles or 01726
 72159 Mrs Grime
Friday fortnightly

STOKE CLIMSLAND
CENTRE of STOKE CLIMSLAND
Tel: 01579 370493
Contact: Helen Adam
1st Saturday monthly, 9 a.m.-1
 p.m.

DEVON

BUCKFASTLEIGH
TOWN CENTRE
Tel: 01803 762674
Contact: Richard Rogers
Thurs weekly, 10 a.m.-1 p.m.

CREDITON
MARKET SQ
Tel: 01884 234362
Contact: Stephen Hill
1st Sat monthly, 10 a.m.-1 p.m.

CULLOMPTON
STATION RD CAR PARK
Tel: 01404 841 672
Contact: Barry Collins
2nd Sat monthly, 10 a.m.-1 p.m.

EXETER
FORE ST/SOUTH ST
Tel: 01392 265757
Contact: Michael Walsh/George
 Dumble, Exeter City Council
2nd & 4th Wednesday
 monthly, 9 a.m.-3 p.m.

KINGSBRIDGE
TOWN SQ
Tel: 01803 8861202
Contact: Carol Trant, South
 Hams DC
1st Saturday monthly, 10 a.m.-
 2 p.m.

OKEHAMPTON
CHARTER HALL, TOWN
 CENTRE
Tel: 01837 53158
Contact: Derek Brown
3rd Saturday monthly and 1st
 Wednesday monthly,
 9 a.m.-2 p.m.

PLYMOUTH
NEW GEORGE ST outside
 Pannier Market
Tel: 01752 668000
Contact: Gerrard Couper
2nd Saturday monthly, 9.30
 a.m.-4.30 p.m.

TAVISTOCK
part of PANNIER MARKET
Tel: 01822 611003
Contact: Keith Spieres
Daily Tuesday to Saturday

DORSET

BRIDPORT
ARTS CENTRE
Tel: 01308 459050
Contact: Tim Crabtree
3rd Saturday each month,
9.30 a.m.-2 p.m.

HIGHCLIFFE
LYMINGTON RD
Tel: 01202 529248
Contact: James Hyde
Wednesday weekly,
9 a.m.-2 p.m.

POUNDBURY
DORCHESTER
Tel: 01308 459050
Contact: Tim Crabtree
1st Saturday monthly,
10 a.m.-2 p.m.

CO. DURHAM

BARNARD CASTLE
MARKET SQ
Tel: 01833 690666
Contact: Chris Dauber
1st Saturday monthly,
10 a.m.-4 p.m.

DURHAM CITY
MARKET PLACE
Tel: 0191 384 6153
Contact: Eileen Wood, Durham
Markets Ltd
3rd Thursday monthly,
10 a.m.-4 p.m.

ESSEX

MALDEN
WHITEHORSE LANE CAR PARK
Tel: 01621 893147
Contact: Aj Collinson
Every Sunday

WITHAM
THE GROVE SHOPPING
CENTRE
Tel: 01376 519440
Contact: Wendy Harlow
May 9, 25; June 13, 27; July 11,
25; August 8, 22; Sept 12,
26; Oct 10, 24; Nov 14, 28;
Dec 1, 12. 9.30 a.m.-2 p.m.

GLOS

CIRENCESTER
CATTLE MARKET
Tel: 01285 643643
Contact: Alison Brown
2nd Sat. monthly, 9 a.m.-1 p.m.

STROUD
CORNHILL MARKET PLACE
Tel: 01453 753358
Contact: Clare Gerbrands
1st & 3rd Saturday monthly,
9 a.m.-3 p.m.

HANTS

ALDERSHOT
UNION ST, TOWN CENTRE
Tel: 01962 845135
Contact: Francis Fee, Hampshire
CC
July 23rd, October 8th,
10 a.m.-2 p.m.

ALTON
TOWN CENTRE
Tel: 01962 845135
Contact: Francis Fee,
Hampshire CC
July 2nd & September 3rd,
10 a.m.-2 p.m.

ANDOVER
HIGH ST July 9, September 17,
10 a.m.-2 p.m.
WEYHILL FAIR SITE June 11,
August 20, October 22,
10 a.m.-2 p.m.
Tel: 01962 845135
Contact: Francis Fee,
Hampshire CC

BASINGSTOKE
TOWN CENTRE
Tel: 01962 845135
Contact: Francis Fee,
Hampshire CC
August 13, October 29,
December 17,
10 a.m.-2 p.m.

EASTLEIGH
TOWN CENTRE
Tel: 01962 845135
Contact: Francis Fee,
Hampshire CC
April 21, June 16, August 18,
October 20, November 17,
December 1, 10 a.m.-2 p.m.

FAREHAM
TOWN CENTRE
Tel: 01962 845135
Contact: Francis Fee,
Hampshire CC
April 1, May 6, June 3, July 1,
August 5, September 9,
October 10, 10 a.m.-2 p.m.

HAVANT
POTASH TERRACE CAR PARK
Tel: 023 9223 3562
Contact: Tony & Carol Martin
1st Saturday monthly,
9 a.m.-2 p.m.

HYTHE
TOWN CENTRE
Tel: 01962 845135
Contact: Francis Fee,
Hampshire CC
September 30, 10 a.m.-2 p.m.

LEIGH PARK
BASING RD CAR PARK
Tel: 023 9223 3562
Contact: Tony & Carol Martin
Last Sat monthly, 9 a.m.-2 p.m.

PETERSFIELD
TOWN CENTRE
Tel: 01962 845135
Contact: Francis Fee,
Hampshire CC
April 2, June 4, Aug 6, Oct 1,
Nov 11, Dec 3,
10 a.m.-2 p.m.

RINGWOOD
TOWN CENTRE
Tel: 01962 845135
Contact: Francis Fee,
Hampshire CC
June 10, 10 a.m.-2 p.m.

WINCHESTER
MIDDLE BROOK ST
Tel: 01962 845135
Contact: Francis Fee,
Hampshire CC
Last Sunday monthly May to
Sept and Dec 10,
10 a.m.-2 p.m.

HERTS

HATFIELD
WHITE LION SQ
Tel: 01707 357377
Contact: Margaret Donovann
1st Saturday monthly,
9 a.m.-4.30 p.m.

TRING
CATTLE MARKET, BROOK ST
Tel: 01442 825097
Contact: David Younger
Saturday weekly, 9 a.m.-2 p.m.

KENT

TUNBRIDGE WELLS
CIVIC WAY in front of Town Hall
Tel: 01892 526121
Contact: Paul Stookes,
   Tunbridge Wells BC
2nd Saturday monthly,
   9 a.m.-1 p.m.

WYE
THE GREEN
Tel: 01233 8132998
Contact: Richard Boden
1st & 3rd Saturday monthly,
   9 a.m.-1 p.m.

LANCS

LANCASTER
CHURCH ST
Tel: 01524 66627
Contact: Jean Wilcock

LEICS

HINCKLEY
THE MARKET PLACE
Tel: 01455 891010
Contact: Karl Letten
3rd Thursday monthly,
   9.30 a.m.-2.30 p.m.

MELTON MOWBRAY
CATTLE MARKET
Tel: 01664 502330
Contact: Darryl Rowse / Ashley
   Baxter, Melton BC
Friday weekly, 9 a.m.-12 p.m.

LINCS

LINCOLN
CITY SQ
Tel: 01507 568885
Contact: Susan Smith
1st Friday monthly, 9 a.m.-4 p.m.

SLEAFORD
MARKET PLACE
Tel: 01507 668885
Contact: Susan Smith
1st Saturday monthly,
   9 a.m.-2 p.m.

STAMFORD
RED LION SQ
Tel: 0771 219976
Contact: Paul Gibbins
Friday fortnightly,
   8.30 a.m.-3 p.m.

LONDON

BROMLEY
HIGH ST
Tel: 020 8466 0719
Contact: James Findlater
Friday weekly, 9 a.m.-5 p.m.

CAMDEN LOCK
CAMDEN LOCK MARKET
Tel: 020 7704 9659
Contact: Nina Planck,
   Wheatland Farmers' Markets
   Ltd
Friday weekly, 11 a.m.-3 p.m.

ISLINGTON
ESSEX RD opposite Islington
   Green
Tel: 020 7704 9659
Contact: Nina Planck,
   Wheatland Farmers' Markets
   Ltd
Sunday weekly, 10 a.m.-2 p.m.

NOTTING HILL
behind WATERSTONES
Tel: 020 7704 9659
Contact: Nina Planck,
   Wheatland Farmers' Markets
   Ltd
Saturday weekly, 9 a.m.-1 p.m.

SWISS COTTAGE
AVENUE RD next to Camden
   Library
Tel: 020 7704 9659
Contact: Nina Planck,
   Wheatland Farmers' Markets
   Ltd
Wednesday weekly, 11 a.m.-4
   p.m.

NORTH'LAND

ALNWICK
MARKET PLACE
Tel: 01670 825895
Contact: Brian Crosbie
Last Friday monthly,
   10 a.m.-4 p.m.

HEXHAM
HEXHAM AUCTION MART
Tel: 01434 270393
Contact: Julie Charlton
2nd Sat monthly, 10 a.m.-2 p.m.

MORPETH
TOWN HALL
Tel: 01670 514351
Contact: Jim Pendrich, Castle
   Morpeth BC
1st Sunday monthly,
   10 a.m.-3 p.m.

NOTTS

MANSFIELD
THE BUTTERCROSS MARKET
Tel: 01623 463073
Contact: Jan Clark-Humphries
3rd Tuesday monthly,
   10 a.m.-4 p.m.

NEWARK
RIVERSIDE PARK
Tel: 01636 655720
Contact: Craig Black
May 25, June 11, 22, July 27,
   Aug 24, Sept 28, Oct 26, Nov
   23, Dec 14, 9 a.m.-1 p.m.

SOUTHWELL
THE MARKET PLACE
Tel: 01636 655720
Contact: Craig Black
June 9, July 14, Aug 11, Sept 8,
   Oct 13, Nov 10, Dec 8,
   9 a.m.-1 p.m.

OXON

BICESTER
SHEEP ST
Tel: 01869 252915
Contact: Anne Wilson
2nd Thursday monthly, July to
   October, 8.30 a.m.-1.30 p.m.

SHROPSHIRE

LUDLOW
MARKET SQ
Tel: 01584 890243
Contact: Elizabeth Bunny
July 13, Aug 10, Oct 12,
   9 a.m.-12 p.m.

OSWESTRY
THE BAILEY HEAD
Tel: 01691 680222
Contact: David Preston
Last Friday monthly,
   9 a.m.-3 p.m.

SOMERSET

BATH
GREEN PARK STATION
Tel: 01761 490624
Contact: Keith Goverd
1st & 3rd Saturday monthly,
9 a.m.-3 p.m.

CHARD
MAIN ST
Tel: 01460 78223
Contact: Roger White
4th Friday monthly,
9.30 a.m.-1 p.m.

CREWKERNE
FALKLAND SQ
Tel: 01460 78223
Contact: Roger White
3rd Saturday monthly,
9 a.m.-1 p.m.

FROME
CHEESE & GRAIN MARKET
Tel: 01460 78223
Contact: Roger White
2nd Saturday monthly,
9 a.m.-1 p.m.

GLASTONBURY
ST. JOHN'S CAR PARK
Tel: 01460 78223
Contact: Roger White
4th Saturday monthly,
9 a.m.-1 p.m.

WESTON SUPER MARE
TOWN SQ
Tel: 01934 634850
Contact: Graham Quick
2nd Saturday monthly,
9 a.m.-2 p.m.

WINCANTON
MEMORIAL HALL, HIGH ST
Tel: 01460 78223
Contact: Roger White
1st Fri monthly, 9 a.m.-1 p.m.

YEOVIL
LOWER MIDDLE ST
Tel: 01460 78223
Contact: Roger White
2nd Thurs monthly, 9 a.m.-1
p.m.

STAFFS

STAFFORD
MARKET SQ
Tel: 01785 248394
Contact: Karen Davies
2nd Saturday monthly, 9.30
a.m.-4 p.m.

SUFFOLK

BARSHAM
THE GRANGE FARM CENTRE,
BARSHAM, BECCLES
Tel: 01502 575218
Contact: Liz Harvey
10 a.m.-3 p.m.

BURY ST EDMONDS
TOWN CENTRE LIVESTOCK
MARKET
Tel: 01379 898357
Contact: Philip Brown
4th Saturday monthly,
9 a.m.-2 p.m.

LONG MELFORD
KENTWELL HALL
Tel: 01787 310207
Contact: Judith Phillips
June 3, July 29, Sept 30, Nov 4,
Dec 2, 9 a.m.-2 p.m.

LOWESTOFT
THE TRIANGLE CENTRE, HIGH ST.
Tel: 01502 523338
Contact: Chloe Veale, Waveney
DC
June 17, Aug 19, Oct 21, Dec
18, 10 a.m.-2 p.m.

NEEDHAM MARKET
ALDER CARR FARM
Tel: 01449 720820
Contact: Joan & Nick
Hardingham
May 20, June 17, July 15, Aug 19,
Sept 16, Oct 21, Nov 18, Dec
16, 9 a.m.-2 p.m.

WICKHAM
EASTERN FARM PARK
Tel: 017288 746475
Contact: Jill Kerr
June 24, July 22, Aug 19, Sept
16, 9.30 a.m.-2 p.m.

WOODBRIDGE
COMMUNITY CENTRE
Tel: 01379 384593
Contact: Ian Whitehead
June 10, July 8, Aug 12, Sept 9,
Oct 14, Nov 11, Dec 9,
9.30 a.m.-2 p.m.

SURREY

GUILDFORD
HIGH ST
Tel: 01483 444540
Contact: Dave Harnett,
Guildford BC
July 4, Sept 26, 10.30 a.m.-3.30
p.m.

WALLINGTON
OLD TOWN HALL & LIBRARY
GARDENS
Tel: 020 8770 6255
Contact: Matthew James,
Sutton BC
2nd Saturday monthly,
9 a.m.-2 p.m.

E. SUSSEX

BRIGHTON
BARTHOLOMEW SQ
Tel: 01243 814369
Contact: Andy Turner-Cross
Weekly from May

HAILSHAM
Tel: 01323 842488
Contact: Carol Burbridge
2nd Saturday monthly March-
Dec, 9 a.m.-1 p.m.

HASTINGS
ROBERTSON ST
Contact: Monica Adams-Acton,
Town Centre Manager
Wednesday weekly,
8 a.m.-4.30 p.m.

HEATHFIELD
STATION RD WEST CAR PARK
Tel: 01323 440295
Contact: Katy Thomas
3rd Saturday monthly April-
December, 9 a.m.-1 p.m.

LEWES
CLIFFE PEDESTRIAN PRECINCT
Tel: 01273 480111
Contact: Dodie Horton
1st Saturday monthly,
9 a.m.-1 p.m.

UCKFIELD
HIGH ST & LUXFORD FIELD
Tel: 01825 766670
Contact: Cathie Corbin
Aug 12, 10 a.m.-4 p.m.

W. SUSSEX

ARUNDEL
MARKET SQ, TOWN QUAY
Tel: 07932 535460
Contact: Jane O'Neill
1st Thursday & 3rd Saturday
monthly, 9 a.m.-1 p.m.

CHICHESTER
THE CATTLE MARKET CAR PARK
Tel: 01243 785166
Contact: Sally Burgess
Friday fortnightly, 8.30 a.m.-3
p.m.

Farmers' markets

HORSHAM
CARFAX, CENTRE OF
 HORSHAM
Tel: 01405 215424
Contact: Nick Shields, Horsham
 DC
Saturdays, 9 a.m.-5 p.m.

STEYNING
HIGH ST CAR PARK
Tel: 01403 711057
Contact: Derek Crush
1st Saturday monthly,
 9 a.m.-1 p.m.

WARWICKS

KENILWORTH
HIGH ST
Tel: 01789 414002
Contact: James Pavitt

STRATFORD UPON AVON
ROTHER ST MARKET
Tel: 01789 414002
Contact: James Pavitt
2nd Saturday monthly,
 9 a.m.-2 p.m.

WARWICK
MARKET PLACE, TOWN
 CENTRE
Tel: 01789 414002
Contact: James Pavitt
3rd Friday monthly,
 9 a.m.-2 p.m.

W. MIDLANDS

BIRMINGHAM
VICTORIA SQ/NEW ST
Tel: 0121 303 5449
Contact: Nicci Boore,
 Birmingham City Council
1st Wednesday monthly,
 10 a.m.-6 p.m.

SOLIHULL
HIGH ST
Tel: 01564 772194
Contact: E. Geoff Tompstone
1st Friday monthly,
 9 a.m.-4 p.m.

WILTS

BRADFORD UPON AVON
WESTBURY GARDENS
Tel: 01225 712333
Contact: Peter Dunford
3rd Thursday monthly,
 9 a.m.-2 p.m.

CALNE
HIGH ST
Tel: 01249 706529
Contact: Andrew Gaskell, North
 Wiltshire DC
1st Tuesday monthly,
 9 a.m.-2 p.m.

CHIPPENNHAM
NEELD HALL
Tel: 01249 706529 Contact:
 Andrew Gaskell, North
 Wiltshire DC
3rd Tuesday monthly,
 9 a.m.-2 p.m.

DEVIZES
MARKET PLACE
Tel: 01380 724911
Contact: Caroline Lightfoot,
 Kennet DC
1st Saturday monthly,
 9 a.m.-2 p.m.

MARLBOROUGH
TOWN HALL: June 17, Sept 16,
 Oct 21, Dec 9.
ST PETER'S CHURCH: Nov 11
Tel: 01672 513950
Contact: Jo Ripley

MELKSHAM
RIVERSIDE adjacent to QUEEN
 MARY GARDENS
Tel: 01225 712333
Contact: Peter Dunford
2nd Friday monthly,
 9 a.m.-2 p.m.

TROWBRIDGE
FORE ST
Tel: 01225 712333
Contact: Peter Dunford
4th Fri monthly, 9 a.m.-2 p.m.

WARMINSTER
BY THE LIBRARY
Tel: 01225 712333
Contact: Peter Dunford
3rd Fri monthly, 9 a.m.-2 p.m.

WESTBURY
EDWARD ST
Tel: 01225 712333
Contact: Peter Dunford
1st Fri monthly, 9 a.m.-2 p.m.

WOOTTON BASSETT
HIGH ST
Tel: 01249 706529
Contact: Andrew Gaskell, North
 Wiltshire DC
4th Sat monthly, 9 a.m.-2 p.m.

WORCS

BROMSGROVE
MARKET HALL, ST JOHN'S ST
Tel: 01527 881327
Contact: Peter Michael
Thursday fortnightly
 8.30 a.m.-2 p.m.

KNIGHTWICK
TEME VALLEY MARKET, THE
 TALBOT AT KNIGHTWICK
Tel: 01886 821235
Contact: Mrs J. Clift
2nd Sunday monthly,
 11 a.m.-1.30 p.m.

YORKS

MALTON
THE MARKET PLACE
Tel: 01751 473780
Contact: Chris Woodfine
Monthly, weekly in summer,
 9 a.m.-2 p.m.

MURTON
YORK LIVESTOCK CENTRE
Tel: 01904 489731
Contact: Richard Tasker
June 17, July 15, Aug 12, Sept 6,
 Oct 21, Nov 25, Dec 16,
 9 a.m.-2 p.m.

SHEFFIELD
WHIRLOW HALL FARM,
 WHIRLOW LANE
Tel: 0114 236 7430
July 11, Dec 16, 10 a.m.-4 p.m.

Wales

MON

USK
THE MEMORIAL CLUB or
 CONSERVATIVE CLUB
Tel: 01600 860730
Contact: Steve Sheerman

INDEX

Index

Index

Index

Index

THE ORGANIC
DIRECTORY
<u>ONLINE</u>

As from June 2000, *The Organic Directory* will also be published online on the Soil Association's website at:

www.theorganicdirectory.co.uk

Future editions of *The Organic Directory* in book form will be compiled from the online database.

If you think your company or organisation should be included in *The Organic Directory*, or if you want your details to be amended, fill in the form at:

www.mamba.demon.co.uk/organic

There is no charge for inclusion in *The Organic Directory*, although we have a section of advertising space in the printed version, and will explore possibilities with the online edition.

We always welcome your suggestions as to how we can improve *The Organic Directory*. Please email them to Clive Litchfield at:

organiceco@aol.com

or write to him c/o Green Books Ltd, Foxhole, Dartington, Totnes, Devon TQ9 6EB.